WHY »NOT?

CRISPIN BOYER

NATIONAL
GEOGRAPHIC

WASHINGTON, D.C.

CONTENTS

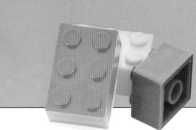

WHY ask

WHY NOT?

Why is the sky blue? Why do people say "bless you" after you go *ahhh-chooooo?* Why did we send astronauts to the moon?

Hey, good questions—all answered in the book *Why? Over 1,111 Answers to Everything*. Now it's time for the flip side: *Why Not?*, a brand-new book with a fresh batch of questions and answers—except with a twist. Why *isn't* the sky green? Why *don't* we say "bless you" after people burp as well as sneeze? Why *haven't* we colonized the moon (or Mars, or the bottom of the ocean)? If you ever wondered why something *isn't* true or *doesn't* make sense, this is the book for you!

Why Not? is your bottomless source of answers to all your burning questions—and questions you didn't even know you had. Why *don't* we ride those old bicycles with the huge front tires anymore? (Believe it or not, those extraordinary bikes are called "ordinary bikes.") Why *can't* cats and dogs get along? (Hint: It's kind of our fault.) Why *didn't* ancient Egyptians live in those pyramids? (The deadly traps might've had something to do with it.) Why *don't* we travel in flying cars and jetpacks? (Be patient—they're in the works!) Inside you'll find the answers to these questions and many more, some serious, some silly, all meticulously researched—spread across hundreds of topics. Just keep in mind that discoveries are being made all the time, and theories are constantly evolving. Although this book packs the most up-to-date answers now, things might be different 10 years from now. In the meantime, are you ready for too much information? Hey, why not!

WHY?

WHY NOT?

What TO WATCH OUT FOR IN *WHY NOT?*

QUESTIONS

Every page is crammed with questions related to the same topic, with answers often leading to more questions. And just because the book is called *Why Not?* doesn't mean we won't also ask why—and who, what, where, when, and how, too. So—go ahead! Why not ask a few more?

SAY WHAT?!

Scattered among the questions you'll find these weird-but-true facts.

MYTH MASHED

Sometimes what you think you know isn't always so. Myth Mashed blurbs will show that some well-established "facts" are actually fiction.

PERSONS OF INTEREST

Explorers, scientists, celebrities, pioneers—meet the very important people who helped solve each chapter's mysteries in these profiles.

Q:TIPS

Here you'll find some helpful advice related to the topic at hand.

SILLY QUESTION, SERIOUS ANSWER

Why is your innie not an outie? Why don't trees scream when we cut them down? No question is too zany for *Why Not?*, and the answers are always given the scientific treatment. So next time your friend starts a joke by asking a question, you might have a real answer.

ANIMALS

IMAGINE COMMANDING YOUR POOCH to speak and hearing a "Yeah, what?" instead of a "woof-woof!" What burning questions would you have for your conversational canine? "What do you dream about?" Or maybe just "Where have all my socks gone?!?" Unfortunately, however, as much as we would love to talk to Fido (and get those socks back), we can't play 20 questions with our furry (and hairy, feathered, or scaly) friends. So in this chapter we'll do the deep digging for you, as we decode and explore the lives of dogs and cats, bugs and bears, eagles and whales, and more creatures that soar, swim, crawl, and slither. By the end of your safari through the next 30 pages, you'll know why fish don't get seasick, why spiders don't get stuck in their own webs, and why cuddly-looking koalas would not make great pets. Get ready to talk to the animals. Things are about to get wild!

WILD THINGS

WHY aren't baby animals as helpless as BABY HUMANS?

Newborn wildebeests can walk within minutes and keep up with their herd in a matter of days. Sea turtle hatchlings dig themselves from their beach nests and scramble into the sea before they're even a day old. Even chimpanzees, our closest evolutionary relatives, reach adulthood in half the time it takes a typical human kid to graduate high school. So why are human babies so helpless compared to the offspring of wild animals? Amazingly enough, scientists believe it's because we're so brainy!

Outstanding
ANIMAL PARENTS

What does being smart have to do with being helpless as babies?

Human brains—particularly the gray matter responsible for problem-solving, speech, learning, emotions, and memory—are far larger and more complex than those of even the most intelligent animals such as dolphins and elephants. But a big brain requires a big head, and big heads pose a danger to moms during childbirth. So evolution (more on that in a bit) came up with a compromise: We humans are born at a very early stage in our development compared to other animals, while our heads are still small enough to limit the risk to Mom during childbirth. To make up for our early exit from Mom, our brain then continues to develop outside the womb, through our childhood, and into adulthood (even into our mid-20s!). The trade-off is that newborn human babies are as helpless as ... well, little babies, needing constant care from Mom and Dad. Most animals, on the other hand, are born with brains much farther along in development—to the point where the animals are ready to stand, walk, and in some cases even fend for themselves in a dangerous world.

SILLY QUESTION, SERIOUS ANSWER

Why don't eggs from the super-market hatch baby chickens?

Female chickens—called hens—lay eggs like clockwork, typically one a day. But for an egg to be fertilized (or capable of making a baby chicken), hens need to mate with a male chicken (a rooster). Some commercial chicken farms that sell eggs don't let roosters into the henhouse (well, unless they want more chickens), which means those eggs will never hatch a chick no matter how long you sit on them. (Some grocery stores sell specially marked "fertilized" eggs for customers to hatch at home if they want baby chickens.)

ELEPHANTS

Born blind and helpless, baby elephants need a lot of TLC from their moms. Lucky for them, they get an entire herd of moms to raise and protect them! Female elephants travel in groups of sisters, aunts, and cousins, all led by the eldest mother, called the matriarch. All the ladies take turns looking after the little ones, leading them by linking trunks to tail and surrounding them to form a wall of muscle between the babies and predators. (Male elephants, meanwhile, travel in their own separate "bachelor" groups.)

EMPEROR PENGUINS

After a mama penguin lays her eggs, the papa incubates them for two months in the Antarctic dark while the mother travels up to 60 miles (97 km) to find food. When the female returns with food in her belly to feed the baby, the air explodes with squawks and peeps as the father and chicks call out for a family reunion—and some tasty upchucked fish.

ALLIGATORS

You might be alarmed to see a baby alligator in the jaws of a monster adult, but chances are the little reptile couldn't be safer! Despite being cold-blooded, alligator mothers are warmhearted when it comes to their babies. They'll defend their little ones from hungry fish, snapping turtles, birds, skunks, and other predators for up to a year and ferry them around on their backs—and even in their scary-looking jaws!

WOLF SPIDERS

You might think good parenting is rare in the spider world, and you'd be right: Most spiderlings are left to fend for themselves when they hatch. But wolf spider mothers are unique in that they actually care for their young. Hatchlings skitter onto the mother spider's back, where they lock legs and hold tight while Mom takes them on spidey-back rides for protection and food. It might not make for a pretty family portrait, but the baby spiders get a leg up in the bug-eat-bug world.

WHY don't snakes HAVE LEGS?

Scientists recently discovered why snakes don't sprout legs as they develop in their eggs, and it all comes down to genes. (You'll learn all about these itty-bitty strips of chemicals later in chapter 5.) Genes contain instructions that tell cells how to build body parts. All snakes carry the gene to grow limbs, but it's switched off early in the baby snake's development, which is why baby snake bodies don't grow legs in their eggs.(Pythons actually sprout nubs of hind legs through their scaly skin—proof they have the leg-growing gene). As for why snakes evolved to slither on scaly bellies, scientists have some theories: One is that snakes evolved from lizards that dug through the dirt to find food. Legs get in the way when you're trying to squeeze through tunnels, so snake legs became smaller over time until they finally vanished.

MYTH MASHED

Why CAN'T SNAKES HEAR?

This myth sure makes sense. Snakes don't have ears! Or do they? Scientists studying snake hearing determined that although snakes don't possess ear canals and eardrums like humans and other animals, they do have sound-sensing organs hidden inside their scaly noggins. These inner ears are attached to the snake's skull and can sense vibrations in the ground and even in the air.

Why don't polar bears freeze to death?

The largest meat-eating land animal is supremely adapted to living in one of the coldest environments on Earth—the Arctic Circle—where temperatures average minus 29°F (-34°C) in the winter. Each strand of polar bear fur is a hollow tube that holds air and traps heat. Beneath this fur is a thick slab of insulating flab. Polar bears are so well adapted to life in the cold, in fact, that they need to be careful they don't overheat! When bears start to feel the burn after chasing prey on a balmy Arctic day, they take a refreshing dip in seawater that's a brisk 29°F (-1.5°C).

EXTREMELY OFFENSIVE ADAPTATIONS

PISTOL SHRIMP: Awesome Claw
By snapping shut its oversize claw at lightning speed, this crustacean (which is no bigger than your little finger) creates a tiny bubble that bursts louder than a thunderclap, stunning nearby fish. Each busted bubble is accompanied by a flash of light nearly as hot as the sun's surface!

CONGA ANT: Bullet-Like Bite
The bite of the conga ant, which scurries through the rain forests of Central and South America, causes a throbbing, fiery pain that victims compare to being shot; hence, this insect's alternate name: the bullet ant. It's been ranked as the most painful insect bite in the world!

EXTREMELY DEFENSIVE ADAPTATIONS

SPANISH RIBBED NEWT: Toxic Spikes
When push comes to shove and predators attack, this fearless amphibian forces its own ribs through its poison-smeared skin to create a row of poisonous spikes.

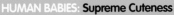

INDIAN GRAY MONGOOSE: Cobra-Proof Bodies
Mongooses are famously feisty in the face of Indian cobras, one of the "big four" serpents responsible for the most human snakebite deaths in India. Mongooses have a slight immunity to the cobra's venom and thick fur that resists punctures from snake fangs. They can shake off a strike and keep fighting!

EXTREMELY ADORABLE ADAPTATIONS

PEACOCK SPIDERS: Fancy Dance Moves
The world's prettiest spider has smooth moves to back up his fabulous looks. "Sparklemuffin" is the pet name scientists have given a new species of peacock spider, a tiny arachnid unique to eastern Australia. The males of this species evolved with brightly colored bodies and killer dance moves to impress any potential mates that creep close.

HUMAN BABIES: Supreme Cuteness
Evolution has wired our brains so that any creature with a big head, large eyes, and button nose (traits most human babies have in common) triggers our perceptions of cuteness, which makes us more willing to drop everything to care for them. Babies who are considered extra cute get bonus attention, studies show.

PERSON OF INTEREST

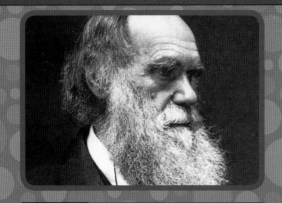

WHO?
Charles Darwin

WHAT is he famous for?
Developing the theory of natural selection

WHEN?
1859

WHERE?
England

WHY is he important?
When he returned home from a five-year expedition aboard the sailing ship H.M.S. *Beagle,* this self-taught naturalist pondered his notes and illustrations of creatures glimpsed around the world. He saw that similar species collected from different locations had curiously odd characteristics compared with one another. These differences seemed key to each animal's survival in its unique environment. A revolutionary theory began to form in Darwin's mind: the theory of natural selection, in which nature favors changes that help a species survive and reproduce, which in turn passes on successful adaptations to the next generation. Eventually, all these adaptations add up until one species evolves into a new one. Darwin's theory explains how all plants and animals—including humans—slowly change (or evolve) over time to improve their chances of survival.

Why don't woodpeckers get headaches?

Because they evolved with built-in helmets! These handsome head bangers spend the day hunting for insects by drumming away on tree trunks. Scans of woodpecker skulls revealed spongy platelike bones that absorb impacts like a bike helmet. They even have a special bone that wraps around the skull and acts as a sort of seat belt for the brain. Such specialized skulls have inspired the designs of real-life helmets.

WHY don't most animals recognize themselves in the MIRROR?

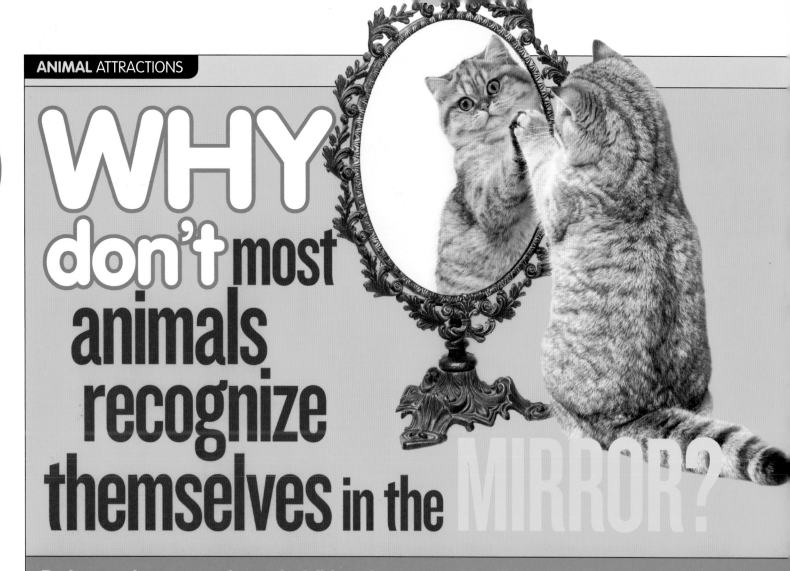

Park a pooch or a cat in front of a full-length mirror and you'll get mixed results—or no results at all. Daisy might sniff at her reflection, give a halfhearted woof, or just bolt for the door. Mr. Kitty might pounce at the mirror or go back to preening his fur. Both animals are incapable of recognizing themselves in the mirror, and they're hardly alone. In fact, only a handful of animals—including humans, great apes (such as gorillas, chimps, and orangutans), elephants, dolphins, and magpies—have the ability to reflect on their reflections. Part of the reason is how animals sense the world. Scent is as important to dogs and cats as sight, for instance, so they don't recognize their scentless reflection as anything familiar. More importantly, self-recognition is a hallmark of higher intelligence: an ability to see oneself as a unique individual and identify one's own movements in a mirror. This ability requires a sophisticated processing of information rather than simple instinct. It's no coincidence that animals capable of recognizing their reflection are considered among the most intelligent in the animal kingdom.

SAY WHAT?!

DOGS CAN'T RECOGNIZE THEMSELVES IN THE MIRROR, but they are able to identify other dogs and animals on TV, according to a study done in 2013. That's why your pooch might turn into a couch potato when you change the channel to a wildlife documentary. Dogs even have their own channel—DogTV—a high-def network of shows tailored to your pup's peepers and moods. Clips of dogs lounging in meadows or reacting calmly to the mail carrier might not seem like must-see TV to you, but such shows could help your pup stay calm when you're not home or learn how to react when a visitor rings the doorbell.

How do scientists know whether animals can recognize their own reflection?

If you spotted a smudge of schmutz on your cheek in the mirror, wouldn't you try to wipe it off? Scientists believe that only animals that can recognize their reflection would have that same compulsion. That's the basis of the "mark test": Test subjects are marked with a sticker or spot of ink, then placed in front of the mirror. Animals capable of recognizing themselves will scratch off the mark. Recently, scientists have learned that some less brainy primates can learn to recognize themselves through repeated exposure to mirrors. Incredibly smart animals like elephants, dolphins, and great apes will actually pose in funny ways to peer at otherwise unseen parts of their bodies.

Why don't migrating animals just stay put?

Do you sit at the dining table when you're done eating or hang out in bed all day when you wake up in the morning? No way. You have stuff to do! Many species of birds, mammals, fish, reptiles, amphibians, and insects move around—or migrate, sometimes in massive groups and over incredible distances—for the same reasons: Because they have stuff to do and because wherever they are doesn't have whatever they might need. Animals typically migrate for three reasons: to find food, seek more hospitable climates, or breed. Polar bears migrate north to find sea ice and seals each fall. Pacific salmon leave the ocean and swim up streams in a treacherous final journey to lay their eggs at their spawning spot. The urge to migrate—often instinctive, or preprogrammed into an animal's brain—is itself an adaptation for survival, and many migrating animals have evolved with neat tricks to make the long trips less risky. The wandering albatross has a wingspan of up to 11 feet (3.4 m)—the widest of any bird—to soar for hours on seasonal sea breezes without ever flapping its wings. Migrating animals can navigate by the stars or even track Earth's magnetic field with a sixth sense called "magnetoreception." For these animals, there's no place like home because no place is home—at least not all year round.

Going Places
GREAT MIGRATIONS

BLUE WILDEBEESTS

DISTANCE TRAVELED ANNUALLY: 1,000 miles (1,609 km)

WHY DO THEY MIGRATE? Each dry season, more than a million of these hoofed animals embark on one of nature's most perilous journeys and greatest spectacles. Joined by thousands of zebras and gazelles, dodging the jaws of lions and crocodiles, they journey north to find greener pastures and water to drink.

HOW DO THEY NAVIGATE? By following the fresh scent of rain on the horizon of dry, grassy plains in central, southern, and eastern Africa

MONARCH BUTTERFLIES

DISTANCE TRAVELED ANNUALLY: 5,000 miles (8,047 km)

WHY DO THEY MIGRATE? The only butterflies that migrate like birds, monarchs travel south each winter to escape the freezing temperatures of northern North America.

HOW DO THEY NAVIGATE? By watching the position of the sun and comparing it with their internal clocks

HUMPBACK WHALES

DISTANCE TRAVELED ANNUALLY: 12,000 miles (19,312 km)

WHY DO THEY MIGRATE? Feeding grounds often make terrible breeding grounds, so humpback whales fatten up in icy Arctic waters and then travel to tropical seas to raise their young.

HOW DO THEY NAVIGATE? By tracking the position of the sun and stars, as well as Earth's magnetic field

ARCTIC TERN

DISTANCE TRAVELED ANNUALLY: 44,000 miles (70,811 km)

WHY DO THEY MIGRATE? These small seabirds rack up more mileage than any other migrating animal each year as they soar along a zigzagging route, reaching nearly from the South Pole to the North Pole, all part of a nonstop flight to find richer feeding grounds.

HOW DO THEY NAVIGATE? By following the flow of air currents, which explains their zigzagging route (flying across or directly into the wind would wear out these little birds). Scientists also suspect that migrating birds have chemical reactions in their eyes that actually allow them to see Earth's magnetic field!

WHY don't animals need to brush THEIR TEETH?

Brush, floss, repeat. Why are human mouths so high-maintenance when lions and tigers and crocs and kangaroos go their entire lives without once reclining in a dentist's chair? For a few reasons, starting with our diet. Humans consume a variety of foods, and some of it wages war on our pearly whites. We eat a diet rich in carbohydrates (found in breads, fruits, potatoes, cereals, candies, cookies, and sweet drinks), and these foods pack sugars that provide a feast for the bacteria living in our mouths. When dentists break out the power tools to jackhammer that brownish coat of slime known as "plaque" from your choppers, they're evicting these mouth-dwelling bacteria before they can decay your teeth and infect your gums. Animals in the wild typically don't eat such a carbohydrate-rich diet.

YUCK MOUTHS
NATURE'S nastiest MAWS

PACU FISH: Get a load of these choppers! The Pacu fish of the Amazon River looks like its close cousin the piranha until you peek into its mouth—revealing a set of pearly whites that look shockingly like human teeth! The fish evolved its freaky smile to chomp on nuts that fall into the water.

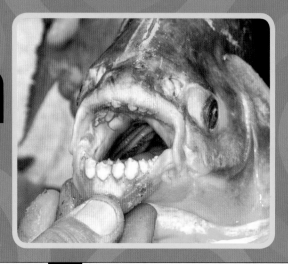

LEATHERBACK SEA TURTLES:
Ask the world's largest turtle to open wide and say "ahhh," and you'll see a mouth straight out of a monster movie, crammed with spiky teeth that line the walls of its throat. The spikes help the gentle leatherback snap up slippery jellyfish, its favorite food.

How Animals
TREAT THEIR TEETH

SHARKS: AWESOME JAWS

Humans only get two sets of teeth to last their entire lives, but sharks get thousands so they can afford to lose a few. Their upper and lower jaws are stacked with rows of razor-sharp choppers. If one tooth tumbles out, a new one shifts from behind to take its place. Sharks lose and replace as many as 2,000 teeth each year!

NARWHALS: TOOTH TOUCHÉ!

Male members of these marine mammals are famous for their unicorn-like horns that grow up to 8.8 feet (2.7 m) long. Just like the tusks of elephants and walruses, narwhal horns are actually

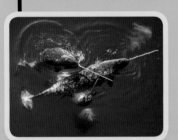

teeth. Scientists think narwhals use this tusk for sensing changes in temperature, pressure, and salinity (salt) levels in their icy Arctic Ocean habitat. They keep their tusk scrubbed clean by rubbing it against the tusk of other narwhals. Imagine plunging your choppers into Arctic waters, then brushing them clean by gnashing them against a buddy's!

MACAQUES: BOSSY FLOSSERS

A group of long-tailed macaques in Thailand regularly perform a dental chore you would probably rather ignore ... they floss their teeth! And you'll never guess where they get their dental floss: These sacred monkeys live in an ancient Buddhist shrine, where they're subject to much pampering by the resident monks and visitors. The monkeys will pluck the hair from tourists, then pull these strands very carefully through their teeth.

BEAVERS: USE THEM AND LOSE THEM

Beavers are too busy to worry about dental hygiene. Fortunately, their jobs come with a great dental plan. Like all rodents (yes, beavers are rodents just like mice and guinea pigs), beavers have incisors that constantly grow throughout their lives. But beavers treat their teeth like chain saws, gnawing through tree trunks to get timber for constructing dams and waterfront dens. Constant chewing keeps their teeth sharp and—just as importantly—prevents them from growing dangerously long.

CROCODILES: DARING DENTISTS

Nile crocodiles preserve their winning smiles with the help of the world's bravest dentists: Egyptian plovers. These plucky little birds peck scraps from the teeth of dozing crocodiles, who open wide while dozing on riverbanks. The big croc and little bird have what's called a "symbiotic relationship," meaning both benefit from their interactions. The croc gets a cleaning and the plover gets a meal. It's win-win!

KOMODO DRAGONS: These lethal lizards—the world's largest—have rancid mouths teeming with more than 50 strains of toxic bacteria, as well as venomous fangs just like snakes. Just one nip is all it takes for a dragon to infect its prey with poisonous saliva; it then patiently follows the stricken animal until it dies of blood loss or poisoning.

WHY don't animals use TOOLS like we do?

Don't be too sure they don't. Until the 1960s, scientists believed humans were the only animals able to craft and wield tools to accomplish tasks. But then a British zoologist named Jane Goodall watched a chimpanzee in Africa strip a twig of its leaves, jam it into a termite mound, then use it like a spoon to slurp termites out of the ground. Hers was the first scientific observation of tool use in wild animals, but it wasn't the last. Creatures across the animal kingdom use tools for all kinds of purposes, from hunting to playing to just getting around. Some of these behaviors are instinctive or are abilities they're born with (such as when hermit crabs use discarded shells as mobile homes). But some tool skills are taught by parents to their offspring, like the macaques' teeth-flossing techniques on the previous page.

SAY WHAT?!

HUMANS ARE NOT THE ONLY SPECIES THAT HAS EXPERIENCED A STONE AGE, that prehistoric period in which our ancestors relied on stone tools to make life easier. Chimps, capuchins, and macaques have been using stones as hammers to crack open nuts for thousands of years—maybe longer. Scientists say these animals are currently living in their Stone Age. Could their technology be catching up to ours?

GOING TO WORK
What tools DO THESE ANIMALS USE?

BOLAS SPIDERS? STICKY BOMBS!

These little spiders instinctively make their own hunting tool: sticky blobs of silk at the end a web line. When a tasty insect flies by, the bolas spider swings the blob at the bug and—splat!—reels in its stuck supper.

DECORATOR CRABS? FASHION ACCESSORIES!

These fab crabs create elaborate camouflage using objects in their environment: plants, sponges, rocks, shells, corals, driftwood, and even bits of castaway human trash such as torn T-shirts and soggy flip-flops. They stick all this stuff to their backs and claws so they can hide in plain sight when predators swim too close.

CROWS? CARS AND STICKS!

Among the smartest birds, crows will drop nuts into traffic, then swoop down to eat the meat from the cracked shells crushed by cars. Crows without access to freeways—such as those on the Pacific island of New Caledonia—use their beaks to fashion hooks from sticks to scoop food from hard-to-reach places. They learn how to make these hooks by watching other crows and even carry their prized tools around with them.

OCTOPUSES? COCONUTS!

Equipped with a more complex brain than other invertebrates (animals without a backbone, such as insects, worms, and snails), octopuses are excellent problem solvers and known tool wielders. Some smaller octopuses stack two halves of coconut shells and haul the shells around with them. When predators swim too close, the octopuses climb into one shell and pull the other half over their heads, creating a mobile fortress.

ELEPHANTS? PAINT BRUSHES!

These brainy mammals live in complex social groups and communicate using sounds too low for humans to hear. They also use their flexible trunk to turn tree branches into back-scratchers, drop rocks onto electric fences to short them out, and even paint pachyderm masterpieces when given a few art supplies!

DOLPHINS? ALL SORTS OF STUFF!

Who says you need hands to be handy with tools? Dolphins, considered the second most intelligent animals (after you, of course), demonstrate a humanlike ability to adapt to different situations. Dolphins in Australia grab sponges to protect their nose when they dig in the seafloor for food. In the country of Myanmar, fishermen signal Irrawaddy dolphins to drive schools of fish into the fishermen's nets. These special dolphins don't do it for free; they snap up fish that get away.

WHY don't birds

perched in trees lose their grip

when they FALL ASLEEP?

Does the thought of snoozing on the top bunk of a bunk bed keep you up at night? What if you roll off the edge?! Now imagine you're a bird picking the perfect perch for the evening. Curling up on the ground is out of the question: You'd become the easiest of pickings for predators! But flying birds (as opposed to flightless birds such as penguins and ostriches) have no fear of falling when they slumber in a tree's tippy-top branches because their feet can pull off a nifty feat. Most flying birds have four toes on their talons: three that face forward and one pointing backward like a claw-tipped thumb. When a bird crouches on a perch, cords of tissue called tendons in its legs grow taut and automatically tighten the bird's grip on the branch. This locking system doesn't require any effort on the bird's part, unlike your own hands, which require muscle power to hold a tight grip. The talon stays closed until the bird straightens its legs to launch into the air at the start of its day.

SAY WHAT?!

YOU ACTUALLY HAD A TAIL ONCE, BUT IT DIDN'T STICK AROUND FOR LONG. At around four weeks old, a human embryo develops a tiny tail that typically dissolves within eight weeks. Very rarely, and for reasons scientists don't understand, these tails don't melt away, and the baby is born eight months later with a nub of a tail up to five inches (13 cm) long. It doesn't provide any of the gripping abilities of prehensile tails, however, and doctors typically remove these tails with a simple operation.

So why don't
bats fall when they hang upside down?

In many ways, bats live like a bird in reverse. These flying mammals are active at night (instead of during the day like birds) and they sleep during the day upside down (instead of right-side up like birds). But like a bird's talons, bat feet lock automatically on branches when they sleep. In fact, a bat actually needs to exert muscle power to open its feet, which are normally locked in a grip when the muscles are relaxed. Bats hang upside down because, unlike birds, they aren't strong enough to take off from an upright position. By hanging upside down, they can drop right into the air and start flying.

Why don't
mountain goats take a tumble?

Watching a family of mountain goats casually scramble up a sheer cliff face, with nothing below but a 10,000-foot (3,048-m) drop, is enough to make anyone with even a mild fear of heights hold their breath. But these nimble animals—which aren't really goats but are related to them and antelopes—are remarkably sure-footed in their high-altitude habitats on the peaks of the Rocky Mountains. Their hooves have rough pads that grip rocks like the soles of climbing shoes, and their two toes can open wide to improve balance or close tight to get a grip. Mountain goats evolved with these natural climbing and leaping—up to 12 feet (3.7 m)—abilities to scramble high out of the range of predators such as wolves, cougars, and bears.

Why can't
all animals hang from their tails?

Animal tails perform all kinds of important tasks, from helping with balance to swatting away flies to communicating with other animals. But only one tail type has evolved into a bonus arm for the backside. Called a "prehensile tail," it can grasp objects and (in many cases) support the animal's weight. The most multipurpose prehensile tail belongs to the New World monkeys of Central and South America, including spider monkeys, howler monkeys, and woolly monkeys. These tree dwellers use their long, flexible tails to dangle from branches, which frees their arms to grab tasty leaves. Their incredible tails are tipped with a hairless "friction pad" that senses pressure and grips like a finger (it even has fingerprint-like ridges). Other animals, including kinkajous, tree pangolins, and chameleons, use their tails to hang out in high tree branches; baby opossums hang from their tails when they sleep. And it's not just tree dwellers that have these astounding appendages: Seahorses wrap their tails around rocks and corals to anchor themselves in strong currents.

WHY don't spiders get STUCK in their own webs?

Spider webs are wonders of the natural world, fashioned from tough silk woven into complex patterns and often dabbed with droplets of a gooey gluelike substance that helps ensnare their supper. Spiders don't succumb to their own traps for several reasons (and not just because they would die of embarrassment). Not only are spiders master web spinners; they're master web walkers! They instinctively know how to tiptoe across their webs, making contact with just a few strands at a time while stepping at just the right angle on their bristly feet to avoid the glue gobs. Spiders' neat-freak habits also help. They're constantly grooming sticky bits from their legs.

Wide World OF WEBS

Not all spiders spin webs, and not all spiders that spin webs spin the same kinds of web. Web varieties include ...

ORB WEBS are the classic sticky webs spun in tree branches to catch flying insects. ▶

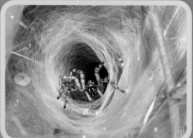

◀ FUNNEL WEBS are thickly woven tubes of silk that narrow at the bottom, where the spider waits for prey that tumbles in from the top. Funnel webs rely on gravity to trap insects and aren't sticky.

COBWEBS are more about quantity rather than quality. They're made from a thick mass of silk anchored by long strings. ▶

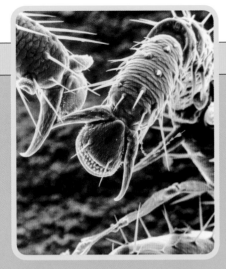

Why don't insects and spiders fall off the wall or ceiling as they crawl around your house?

It's not suction cups that help all sorts of insects and spiders defy gravity as they skitter up walls and across your ceiling. In many cases, the tips of their legs are coated with microscopic hairs that grip tiny bumps and grooves in the wall. These hairs are spread across all six (or in the case of spiders, eight) of their legs, more than enough support for the creature's slight weight. Some insects, including grasshoppers, have sticky help in the form of oily secretions that adhere to smooth surfaces, such as glass and tiles. These super climbers can wander where other bugs cannot.

Why don't mosquitoes just drink water or nectar instead of blood?

They do. Of the more than 3,000 species of mosquito, only about 200 slurp the blood from animals, buzzing from person to person and jabbing them with their needlelike "proboscises." And only the female members of these species drink blood, because it has the protein and iron they need to make their eggs. When they're not making eggs, these mosquitoes drink water and nectar just like the males.

Why don't insects go solo instead of ganging up in colonies and swarms?

There's more than just safety in numbers for colonizing insects such as ants, bees, and wasps—there's smarts in numbers, too. It's on display when individual members of a colony work together to accomplish particularly brainy feats—such as tunneling a new nest or defeating an army of invading insects—that individual members could not. Scientists call this "swarm intelligence," or when a colony of animals works together to form a kind of collective brain. An ant on its own, for instance, is fairly helpless. Even a queen ant isn't any smarter than the other members of the colony (her only job is to lay eggs). But by laying down chemical trails as they travel and reading these trails with their antennae, ants can work together to plot the fastest path to food or summon help to repair a collapsed tunnel.

SILLY QUESTION, SERIOUS ANSWER

Why can't we just exterminate all mosquitoes?

Actually, some scientists don't think that's such a bad idea. Mosquitoes are the world's deadliest animal, responsible for spreading diseases (such as dengue fever and malaria) that kill nearly a million people each year. But scientists aren't sure if doing away with mosquitoes would cause more harm than good. These insects have been slurping the blood of animals since the age of the dinosaurs, becoming a part of the food chain in the process. Mosquitoes make a tasty snack for all sorts of life-forms—bats, birds, fish, frogs, lizards, and even some plants. Removing mosquitoes would knock some ecosystems out of balance. Fish that feed on mosquito larvae would starve, and animals that eat those fish would soon begin to get hungry, too. An absence of mosquitoes would send shock waves up the food chain, all the way to us humans at the top. Researchers in Florida found that wiping out one species of mosquito in a region only opened the door for a species known for transmitting more dangerous diseases. So maybe it's best to not mess with Mother Nature.

SAY WHAT?!

INSECTS AREN'T THE ONLY ANIMALS THAT LIVE IN COLONIES.
A bucktoothed burrowing rodent called the naked mole rat lives in close-knit colonies beneath the sun-baked grasslands of East Africa. Like ants, the rats take on the jobs of worker drones and soldiers, all charged with serving their queen. Unlike an ant queen, however, a mole rat queen is a royal terror, spending her days bullying the other females. A chemical in the queen's pee prevents the other rats from reproducing and usurping her role as mama mole.

WHY can't FISH

breathe on land and breathe underwater?

HUMANS

Like you, most animals that live on land—and a few (including reptiles and marine mammals such as dolphins and manatees) that live in the water—have lungs: a pair of balloon-like organs in their chests. Each is filled with microscopic air sacs that absorb oxygen into your bloodstream with every breath. But lungs only work when filled with air, which is why alligators, sea turtles, whales, and seals must all swim to the surface to suck in a breath. Amphibians in their early stages of development and aquatic animals such as fish, on the other hand, have gills—special organs located behind their mouths. As water passes over them, gills filter oxygen from the water directly into the fish's bloodstream. Gills only work in the water. So unless you spontaneously grow a pair of gills (which by some estimates would need to be 16 feet [5 m] long to provide enough oxygen to your warm-blooded body), you're stuck on dry land with the rest of your mammal friends.

SAY WHAT?!

ONE WAY MANATEES CONTROL THEIR POSITION UNDERWATER IS BY CHANNELING FLATULENCE THROUGH THEIR DIGESTIVE SYSTEM. When they want to dive deeper, they'll even pass gas!

HOW LONG animals CAN HOLD IT

Why can't humans hold their breath underwater like whales, dolphins, alligators, and other record breath holders?

Imagine being able to hold your breath for the length of an entire movie—while you're also munching on popcorn and leaping out of your seat during the scary parts. For sperm whales, such an astounding feat is part of their daily lives. They routinely dive to hunt giant squids in sunless depths two miles (3.2 km) underwater for up to 90 minutes on a single breath. What's their secret? When animals (including you) hold their breath, it's not like their bodies suddenly stop needing oxygen. But marine animals have evolved to make the most of the oxygen stored in their lungs and tissues. When they go deep, breath-holding animals slow their heart rates and maximize blood flow to their brains, hearts, and muscles while restricting blood to the less crucial body parts. And all aquatic breath holders have more of a special protein in their muscles and other tissues called myoglobin. You have it in your body—it's what makes your tissues red—but diving animals have so much more that their tissues are actually black. Myoglobin binds with oxygen, storing it in the tissue for later use. All that extra myoglobin in a diving animal's body acts as a natural scuba tank, locking in air for the tissues to use during deep dives.

SEA TURTLES	4 HOURS (WHEN RESTING)
ELEPHANT SEALS	2 HOURS
SPERM WHALES	90 MINUTES
CROCODILES	1 HOUR
EMPEROR PENGUINS	20 MINUTES
DOLPHINS	15 MINUTES
HUMANS	22 MINUTES (WORLD RECORD SET BY GERMAN FREE DIVER TOM SIETAS)

PERSON OF INTEREST

WHO?
Sylvia Earle

WHAT is she famous for?
Uncovering the mysteries of the deep

WHEN?
Present day

WHERE?
The world's oceans

WHY is she important?
After logging more than 7,000 hours exploring beneath the ocean's waves, this American marine biologist has discovered thousands of species and walked in places where no one has dared to tread. (Earle set a record for the deepest hike when she strolled 1,250 feet [381 m] below the surface of the Pacific Ocean.) In 2009, she started a foundation called Mission Blue to designate protected parts of the ocean similar to national parks on land. She has become an ambassador to the seas, earning the nickname "Her Deepness."

Why can't I breathe underwater through a long snorkel like elephants can with their trunks?

Anyone who has snorkeled knows it's a fun way to peek underwater while breathing comfortably on the surface. But what if you used a superlong one to dive even deeper? You couldn't take the pressure—the water pressure, that is! When you dive even just a few feet deep, the weight of all that water above you builds fast, creating pressure against anything that contains air. That includes your lungs and your ears (which is why they begin to ache when you dive too deep). If you tried to breathe through a long snorkel, your lungs just wouldn't be strong enough to pull the air from the surface against the water pressure that had built around you. In fact,

trying to breathe from such a snorkel could be dangerous, possibly rupturing the blood vessels in your lungs! But elephants are super snorkelers. They can breathe underwater through their long trunk because their lungs have adapted for breathing against the extreme differences in pressure above and below the water. No other mammal has lungs like theirs.

WHY can't I see a GREAT WHITE SHARK at an aquarium?

The ocean's most fearsome fish does not do well in captivity. The first great white kept in an aquarium, caught in 1955, survived for less than a day. Sea World in the 1980s managed to keep a great white alive for 16 days before it died. California's Monterey Bay Aquarium has had the best luck. In 2004, the aquarium managed to keep a great white in one of its largest exhibits for more than six months before the shark attacked other sharks in the tank with her. The aquarium released the great white back to the wild and has since abandoned plans to exhibit the king of all sharks. These top predators don't dwell well behind glass for many reasons. For starters, they need room to roam. Great whites in the wild have been tracked crossing entire oceans. Cooped up in even the largest aquarium tank, they often injure themselves bouncing off the glass, and they have a hard time moving fast enough to keep water flowing over their gills. Great whites are also aggressive hunters and picky eaters, preferring live prey and warm-blooded seals and sea lions to bits of cold fish. When kept in a tank, these sharks simply refuse to eat.

Why aren't whale sharks whales?

Because they're fish—the largest in the world, actually, growing up to 46 feet (14 m) long. Like all fish, whale sharks have gills for breathing underwater, are cold-blooded, and lay eggs. Whales, on the other hand, are mammals, meaning they breathe with lungs, are warm-blooded, and give birth to live young. But whale sharks and whales do share a few things in common besides their titanic size. Like humpback whales, blue whales, gray whales, and other "baleen whales" (so named for the furry plates that line their massive mouths), whale sharks are filter feeders that feast on pinhead-size creatures called krill.

Why don't jellyfish have brains?

Not only are they brainless: They're boneless, heartless, faceless, and even headless! (Oh, and they also eat and poop through the same hole.) Jellyfish aren't fish at all. They're extremely simple creatures related to corals and anemones, and they don't need brains because they react automatically to the world around them. Instead of a brain, they have a simple network of nerves that detect light and prey. Most jellyfish bob about the ocean waiting for prey to bump into them. Some have tentacles bristling with stingers, called nematocysts, that are like tiny harpoons filled with venom. These harpoons launch by the thousands when a jellyfish's tentacle detects certain chemicals on the surface of its prey (typically fish or shrimp, although human skin will trigger them, too). The harpoons lodge in the skin and inject toxins that damage flesh, shut down the nervous system, and can even stop the heart. The most dangerous jellyfish—the box jellyfish of northern Australia—carries enough venom to kill 60 humans! As with everything else jellyfish do, they launch these deadly stingers without a thought.

Why don't fish drown when they sleep?

The same reason you don't suffocate when you drop off to dreamland. Gills provide oxygen for (most) fish whether they're awake and swimming or dozing and still. But sleep in fish isn't quite the same as sleep in humans and other mammals. Fish enter a trancelike state with their eyes open (most fish lack eyelids) and occasionally flick a fin to keep from drifting away. Some fish tuck into cover, such as coral or rocks, for protection. Sharks either stay on the move while they doze—an underwater version of sleepwalking—or sleep in a strong current because they must keep water moving over their gills to breathe.

FEARSOME THREESOME

Terrors OF THE DEEP

BARRELEYE

DEPTH: 2,000 feet (610 m)

This fish's orblike eyes are deep inside its see-through head. Also known as the "spookfish," the barreleye hovers at inky depths of the Pacific, staring upward through its own skin for the silhouettes of prey.

DEEP-SEA ANGLERFISH

DEPTH: 6,000 feet (1,829 m)

Fish that dwell far below the reach of sunlight have evolved with night-lights powered by their own bodies, a phenomenon called "bioluminescence." Deep-sea anglerfish use a bioluminescent bulb as a lure to draw fish within snapping distance of their jaws.

FANGTOOTH FISH

DEPTH: 16,000 feet (4,877 m)

Among the deepest-dwelling creatures ever discovered by scientists, the fangtooth has the largest teeth—relative to its body size—of any fish. If not for special sockets in the fish's upper jaw, the fangtooth would actually pierce its own brain each time it shut its choppers!

MASHED MYTH

Why CAN'T FISH SWIM BACKWARD?

Although some fish can swim only forward, many sea creatures have evolved with a dizzying array of propulsion options. PUFFERFISH wiggle their fins to thrust in all directions: up, down, forward, and backward. SEA ROBINS stroll across the sea bottom on stiffened "pelvic fins" that step forward and backward. MUDSKIPPERS have stiffened fins that work like stubby legs to launch them in short skips across dry land.

WHY can't I SEE IN THE DARK like a cat?

You might stub your toe on the night-stand on the way to the bathroom at midnight, but your startled cat zooms through the gloom of your bedroom as if it's high noon. What's Miss Whiskers' secret to seeing in the dark? Her eyes have it! You see what you see because of the way your brain interprets visual signals transmitted from your peepers, which are packed with specialized cells and structures that focus the light bouncing off everything in view. Crucial to the process: special "photorecep-tor" cells called rods and cones that line the tissue at the back of each eyeball. Rods process light and shadow; cones detect color. Cats have eight times as many rod cells as humans, and all those rods bestow big bene-fits when it comes to stalking prey. Cats have extraordinary night vision (dusk to them is as clear as day), and they can detect rapid movements (another duty of rod cells) in dim light better than we can.

Why don't I have a super sense of smell like a bloodhound?

Just as we have specialized rod and cone cells in our eyeballs to sense light and color, our noses are packed with about 5.5 million special "olfactory sensors" that detect the molecules of whatever we're smelling—such as a sweet rose or spoiled milk—drifting in the air. Humans have evolved a keen sense of smell to sniff out rotten foods and avoid smelly poisonous plants. But we're far from the champion sniffers. The nose of a bloodhound contains 40 times as many olfactory cells as ours, granting these super pooches a sense of smell that's hundreds of times more powerful. That might seem like a nightmare when you have to take out the smelly trash, but dogs also have a more powerful smell-processing center in their brains to glean a lot more information from odors than we can.

Why don't I have super vision like an eagle?

Imagine sitting in the highest seats of a baseball stadium and seeing the laces on the ball without binoculars! Eagles and other birds of prey have this type of super vision thanks to built-in telephoto lenses in each eye. These lenses are concentrations of cone cells that can focus on objects and animals—such as mice and fish—from hundreds of feet in the air.

Why can't I taste things like a catfish?

When you stick a slice of pepperoni pizza in your mouth, up to 8,000 chemical receptors known as "taste buds" on your tongue interpret the pizza's cheesy, salty flavor and transmit that information to your brain, which makes your mouth water and triggers the start of the digestive process. What if you could taste that pizza just by rubbing it on your arm or your feet or your face? The yellow bullhead catfish, a large catfish that lurks on the muddy bottoms of rivers and lakes, has this strange power. From its whisker-like "barbels" to its tail, the catfish's skin is covered with more than 175,000 taste buds. Having a body that doubles as a tongue might seem gross when you're riding the bus, but catfish need all the sensory input they can get in their murky underwater environment. By "tasting" the world around them, catfish can identify yummy creatures living in the mud or darting around them in the dark.

INSTEAD OF A SWEET TOOTH, THE COMMON HOUSEFLY HAS A SWEET TOE! This winged insect buzzes through the air at five miles an hour (8 km/h) and tastes its food with hairlike receptors on its feet. Flies also spit digestive chemicals on their food to help break it up before chowing down. As if you needed another reason to swat houseflies at your next barbecue.

WHY don't we have WHISKERS like other mammals?

Cats and dogs have whiskers, and so do mice, manatees, chimpanzees, and nearly all other mammals. So why don't we sprout them from our upper lips or above our eyes? Beards and mustaches—which some humans begin growing after puberty—don't count. Like eyelashes and eyebrows, whiskers are a particular type of hair with a specific job, which you can probably guess from their scientific name: vibriassae. Whisker follicles are packed with special sensors that detect vibrations. These detectors help animals scan for obstacles or even changes in the in the breeze (a useful skill for staying upwind while hunting so prey can't catch your scent). Whiskers help cats and rats navigate tight spaces and dogs feel their way through the dark. Human hair follicles have touch sensors too (which is why you feel a tickle when someone brushes the hairs on your arms), but they're not nearly as sensitive as animal whiskers. Scientists aren't sure why humans evolved without whiskers while our close relatives the chimpanzees kept theirs. They suspect we lost the ability to grow whiskers as we evolved with larger brains than other primates, but they're not sure why.

SEEING THINGS

FIVE WAYS animals SENSE THE WORLD

We humans get by fine with our five senses—vision, hearing, smell, touch, and taste—but some animals need a little extra perception to survive and thrive in the wild ...

BATS AND DOLPHINS: ECHOLOCATION

These two mammals live in entirely different environments with one similar characteristic: darkness. (Bats are active at night, while dolphins live in the murky ocean.) Both animals complement their sense of sight with echo-location—by sending out sound waves that bounce off obstacles and prey around them. Dolphins will even eavesdrop on each other's echolocation signal to see—or, rather, hear—any fish or other goodies their friends are scanning. Imagine "hearing" your friend's sandwich!

SHARKS AND PLATYPUSES: ELECTRORECEPTION

The heads of sharks (and rays) and the bills of the oddball platypus are covered with special pores that detect the electrical signals given off by all living things. That means sharks can monitor your heartbeat, muscle movements, and even your brain activity!

PIGEONS AND SEA TURTLES: MAGNETORECEPTION

Ever wondered how migrating animals travel thousands of miles without stopping for directions? Pigeons, sea turtles, whales, and other animals that migrate vast distances can detect Earth's magnetic field to maintain their bearings. It's like they have their own built-in compass and GPS system. Female sea turtles use Earth's magnetic field to find their nesting location: their birthplace, the beaches where they travel to lay their own eggs.

PIT VIPERS: INFRARED VISION

Rattlesnakes, water moccasins, cottonmouths, and other venomous so-called pit vipers didn't earn their name because they live in pits; instead, these serpents possess special heat-sensing organs in pits between their nostrils and eyes. The organs detect even the slightest rise in temperature against the background, giving these snakes extra help when hunting at night.

EAGLES AND CHICKENS: ULTRAVIOLET VISION

Eagles and other birds such as chickens have a fourth type of photo-receptor in their eyes that humans lack, enabling them to see colors—including vibrantly purple ultraviolet colors—that you can't. Researchers think birds developed their exceptional color perception and motion-detection vision for hunting in broad daylight.

WHY can't I have one of these COOL CREATURES as a pet?

Kitties and pooches are cuddly and cute, but they're not exactly the wildest pets in the world. The United States alone is home to nearly 180 million cats and dogs, more than half as many pets as there are people who own them. But if you think it would be more fun to have an exotic animal as a pal, think again. There's a reason they don't say pandas are people's best friend ...

Why can't I have a pet koala?

Because they're scarier than they look! A koala snoozing in the crook of a tree might look like a stuffed animal, but you'd be sorry if you tried to cuddle with one of these beloved marsupials of the Australian bush. Their long, sharp claws—supremely adapted for climbing trees—are used as daggers when two male koalas argue over territory or a mate. Squabbling koalas will scratch each other's ears to ribbons. "They're quite ferocious," says Deborah Tabart, head of the Australian Koala Foundation. "Even when you're cuddling them, it hurts when they dig their claws into your back." Male koalas also grunt loudly—a sound sort of like a burp combined with a sneeze—to impress faraway females. Did we mention they're active mostly at night?

Why can't I have a pet sloth?

Because they're power poopers! These so-ugly-they're-cute tree-climbing natives of the South and Central American rain forests live their lives like they're on permanent vacation, sleeping 20 hours a day and creeping so slowly that some sloths actually grow moss on their backs. Their diet—which consists of leaves, flowers, and bits of fruit—is to blame for their slow-motion lifestyle. After all, imagine how sluggish you'd be if all you ate was salad greens but had to climb to every room in your house! But what goes in must come out. Sloths will store a week's worth of doo-doo in their bowels before finally climbing to the ground and unloading a fifth of their weight in feces.

Why can't I have a pet snowy owl?

Because they're illegal to own! If you can't cast levitation spells or attend a school of witchcraft and wizardry like Harry Potter, the least you can do is own a pet snowy owl like the boy wizard, right? Wrong. For starters, keeping an owl as a pet is illegal in the United States unless you have a special permit. But you probably wouldn't want one anyway for a variety of reasons, and not just because—unlike Harry Potter's pet, Hedwig—these owls would probably fetch you something other than the mail. Ferocious night hunters, snowy owls need lots of airspace to stalk prey, and they crave live critters such as mice, moles, and small rodents known as lemmings. They also have a habit of stashing part of their kill for later snacking. Do you really want to dig out a half-chewed lemming from behind your couch?

Why can't I have a pet giant panda?

Because you'd cause an international incident! These bamboo-munching members of the bear family are one of the world's most elusive animals. Only around 2,000 live in the foggy forests of China's mountains. And save for a couple of exceptions, all captive pandas in zoos around the world are considered the legal property of China, lent out for just a limited time. Even if you did manage to secure your own panda, you'd never keep up with its appetite. Bamboo accounts for 99 percent of their diet; each bear spends as much as 16 hours a day devouring nearly 40 pounds (18 kg) of it, gripping the leafy stalks with a thumb-like wrist pad. And though they might look cuddly, pandas are just as powerful and unpredictable as any other member of the bear family.

OK, then: Why can't I have a pet red panda, instead?

Because they'll mark your territory! From the tufts of its fuzzy white ears to its red-ringed tail, a red panda is roughly 12 pounds (5 kg) of concentrated cuteness. But despite sharing the same "panda" name and habitat, red pandas and giant pandas aren't related. Giant pandas are part of the bear family, whereas many scientists link red pandas to the critter cluster that includes raccoons. Like pandas, red pandas are built for the cold and eat up to 30 percent of their body weight each day in bamboo. Like raccoons, they're feisty creatures with sharp claws that will tear up your furniture. Red pandas also need a lot of room to roam— roughly two square miles (5 sq km) of forest. They mark their territory with pee and other secretions that would stink up your house!

WHY don't dogs TALK like humans?

You may have trained Rover to "speak" on command, but there's a big difference between teaching your pup to bark and carrying on a meaningful conversation. Dogs are clever mammals, capable of understanding hundreds of human words and learning how to do all sorts of important jobs, from sniffing out lost hikers to helping people with disabilities. Pooches and people go way back—as far as 30,000 years ago, when humans began tossing morsels to wolves (your pups' ancestors) in return for protection and help with hunting. As a result, dogs are hardwired to be your best friend. Your dog just gets you. But dogs can't carry on a conversation for a variety of reasons. They lack the vocal plumbing to produce human speech, which requires fine control over the lips and tongue to form sounds we recognize as words. Sure, you may have seen online videos of dogs woofing out phrases like "heh-roh" and "I ruv roo," but those are the closest pooches can get to copying human talking.

Do dogs even have a language?

Not like ours. Humans (and a few other hyperintelligent animals, such as dolphins) communicate using a learned language instead of the instinctive barks, yips, grunts, shrieks, and other sounds that most animals are born using. When those clever pups online bark out "heh-roh," they have no idea what those phrases mean. The dogs are really just copycats! They've learned through patient training that these sounds please their owners, who repeat the sounds to their dogs and give them treats when the dogs get the sound right. It's similar to how other animals—such as parrots, elephants, and beluga whales—learn to mimic human speech. But none of these animals is actually talking to us (see sidebar). Human language is incredibly complex, filled with concepts such as nouns, verbs, and past and present tenses. Despite being our best animal buddies and longtime companions, dogs can't grasp these complicated language concepts. But that doesn't mean they don't "ruv roo."

So how do dogs talk to other dogs?

Just because dogs can't talk with us doesn't mean they can't communicate with each other. Dogs are pack animals, descended from wolves, and like wolves they live in a three-dimensional realm of smells. A dog's body is covered with glands that secrete all kinds of interesting odors. Using urine or the pads of their paws, dogs will mark their territory and transmit info about their identity, including age, sex, social status, and much more. So when dogs sniff each other's stinky parts, they're really just getting to know one another.

Mimicking VS. TALKING

THOUGH MANY CLEVER ANIMALS can mimic human speech, for the most part they're just copying our sounds when they do; they don't actually know the meaning of what they're saying. (A clever captive African gray parrot named Alex learned to repeat the words for up to 50 objects and could even count and describe them using simple adjectives.) Scientists think some animals have developed their own language: Dolphins talk using learned "words" spoken in high-speed clicks, and elephants communicate in low-frequency rumbles that humans can't even hear. We've yet to decode these mysterious languages.

POOCH POSTURE

HOW TO READ YOUR dog's mood

Everyone knows that happy dogs wag their tails, but did you know part of the reason behind that wag is to fan scents that other pooches appreciate? Just like their wolf ancestors, dogs rely on both body language and smells to communicate with members of their pack. If you have a dog, you're a member of your pooch's pack! But because you can't make heads or tails of your dog's scents, you can at least make sense of your dog's head and tail with this guide to common pup postures ...

I'M ALERT!

A dog ready for action stands with his head and tail held high and his ears pointed slightly forward. Follow your pup's gaze and you'll see what's got them excited (probably a squirrel or the neighbor's cat).

YOU'RE THE BOSS!

Sloppy posture is the highest form of respect in the dog world. Subordinate dogs crouch and tuck their tails. Sometimes they'll slink to the ground and go belly up, displaying their vulnerable tummies as a sign of surrender.

I'M IN A BAD MOOD!

Ticked-off dogs are easy to recognize. Their furrowed forehead, bared fangs, and tense body posture send a clear message: "Back off!"

I'M CHILL!

Calm pups stand with their tail hanging normally (not drooping), their heads and ears up, and their legs in a relax stance.

LET'S PLAY!

Dogs let you know they're ready to play by sticking their chests to the ground and their rumps in the air. What are you waiting for? Throw the ball!

WHY don't cats and dogs GET ALONG?

It's a rivalry that has been raging for millions of years, long before humans were around to see it. About 20 million years ago in North America, many species of the Canidae family—better known as dogs—suddenly went extinct. Scientists think it's no coincidence that species of felids—aka cats—exploded in variety and population around the same time. In fact, scientists suspect early cats and dogs competed for food and that the cats won. But that was just the first round in a scuffle that's lasted ever since. Dogs got a paw up when they began palling around with humans as far back as 30,000 years; cats, by contrast, have lived with us only for the past 8,000 years or so. Tales of dogs and cats fighting like, well, cats and dogs began appearing in folklore not much later.

So **why can't** our two favorite pets play nice?

It's not that they're on each other's menu. In the wild, coyotes skulking near cities might snack on the occasional stray cat while lions will munch on African wild dogs, but they're just doing what all meat-eating hunters do. (Wolves also eat rabbits and lions eat gazelles, but you never hear anyone describe two enemies fighting "like wolves and rabbits.") The real source of conflict in the cat-and-dog relationship is us, not them. Humans domesticated both cats and dogs, forcing them to share our homes, interact with each other, and compete for our scraps and belly rubs. Cats are solitary animals, while domestic dogs evolved from wolves—pack animals that like to socialize with one another. Think of dogs as the party crashers of the animal kingdom: They tend to bound right up to new people or pets to check them out. Cats, on the other hand, would rather not make a scene. They'll interpret a charging pooch as a threat and break out their claws, or they'll turn tail and flee. Either a fight breaks out or the dog gives chase, replaying a rivalry that's endured since ancient times.

 **How** TO MAKE CATS AND DOGS PLAY NICE

You've seen videos of it online, or maybe even witnessed it in real life: dogs and cats playing together, sharing a lap—sometimes even cuddling! Yes, cats and dogs can set aside their evolutionary differences and coexist peacefully in the same home. Here's how pet experts say you can make it happen ...

Separate the pets

Start by keeping your quarreling pets in separate rooms for a few days so they can get used to each other's smell. (Remember, cats and dogs live in a world of scents.)

Prep your pooch

Make sure your dog obeys commands such as "heel" and "sit" so you can keep him or her under control at all times.

Rein in Fido

Keep your dog on a short leash—literally—when you decide to introduce both animals in the same room. The cat won't run up to the dog, but you need to restrain your dog's natural instinct to charge into an encounter.

Treat them to treats

Make sure to reward both your dog and cat for keeping their cool. Give them treats and belly rubs for acting friendly around their ancestral enemy.

Go slow

Just as with people, first impressions are important with cats and dogs. A scrap on day one will mark the start of a rocky relationship. There's no need to rush introductions until both animals are calm around each other.

Why can't
dogs eat chocolate?

Resist those puppy-dog eyes when your pooch begs for a handout. Many foods people eat—including nuts, cheeses, and avocados—can make Fido sick. And chocolate is the worst! It contains a substance called theobromine that in humans puts a pep in our step. Unfortunately, it can send pups to the vet. Dogs don't have the ability to digest theobromine properly. Too much of it can cause trouble breathing, pain, seizures, and even death. Darker chocolates pack more theobromine than normal chocolate, but even a little—like the chips in a cookie—is bad for little dogs. Big dogs can handle more, but really you should keep all chocolate far out of reach. If Spot accidentally eats some (especially if Spot is a small dog), you should take him to the vet.

Can my cat snack on chocolate?

Just like with dogs, chocolate is dangerous for cats, but chances are Mr. Whiskers won't munch on chocolate unless you cram it in his face. Take pity on your kitty: Cats can't taste sweets! Although humans, dogs, and many other mammals have evolved to crave the sweet taste of energy-giving carbohydrates, finicky cats (including big cats such as lions and tigers) only seek the salty flavor of meat, their primary food.

PUPS VS. KITTIES:
Which Pet Is Supreme?

Eyesight

Dogs are color-blind like cats and suffer from the same nearsightedness as cats (although dogs are better at spotting motion at a distance and have a wider field of view). Still, cats are champs at seeing—and hunting—in the dark.

WINNER: CATS!

Sense of smell

A dog's nose contains about 220 million scent cells, at least twice as many as cats. Bloodhound dogs have been specially bred and trained to find and follow a scent trail to the end, even if the trail is nearly two weeks old and stretches for more than 130 miles (209 km)!

WINNER: DOGS!

Hearing

Cats and dogs can detect sounds that we can't, in part because they aim their pointy ears like satellite dishes to capture fainter noises from farther away. But they're also physically capable of detecting sounds outside the normal range of human hearing. Dogs can hear sounds up to twice as high-pitched as we can, but cats can actually hear sounds up to three times higher-pitched! They use this super hearing to zero in on the squeaks and scampering feet of their rodent prey.

WINNER: CATS!

Agility

Cats can use their sharp retractable claws and superior balancing skills to go where dogs can't, such as high into trees or along the tops of fences. Cats even have a "righting reflex," the ability to spin in midair and land on their paws no matter which way they fall.

WINNER: CATS!

Cleanliness

Dogs have a nasty habit of rolling in repulsive piles of leaves, poop, and even roadkill—often right after their weekly bath (to erase the smell of shampoo, which dogs don't like). Cats, meanwhile, groom themselves throughout the day using their sandpapery tongues to comb food and dirt from their fur (which they sometimes hack up in icky hairballs). Cats are also courteous enough to bury their poop in the litter box or your backyard, a habit they picked up in the wild to hide odors from predators or show respect to more dominant animals (that would be you). Dogs just let it sit until you scoop their poop.

WINNER: CATS!

Smarts

Sorry, cat people. Research shows that mutts edge out kitties when it comes to overall smarts. Pooches have bigger brains, can learn to understand hundreds of human words, and can be trained for all sorts of important jobs. Teaching tricks to cats is tougher, although felines are experts at manipulating their masters with one perfectly pitched meow. Researchers believe that dogs are brainier because they were domesticated sooner and evolved alongside humans and are social animals (which tend to be smarter).

WINNER: DOGS!

Comfort CREATURES

ALTHOUGH DOGS AND CATS are from two different families—the Canidae and Felidae families, respectively—they're not so different from each other. Both mammals are carnivores, meaning they eat meat (which they hunt for in the wild). Instead of sweating through their fur-covered skin, both animals cool off by panting through their mouths. And they've both been companions to humans for thousands of years. Studies show that people with either pet tend to have healthier hearts and lower blood pressure. Whether you're a dog person or a cat person—or both—your furry friends might give you a little extra life.

OUR **PLANET**

EARTH IS A SPECIAL SPOT IN THE UNIVERSE FOR SO MANY REASONS: its sprawling continents and seas, its mind-blowing variety of life-forms, its staggering selection of ice-cream toppings. And though we Earthlings have explored, studied, and mapped the world for thousands of years, we still know more about the surface of the moon than certain parts of our own planet. Prepare to solve our world's mysteries—and unearth many more—as we explore exactly what makes our big ball of soggy rock go 'round.

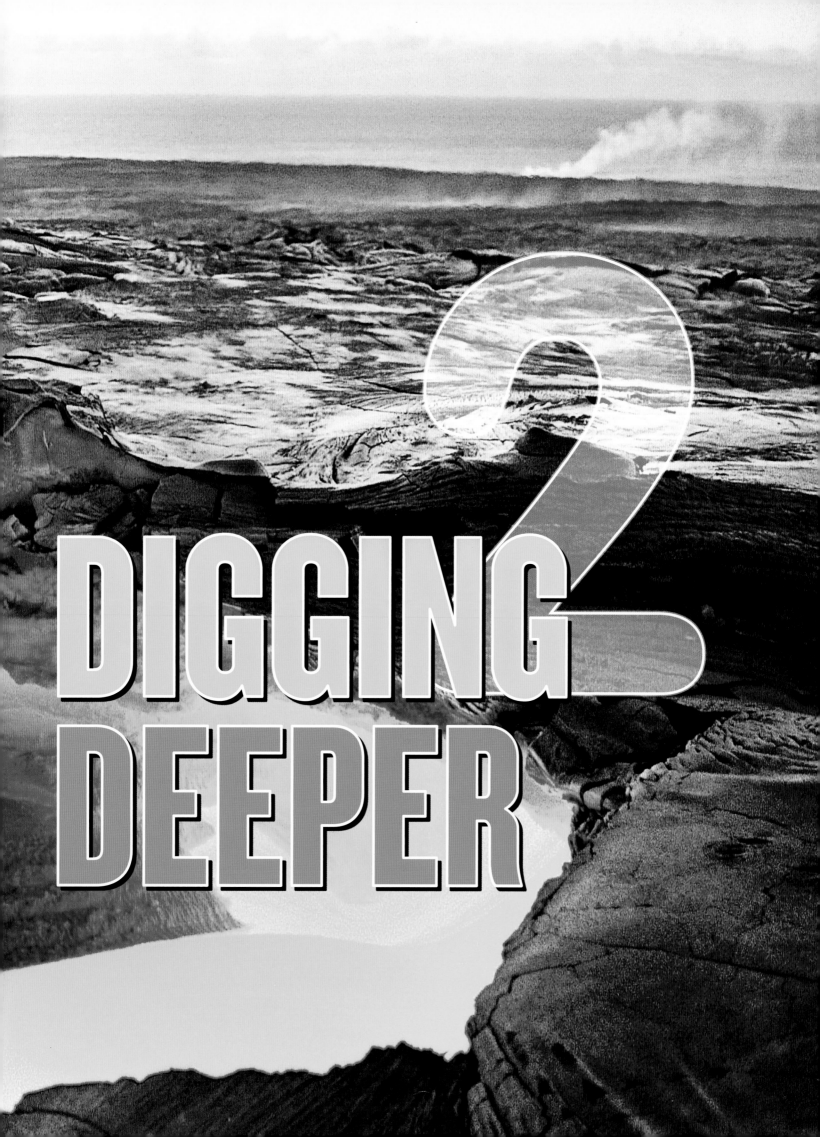

DIGGING DEEPER

2

WHY can't I walk on THE CLOUDS?

Sorry, wannabe skywalkers: You can't stroll on a cloud any more than you can trip over a fog bank. Both clouds and fog are made of the same stuff—itty-bitty drops of water or ice that "condense" out of wet air as it cools. Neither is substantial enough to support even a hair from your head against the relentless pull of gravity, that force of attraction generated by every object in the universe—even a grain of sand or this book in your hands. You can't see gravity's effects on a small scale, but the larger an object and the more matter it contains (its "mass"), the greater its gravitational tug. The Earth is a really, really big object—composed of rocks and metals you'll learn about in this chapter—so the effects of its gravitational field are obvious. It's why up is up, down is down, and you can't walk on your ceiling unless you've been bitten by a radioactive spider. Earth's gravity pulls us and everything around us, including the air we breathe, toward the planet's core.

Why isn't the Earth flat?

Our world isn't shaped like a pizza—or a giant cube or a skinny tube—because of that same force that keeps your sneakers from achieving liftoff. Gravity is what gave Earth (and all known planets in the universe) its shape when our world formed from a swirling cloud of dust and rocks roughly 4.6 billion years ago. Gravity clumped all that space stuff together into a shape that isn't perfectly round (it's actually called an oblate spheroid) but is anything but flat. In fact, a flat, pizza-shaped planet would crumble under its own gravity into a round shape—er, an oblate spheroid—just like Earth.

How CAN WE TELL THE EARTH IS DEFINITELY NOT FLAT?

➔ Circumnavigation: People have flown, sailed, and even walked (with the help of planes and boats) around the world.
➔ Sinking ships: Watch a ship travel over the horizon and you'll see it disappear from the hull up as your view is obstructed by the curvature of the planet.
➔ Height advantage: The higher you climb, the less of the planet's surface blocks your view and the farther you can see.
➔ Moon shadows: During lunar eclipses, when Earth briefly blocks the sun's rays from hitting the moon, our planet's shadow on the moon is curved.
➔ Stargazing: We can see that the moon, the sun, and other planets in our solar system are round, which would imply that our world is also round.
➔ Seeing is believing: We've snapped pictures of Earth from space. (Yeah—it's definitely not flat.)

MYTH MASHED

Why DID PEOPLE THINK THE WORLD WAS FLAT UNTIL COLUMBUS SET SAIL?

Give the people of the past some credit. It was widely accepted that the world was round when explorer Christopher Columbus sailed his fleet over the horizon in 1492. Humans have actually known Earth was round for more than 2,000 years! A Greek mathematician named Eratosthenes even managed to calculate the distance around the planet by measuring the angle of the sun's shadows in two distant places and factoring in the distance between those locations. He made this surprisingly accurate calculation some 1,700 years before Columbus was born.

But what if the Earth were flat?

Even if the laws of physics allowed such a world to exist, life on the surface of a flat Earth would be best described with one word: wacky. Because a disklike world is denser at its middle and less so toward its rim, such a world's gravity would tug everything—including the atmosphere and the oceans—toward the center. The seas would puddle in the middle like a titanic raindrop. Hiking to the outer rim of the disk would feel like traveling up a hill that grows steeper as you near the edge, until you're hanging from the rim with your fingertips—even though the landscape looks flat. See? Wacky.

SAY WHAT?!

DESPITE ALL THE EVIDENCE TO THE CONTRARY, thousands of die-hard science deniers insist our planet is shaped more like a pancake than a basketball. These members of the "Flat Earth Society" have concocted all sorts of theories to explain a world that isn't round. The sun and moon, they say, are actually artificial light sources whirling through the sky to create the illusion of a spherical, spinning planet, and NASA's space missions were all faked on elaborate movie sets.

WHY doesn't the SUN RISE in the west and set in the east?

It has been happening like clockwork since the Earth formed its surface some 4.6 billion years ago. Each morning, the sun rises in the east. Every evening, it sets in the west. All heavenly objects—the moon, the planets, stars, and comets—follow the same east-to-west track across the sky. Of course, it's not these objects that are rocketing over our heads each day. Earth itself is rotating on its axis—one full rotation every 23 hours and 56 minutes—and that spin makes heavenly bodies appear to rise in the east and set in the west to us Earthlings on the ground. Earth and all its neighboring planets spin because they've always spun, ever since they grew from whirlpools of gas and dust billions of years ago. Those whirlpools spun faster and faster as they collapsed under their own gravity to form the planets. With no force to counteract their spinning motion, they retained their rotation from the very beginning.

Earth rotates once every 23 hours and 56 minutes? I thought a day was 24 hours?

Well, it is and it isn't. It takes 23 hours and 56 minutes for Earth to complete one full rotation, which scientists call a "sidereal day." But as our world turns, it is also orbiting the sun, one full trip around each year. Because of Earth's constant orbital motion, it takes about four additional minutes each day for the sun to return to its original position in the sky, for a total of 24 hours. Scientists call this a "solar day," but you can just keep calling it a "day" unless you want to get funny looks.

SPIN ZONE

SIDE EFFECTS OF
our planet's ROTATION

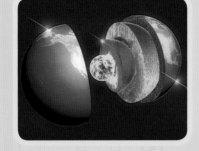

TIME ZONES

The worldwide system of 24 time zones—one for each hour of the day—was created to adjust local time based on Earth's rotation.

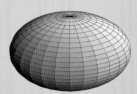

FUNKY IN THE MIDDLE

The planet's rotation gives it a slight bulge around the middle, which is why scientists call Earth an "oblate spheroid."

HIGH TIDES/LOW TIDES

You'll learn elsewhere how the moon's gravitational pull creates a bulge in the oceans on two sides of the planet. Earth rotates beneath these bulges, which creates a high and low tide each day.

FORCE FIELD

Earth's spin interacts with the planet's metal core to create a magnetic field that shields us from solar radiation and all but the strongest storms of charged particles thrown out by the sun. Without this natural force field, we Earthlings would be at greater risk from skin cancers and other life-ruining radiation hazards.

WHIRLED WINDS

The spinning motion of the Earth transfers into a force—known as the Coriolis effect—that affects the oceans and wind patterns. It's why hurricanes spin and ocean currents swirl in massive whirlpools known as gyres.

PLAY BALL

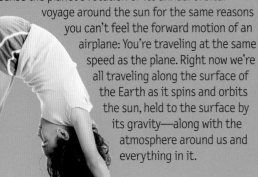

The Coriolis force can even affect sports—although rarely in a way that makes a difference. In American football, Earth's spin can "deflect" a field goal kicked north from the 50-yard line by nearly half an inch to the east. Physicist Neil deGrasse Tyson credited the Coriolis effect with helping the Cincinnati Bengals score a game-winning field goal in 2015.

SAY WHAT?!

A DAY ON EARTH DIDN'T ALWAYS LAST 24 HOURS.

During its earliest formation, the Earth spun once every six to eight hours. Over billions of years, the "tidal pull" of the moon slowed Earth's rotation to its present rate.

Why can't
I feel the Earth moving?

You can tell the Earth is rotating just by watching heavenly bodies move across the sky, but plop on the couch and it sure feels like you're going nowhere. You can't sense the planet's rotation or its annual orbital voyage around the sun for the same reasons you can't feel the forward motion of an airplane: You're traveling at the same speed as the plane. Right now we're all traveling along the surface of the Earth as it spins and orbits the sun, held to the surface by its gravity—along with the atmosphere around us and everything in it.

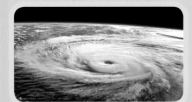

WHY isn't the Earth covered with WATER?

We shouldn't take our dry land for granted. Compared with the overall surface of the Earth, land is actually in short supply! A little more than 70 percent of the planet is covered with water, most of that (97 percent) in the form of salty oceans. But Earth wasn't always this wet. In fact, the planet's surface was once home to a much different kind of sea—a sea of boiling lava! It seethed atop a fireball of asteroids, comets, and other space debris that had clumped into a gooey lump during the Earth's birth nearly 4.6 billion years ago. As the surface cooled and hardened, it formed a rocky crust that split into titanic slabs of rock called tectonic plates (more on those in a bit). Underneath, Earth's interior retained the intense heat of its broiling birth.

So **where** did the oceans come from?

Those comets and asteroids that had formed the Earth's insides were soggy with water, which boiled to the surface and "degassed" into the atmosphere, while icy comets fell from space to deliver even more water. But all this H_2O remained a steamy vapor until atmospheric temperatures finally cooled below water's boiling point about 3.8 billion years ago. Steam turned to rain, which poured and poured and poured in a storm that lasted for centuries. All that rain collected in a shallow ocean that spanned the planet. Much later, tectonic plates began to form "continental crust," which was thicker and therefore higher up than the lower-lying "oceanic crust," where the oceans pooled. Landmasses were born. Life-forms that had evolved in the ocean suddenly had a new realm to conquer.

Why can't we remove the salt from the ocean?

"Water, water everywhere," goes the line from a famous poem about a sailor stranded at sea, "nor any drop to drink." The oceans are far too salty to wet a human's whistle. Roughly 3.5 percent of the weight in seawater comes from salt, and all that sea salt is actually from land. Rain erodes rocks and soil when it splashes against the ground, creating salty sodium and chloride ions that follow streams and rivers into the ocean. All those ions add up. Remove the salt from the ocean and you would create a layer 500 feet (152 m) deep across the entire land surface of Earth. But there's nothing stopping us from removing the salt from parts of the ocean. More than 13,000 "desalination" plants are operating around the world, mostly in places where freshwater is scarce. They use special filters or massive boilers to separate salt from seawater, creating freshwater for drinking and agriculture. But these plants require an enormous amount of energy to operate, and the costs of desalinating the seas extend well beyond a big electric bill. Removing too much ocean salt would upset delicate ecological balances for the plants and algae in the ocean, which produce half of the oxygen we breathe, and absorb nearly one-third of the carbon dioxide that is causing a gradual heating of the planet.

Why isn't the ocean clear and blue everywhere?

You might think it's pollution—or maybe something just as nasty like whale poop—that turns some seas brownish gray or sickly green like pea soup, as opposed to the see-through blue of famously beautiful bodies of water such as the Caribbean Sea or the beaches around Hawaii, U.S.A. But the ocean's mud-puddle-like appearance in many places is not only natural—it's essential to sustaining life in the sea. As the Earth rotates, it sloshes some parts of the oceans from the west to east, churning up nutrients and sediments from the ocean's depths in a process known as upwelling. These nutrients include algae and tiny organisms called zooplankton that form the foundation of the ocean's food chain. Calmer seas such as the Caribbean have coral reefs and landmasses that block the upwelling process. They remain crystal clear but actually contain fewer nutrients, making them a paradise for snorkelers and scuba divers but hardly a buffet for marine life that must migrate to richer waters.

WATER POWER

HOW H₂O shapes THE WORLD…

If you want to see the mightiest earth-moving machine on Earth, just turn on your faucet. It's water! Given enough time, water in the form of rains, rivers, and seas can erode the landscape in amazing ways …

CANYONS

Like all "slot canyons," Antelope Canyon in Arizona, U.S.A., was carved out of sandstone by raging torrents of rainwater over millions of years, and the process continues today. But it's just a line in the sand compared with the Grand Canyon, carved by the Colorado River through 277 miles (446 km) of Arizona, U.S.A., and up to a mile (1.6 km) deep in places.

CAVES

Water seeping through rocks causes a chemical reaction that eats away at the minerals, creating underground cavities known as caves. Combined with the surging power of rivers, this process can open up otherworldly under-worlds. A fast-moving river flowing beneath a mountain in Vietnam carved the world's largest cave—Hang Son Doong—so big it has its own jungle and climate system.

COASTS

The land and the sea are locked in a constant battle—and the land is literally losing ground. Waves pounding against a coastline nibble away at its features. Rocks form cracks that fill with water and expand. Cliffs crumble slowly over time. Hurricanes and other larges storms accelerate the process. The daily cycle of high and low tides spares many beaches—unless they've been stripped of their "sea oats" and other vegetation that helps lock dunes in place.

WHY haven't we COLONIZED the bottom of the ocean?

Imagine peeking at corals swaying in the current outside your bedroom porthole each morning and spying a school of parrotfish on your submarine ride to school. There's no reason why humans couldn't start colonizing the ocean floor—at least some of it—in real life. Such underwater habitats already exist—although on a small scale, in the Florida Keys, U.S.A., and a few other places around the world. The most famous is called the Aquarius Reef Base, a tube-shaped laboratory resting 60 feet (18.3 m) deep atop a wall of coral about 5.5 miles (8.9 km) off Key Largo. Aquarius is hardly a teeming underwater metropolis—it's only about the size of a school bus and can accommodate no more than six people at a time—but here "aquanaut" scientists live for weeks as they study the undersea environment. Air, electricity, and Internet are supplied by a buoy that bobs on the surface above. A series of Aquarius modules could be linked together to form an underwater neighborhood, town, or even a full city. British futurist Philip Pauley has even designed a self-sufficient underwater city (called the Sub-Biosphere) built of connected domes that could house up to a hundred people. Permanent aquanauts could raise crops, which would in turn generate breathable air in each dome.

So **why** are we still living high and dry?

There's just not enough demand to live with the fishes—at least not on a large enough scale. But living underwater comes with extra challenges we don't face on the surface, making it expensive and inconvenient. Habitats need to be thick-hulled and pumped with air to withstand the crushing pressure of all that water above them. Returning to the surface requires hours of "decompression" time to safely rid the body of any dangerous gases that build up in a pressurized environment. Cities built within 60 feet (18.3 m) or so from the surface wouldn't have to worry too much about these problems, but going deeper would require extra precautions and many inconveniences. Unfortunately for undersea builders, the average depth of the ocean is 12,100 feet (3.7 km), where sunlight is a distant memory and the extreme pressure would crush a typical submarine like a soda can.

Two Dangers
OF DEEP LIVING

THE BENDS

Anyone who breathes compressed air below 130 feet (40 m) risks a lethal buildup of nitrogen bubbles in their tissues. These bubbles will expand and cause a painful—potentially deadly—condition known as the bends if a person returns to the surface without making lengthy decompression stops. In other words, returning to the surface after living in the deep isn't as simple as a quick trip to the store.

RAPTURE

Breathing compressed air at extreme depths can cause a disorienting condition known as the "rapture of the deep," which makes it more difficult to think clearly and avoid unnecessary risks. Good decision-making abilities are kind of important when you live deep below the ocean's surface, where small mishaps can turn into major emergencies.

GOING DEEP
three UNDERSEA HABITATS

THE UNDERWATER ROOM PEMBA ISLAND, ZANZIBAR

DEPTH: About 10 feet (3 m)

Aquanauts who just want to dip their toes into the undersea-living experience can spend the night in this deluxe room at Zanzibar's Manta Resort. It's essentially a houseboat with a "basement": a bedroom below the waves. Large windows provide a 360-degree view of the coral heads and their colorful residents. At night, underwater lights switch on to attract squids, sharks, and other creatures as the gentle waves rock residents to sleep.

JULES' UNDERSEA LODGE KEY LARGO, FLORIDA, U.S.A.

DEPTH: 30 feet (9 m)

Once a research laboratory, this habitat has been converted into a secret underwater clubhouse and hotel room complete with a large porthole that overlooks a mangrove habitat teeming with sea life. Guests can stay overnight in comfy bunks for $800—a price that includes the world's only underwater pizza delivery. (Guaranteed fresh, fast, and not soggy—or it's free!)

AQUARIUS REEF BASE KEY LARGO, FLORIDA, U.S.A.

DEPTH: 60 feet (18.3 m)

Scientists must don scuba gear to reach the front door (actually, an open pool called a wet porch at the bottom of the habitat) to enter this underwater laboratory off the Florida coast. Once inside, they have all the comforts of home—movies! Internet! breathable air!—as they study the nearby reef ecosystem while conducting experiments about life underwater. Visiting astronauts sometimes mingle with the aquanauts to practice living in a tight, closed environment similar to a spaceship.

WHY can't I walk all the way around THE WORLD?

When American Steve Newman returned to his family's porch in Ohio, U.S.A., in April 1983, he had become the first person to walk by himself around the planet, strolling through 20 countries and racking up roughly 21,000 miles (33,796 km) during a four-year hike. Of course, when he hit the Atlantic and Pacific coasts, he had to stow his hiking shoes and hop aboard a ship for the trip to the next continent. If he had started his walk 260 million years ago, though, Newman could have strolled across the world's major landmasses without ever getting wet. Remember, Earth's surface is divided like a jigsaw puzzle into titanic tectonic plates. Composed of continental crust and oceanic crust and the upper bit of the next layer down known as the mantle (collectively known as the lithosphere), these plates float on a sea of hot melted rock and metals. They're always slowly moving—about as fast as your fingernails grow—a phenomenon known as continental drift. About 260 million years ago, all the plates with landmasses (known as continents) were smashed together into one supercontinent known as Pangaea before starting to break up—a process called rifting—around 220 million years ago into the configurations we see today.

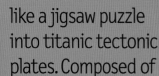

Why don't islands float?

Well, technically they do—along with everything else on the planet's crust—atop molten magma broiling beneath the tectonic plates. But it's reasonable to think islands float in the ocean because they look disconnected from the larger landmasses. Not true. In a sense, islands are like the tips of icebergs: Most of their mass lies hidden below the ocean's surface. But icebergs, even those larger than the U.S. state of Rhode Island, still float. Islands, on the other hand, are outcrops of rocky crust that extend all the way down to the tectonic plate they ride on. Greenland, the world's largest island, is embedded in the same plate as North America. The island chain of Hawaii, U.S.A., is built atop lava erupting from a "hot spot" of undersea volcanoes in the middle of a tectonic plate. If you drained the ocean around Mauna Kea, a volcano that rises 13,680 feet (4,170 m) above the island of Hawaii, U.S.A., you'd find the tallest mountain in the world: higher from base to summit than Mount Everest.

Will I ever be able to walk around the world?

Sure, or at least most of it—and only if you live for another 100 million years. According to one scientific estimate, that's when the American and Asian continents will once again join into a supercontinent called Amasia. You'll want to bundle up: Amasia is projected to form across the North Pole.

WHEN continents COLLIDE (OR DIVIDE) ...

Mountain ranges! Volcanoes! New stretches of seafloor! Grand geographic features form as tectonic plates creep across the globe. Here's how tectonic drift shifts more than just the landmasses on a map ...

MOUNTAINS form when two plates of continental crust collide, compressing the crust at the point of impact and pushing it upward. The Himalayan mountains, for instance, formed from the slow-slow-slow-motion collision of the Indian tectonic plate with the Eurasian plate.

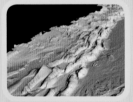

NEW SEAFLOOR FORMS when two plates of oceanic crust drift apart, allowing magma to bubble up from below and harden into new crust. This process happens along mid-ocean ridges, where oceanic crust is the thinnest.

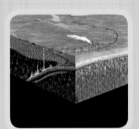

EARTH'S CRUST IS RECYCLED when plates of continental crust collide with oceanic crust, which gets shoved downward to the mantle in a process called subduction. Once it reaches the mantle, oceanic crust melts and returns to the surface as magma in mid-ocean ridges, where it's recycled into new crust.

THE EARTH SHAKES when plates grind against each other, a scary phenomenon you'll read about on the next page ...

WHY can't we predict EARTHQUAKES?

Natural disasters such as hurricanes and floods are easy to track because they form in plain sight. Earthquakes, on the other hand, happen deep underground, most of them 50 miles (80 km) or less below the planet's surface, with no telltale warnings or signals. Remember, Earth's crust—its outermost layer—is divided into titanic slabs of rock called tectonic plates that fit together like jigsaw puzzle pieces and are always on the move. The plates grate against each other along fractures known as faults, gradually releasing pressure with thousands of daily quakes too slight for us to sense. But when that pressure builds over decades or centuries, the plates can slip and release devastating seismic waves that race through rock, sand, and soil like ripples in a pond. This sudden burst of energy is what causes the most powerful quakes, but it happens too quickly and among the "noise" of common quivers for geologists to predict exactly when the next big one will rock the world.

So we have no idea when major earthquakes will strike?

Not quite. Scientists can forecast when earthquakes might happen along a particular fault by noting how long they haven't happened. Remember, earthquakes release the pressure built up between two grinding plates. More time between major quakes means more pressure has built up and that the fault is overdue for some serious slippage. Geologists studying faults can figure out the average number of years between major quakes, then calculate the probability—or chances—of a big one happening over the next few decades. The odds are low, for instance, of a major quake striking the northern San Andreas Fault in Northern California in the next 30 years because a big one happened relatively recently, in 1906, releasing the pressure from that particular fault line. Geologists are always studying earthquakes and sifting through the noise for warning signals—such as magnetic pulses generated by stone under stress and swarms of minor quakes in a particular region—to create an accurate prediction system. But for now, long-term forecasts are the best they can offer.

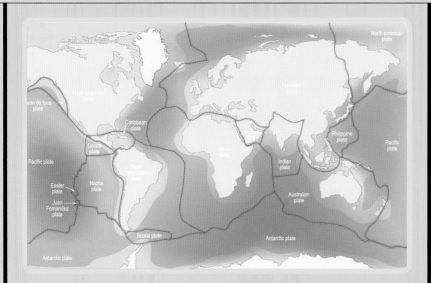

CONTINENTS VS.
tectonic PLATES

You might think each of the seven continents—North America, South America, Africa, Europe, Asia, Australia, and Antarctica—is its own tectonic plate. Not true! The continents are actually landmasses embedded in much larger tectonic plates made of both continental and oceanic crust, the entire slab creeping across the globe to the beat of continental drift. Geologists don't like the term "continents" to describe the major landmasses because continental borders are in many cases arbitrary, just lines drawn on a map. Asia and Europe, for instance, ride atop the same tectonic plate even though any atlas will label them as two separate continents. Australia is embedded in the same plate as India, but Australia is considered its own continent while India is part of Asia. One thing all seven continents have in common, however, is that they ride so high on the continental crust that they're never recycled in undersea subduction zones. That means each continent is a trove of geological treasures. In western Australia, home to the oldest hills on Earth, geologists dug up crystals that formed 4.4 billion years ago. That makes them nearly as old as the planet! Such ancient minerals provide a snapshot of the Earth's earliest days. By studying these crystals and other rocks on the continents, geologists have confirmed how Earth cooled and eventually became hospitable to life.

How OLD IS ...

PERSON OF INTEREST

WHO?
Alfred Wegener

WHAT is he famous for?
Predicting how the continents drift

WHEN?
Early 1900s

WHERE?
Germany

WHY is he important?

Using global positioning systems, scientists have not only confirmed that the continents creep across the planet—they can even monitor their speed and direction. But such technology didn't exist in 1912, when German scientist Alfred Wegener proposed his controversial theory that the continents are always in motion. Before Wegener, geologists thought Earth's surface changed over time because it shriveled, revealing new mountain ranges like wrinkles on a drying plum. But Wegener wondered at how, when viewed on a map, the Earth's seven continents seemed to fit together like jigsaw pieces: North and South America slid into place alongside Africa and Europe. Scouring the continents' coasts, Wegener found fossils of similar plants now separated by a vast ocean. He saw this as evidence that the continents were once joined in the supercontinent now known as Pangaea, but fellow scientists scoffed at his theory. It wasn't accepted for another 50 years.

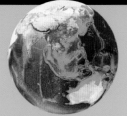

... Earth?
4.6 billion years old

... the moon?
4.5 billion years old

... the ocean?
3.8 billion years old

... oxygen in the atmosphere?
2.5 billion years

WHY isn't all rock "HARD AS A ROCK"?

Rocks come in all sizes and in varying degrees of hardness, depending on which minerals they're made from. Minerals are defined as naturally occurring nonliving solids, but just think of them as the building blocks of rocks. Most rocks on Earth (and elsewhere) are made of minerals smashed together by processes we'll cover below. Granite, for instance, is made of the minerals quartz, mica, and feldspar. A rock's hardness or durability depends on its mineral composition and what's keeping these minerals together. Diamonds are the hardest mineral on Earth (the only thing that will scratch a diamond is another diamond); the softest mineral is called talc. Rocks made out of talc practically crumble in your hand. Who knew rocks were so interesting? Minerals even come in different species, each defined by the unique crystal structure of their tiniest parts. Geologists have discovered about 2,500 species of minerals, but collecting them all isn't easy. Most minerals are rare. Many are valuable. Not all of them are as "hard as a rock"—and hardly any of them are as dull as a box of rocks.

SET IN STONE

THREE KINDS OF rock

SAMPLES

IGNEOUS ROCKS form when magma (or hot liquid rock) cools and becomes solid. Igneous rocks that form underground—such as granite—cool slowly and come in a larger variety of colors and crystal sizes. Magma that cools above ground as lava can be sharp and porous or black and glassy (such as a rock known as obsidian, once prized as a cutting tool), depending on how quickly it cools. Most of the rocks on Earth are igneous rocks.

DIORITE **GRANITE** **OBSIDIAN**

SEDIMENTARY ROCKS form when itty bits of shells, sand, and pebbles of bigger rocks that have been worn down by wind and rain build in layers that harden over millions of years underground. The second most common type of rock, sedimentary rock is also the softest. Chiseling into its layers can reveal the fossils of shells, plants, and animal skeletons that were buried and incorporated into the rock long ago.

FLINT **LIMESTONE** **SHALE**

METAMORPHIC ROCKS were once either igneous rocks or sedimentary rocks that wound up underground through the rock cycle (see sidebar) and were changed—or metamorphosed—into new types of rock from the intense heat and pressure.

MARBLE **SLATE** **GNEISS**

ROCKS AROUND THE CLOCK

THE rock CYCLE

Rocks might look like they're going nowhere fast, at least from your perspective as a human whose life span is barely a blip in the million-year time scales of geological processes. But actually all rocks on Earth are undertaking a trip—known as the rock cycle—millions and even billions of years in the making. Through erosion (in which rocks are worn down by wind and water), volcanism, and the shifting of tectonic plates, rocks make their way deep underground where they're subjected to intense heat from pressure, friction, or the planet's molten core. This heat melts the rock into magma, which is injected back to the surface through volcanoes. Or it bakes the minerals into new types of metamorphic rock that are thrust back to the surface through newly forming mountains. Erosion once again goes to work on these rocks, wearing them down, and the rock cycle begins again.

WHY isn't this mineral ...

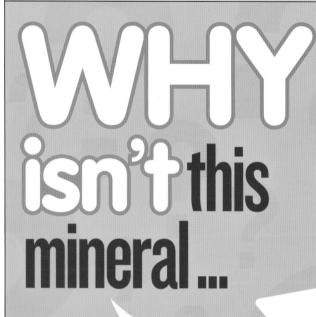

Because the mineral on the left is quartz, one of the most common minerals on the planet.
(Those grains of sand between your toes on the beach? They're bits of quartz.) The mineral on the right is a diamond, one of the world's rarest and most valuable minerals. They are forged a hundred miles below your feet, where the molten temperatures and intense pressure of Earth's mantle put the big squeeze on carbon, one of the planet's most common elements. Clusters of carbon atoms mash together over billions of years into a dense and rigid pattern. The end result: diamonds. Eventually, lava pushes veins of these rocks toward the surface, where they look more like pieces of glass than glittering jewels—until a jeweler cuts and polishes them. Diamonds are valuable for their uses in jewelry and in industry as the virtually indestructible tips of cutting tools.

SAY WHAT?!

IN THE GRAND SCHEME OF ROCKS AND MINERALS, GOLD IS EXCEEDINGLY RARE.

According to estimates, all the gold ever mined in the world would fill only two Olympic-size pools.

If diamonds are the world's hardest natural substance, then how do people cut diamonds?

With other diamonds, of course—typically in the form of diamond dust applied to the blades of powerful jewel-cutting saws.

... worth as much as this mineral?

Why can't we turn lead into gold?

Most of the metals we use in everything from cars to power lines to skyscrapers are mined from especially valuable minerals known as ores, which supply iron (the source of steel), copper, nickel, aluminum, zinc, and more. Gold, mined in rocks and rivers as flakes and nuggets, is one of the most valuable metals because it's rare and does not tarnish or rust like other metals. For centuries, primitive scientists who called themselves alchemists attempted strange experiments using a mythical material they called the philosopher's stone to "transmute" lead into gold for kings and other rich patrons. Today we know that gold and lead are both elements, or unique substances that cannot be changed or broken down because they are the building blocks of all things. The only way to transmute them is to harness the same process that created them in the first place, typically within stars. Scientists can actually transform one element into another—including lead into gold—using modern particle accelerators to smash apart the tiniest parts of elements, but the process requires so much energy and produces so little gold that it's hardly worth it.

Why can't we dig a hole to the center of the Earth?

An expedition to the sun would be easier—although no less deadly at the destination. (Earth's core is actually hotter than the surface of the sun.) Engineers have yet to devise a drilling machine that can withstand the intense pressure and searing heat that begins just a few miles beneath your feet—and only gets more intense as you dig though magma and rock to reach Earth's Mars-size core of molten metals roughly 3,958 miles (6,370 km) straight down. The deepest hole ever dug—the Kola Superdeep Borehole in northwest Russia—is just 7.6 miles (12.2 km) deep, hardly scratching the surface of Earth's crust. The drilling operation ground to a halt in 1992 when the drill hit a pocket of extreme temperatures.

WHY can't I WALK ON LAVA?

Surprise! People actually walk on lava every day without so much as a toasted pinkie toe. A quick lesson in lava will explain why. Earth's crust is floating on a sea of molten, or hot liquid, rock called magma, which is known as lava when it bubbles to the surface through undersea vents or one of nearly 2,000 active volcanoes wherever two tectonic plates meet. From that point, lava emerges into daylight in several flavors, not all of them lethally hot...

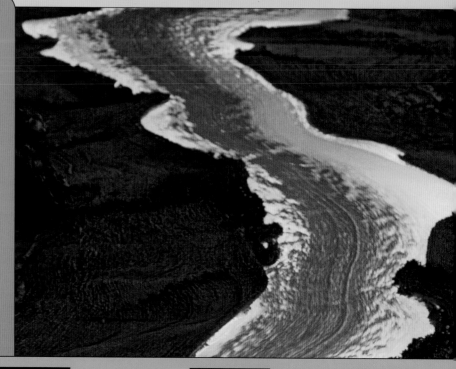

SOLID LAVA

In effusive volcanoes—or the kinds that don't blow their tops in explosive eruptions—lava flows at a steady rate, often forming new mountains and islands after it cools (the islands of Hawaii, U.S.A., were formed from it, in fact). Even after it has cooled off, lava is still called lava—or igneous rock, if you want to get fancy.

WHAT IF I STEPPED ON IT? Lava rock won't scorch your soles, but you wouldn't want to stroll on it barefoot. Its rough edges are sharp!

PAHOEHOE LAVA

This type of lava, pronounced "paw-hoey-hoey," usually flows at a snail's pace (in thin clumps called tongues). And like a snail, it forms a hard shell: Pahoehoe lava's top layer cools into a thin skin of rock that blocks the intense heat of its red-hot interior.

WHAT IF I STEPPED ON IT? Depends on how hard you trod and how long you linger. A quick step barely dents the outer skin. Prolonged pressure, however, will break it, causing flames to flare up around your foot, setting fire to your sneakers and everything attached to them if you don't retreat!

MAGMA

Before lava leaves the ground, it's called magma, and this is the hottest rock of all, around 2000°F (1093°C) near the surface. (Cookies bake at 350°F [177°C].) At 2,000 degrees, rock melts.

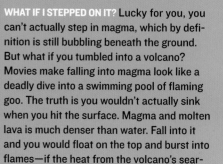

WHAT IF I STEPPED ON IT? Lucky for you, you can't actually step in magma, which by definition is still bubbling beneath the ground. But what if you tumbled into a volcano? Movies make falling into magma look like a deadly dive into a swimming pool of flaming goo. The truth is you wouldn't actually sink when you hit the surface. Magma and molten lava is much denser than water. Fall into it and you would float on the top and burst into flames—if the heat from the volcano's searing interior hadn't already set you ablaze.

Why can't I step out of quicksand?

In the movies it all happens so quickly: After one wrong step into a pool of muddy muck, the unlucky adventurer begins to sink, first to his knees, then his waist, then to his neck, and then ... bloop. Quicksand claims another victim! Real-life quicksand isn't quite the death trap, although it's not something you'd want to wade into. This nasty goop forms wherever water mixes with sand or clay in just the right ratio to make the whole mix loose and mushy. Anyone unfortunate enough to step into quicksand slowly begins to sink as the weight of their body displaces—or squeezes out—the water beneath and around them. With the water displaced, the sand becomes hard, almost like a quick-drying cement, making it nearly impossible to pull out sinking feet and legs. (According to one study, trying to pluck your foot from quicksand is like lifting a medium-size car.) Fortunately, quicksand is about twice as dense as the human body, meaning you would float on it. Victims sink only so far—to the knees or waist depending on their size and weight.

DANGER

QUICKSAND STAY AWAY

cemex Caring for your safety

Q: tips

How TO ESCAPE FROM QUICKSAND

Quicksand forms near beaches, rivers, and bogs and often blends in with the surrounding terrain. Here's how to get out of this mess ...

Don't panic!

The more you struggle, the more water you'll displace from the quicksand and the deeper you'll sink, meaning more of your body could get stuck.

Lean back and relax!

Spreading out your weight on the quicksand will help you float above it.

Call for help!

Pulling yourself from quicksand is no easy task. Scream for assistance or call for help on your phone if it hasn't sunk into the muck. Rescue personnel around quicksand-prone areas typically have specialized training and tools to pull you free.

Wiggle for freedom!

If no one shows up, you'll need to save yourself (otherwise you could die from exposure or the rising tide if you're on a beach). Start by wiggling one foot and then your leg to create small gaps around your body. These gaps will fill with water, softening the hard sand that's locking your body in place. Eventually, if you keep a cool head and work slowly, you'll be able to free one leg, then another, then crawl out of the quicksand. And watch your step from now on!

space STONES

Not all rocks found on Earth are actually from around these parts. Some originated in the asteroid belt, a stretch of space between the orbits of Mars and Jupiter where more than a million pint-size planetoids orbit the sun. When these roving rocks get caught by Earth's gravity and fall into the atmosphere, they're called meteors. But fear not: Most are small. As much as 22 million pounds (almost 10 million kg) of meteors burn harmlessly in Earth's atmosphere each day, appearing to us as shooting stars. Any piece of space debris that survives its fiery free fall is known as a meteorite once it touches down. Just like Earth rocks, meteorites are made of minerals, typically iron ore. Some scientists believe the asteroid belt is made of the remnants of a planet that never formed. Each dropped rock is an unused building block of another world.

CRYSTAL castle

The crystal structures that make up minerals (which in turn make up rocks) aren't always tiny. Gypsum crystals inside the Cave of Crystals in Mexico are larger than power poles—the largest is 39 feet (12 m) long and 13 feet (4 m) around. These crystals formed over half a million years from mineral-rich water kept at intense temperatures by a molten-rock chamber below the cave, about a thousand feet (305 m) underground. The chamber might look like a cool place to snap some amazing crystal selfies, but you wouldn't want to linger longer than 15 minutes—or you might never leave. The cave is so hot (120°F [49°C]) that geologists must wear special cooling suits to study this beautiful but hostile environment.

GOLD VS. FOOL'S GOLD

Despite tales of deception and desperation from the gold rush days of the Wild West, gold miners rarely confused iron pyrite with gold nuggets. Pyrite—better known as fool's gold—has a cubelike mineral structure that's easy to ID from genuine golden flakes and nuggets. Pyrite is also shinier, proving all that glitters is actually not gold. Can you tell the gold from the fool's gold here?

PYRITE

GOLD

ROCK STARS

When an air bubble forms inside a layer of rock, minerals seep into this hollow spot and form a hard shell around the edges. Minerals continue to seep through this shell and form crystals over millions of years. The result is a geode, a cool rock formation coveted by collectors. You might even have one, cracked open to display its glittering crystal innards.

LIVING rocks

Not all rocks are made of minerals. Coal is formed from plants and animals that lived—and died—hundreds of millions of years ago. Their decomposing bodies spent the ages buried deep underground, squeezed by the intense heat and pressures of the Earth's interior until they baked into a "fossil fuel" we can burn to create electricity.

Acasta Gneiss
WORLD'S OLDEST DISCOVERED ROCKS

Rocks from an outcrop called Acasta gneiss in Canada's Northwest Territories might look about as exciting as, well, a box of rocks, but they're actually from the world's oldest known exposed rock formation. Scientists believe this metamorphic slab may have formed more than four billion years ago!

Amber—another type of organic, or once living, rock—forms from tree sap that dried and hardened thousands or even millions of years ago. It's treasured as a jewelry gemstone and for its preservative qualities. Bugs and other small animals trapped in amber are protected from decomposition, giving scientists who study extinct species a window into the distant past.

WHY isn't the SKY ORANGE?

Actually, the sky was orange until about 2.5 billion years ago, but if you jumped back in time to see it, you'd double over in a coughing fit. Way back then, the air was a toxic fog of vicious vapors: carbon monoxide, carbon dioxide, nitrogen, cyanide, and methane. This last gas gave the sky an orange tint and the land a strange glow. But then something happened that would change the sky—and the planet—forever. Blue-green microbes called cyanobacteria formed in the ocean that were capable of a special trick that transformed the planet: photosynthesis. Later used by plants, this natural process converts sunlight and carbon dioxide into energy, creating oxygen as a by-product. Fed by nutrients in the sea and powered by the sun, cyanobacteria exploded across the ocean, pumping more and more oxygen into Earth's atmosphere. Slowly, over the next two billion years, oxygen in the atmosphere rose to its present levels, and the sky took on the blue hue on view today.

So **why** is the sky blue?

The light shining from the sun is made of all the colors of the rainbow, and each color travels on its own special type of wave, called its wavelength. When light hits the air molecules in our atmosphere, its colors are scattered in all directions. Blue light is scattered more because of its short, choppy wavelength, making it the color we see the most. At sunrise and sunset, when the sunlight must travel though a thicker chunk of atmosphere to reach our eyes, blue light is scattered completely out of our field of vision, and we're typically left seeing brilliant red and orange colors.

WONDER WEEDS

WONDER WEEDS

THREE WAYS PLANTS ARE LIKE people

THEY SENSE THE WORLD!

Plants lack eyes, ears, noses, and tongues, but that doesn't mean they're cut off from the world. In fact, scientists think plants pack as many as 20 different senses. They can smell and taste chemicals in the air and on their own bodies. They detect light and shadow to grow in the direction of the sun. Plant roots can sense solid objects underground and veer around them as they sprout. Plants can even hear the sound of flowing water or the munching of hungry insects. In one experiment, a scientist played the sound of a leaf-chomping caterpillar next to a plant, which immediately began deploying chemicals to defend itself!

THEY BREATHE!

Ninety-nine percent of all living things on Earth are plants, and all that greenery "breathing" together—exchanging carbon dioxide with oxygen through photosynthesis—works like the planet's lungs. Scientists watch carbon levels drop every June through November in the Northern Hemisphere when trillions of leaves open and begin inhaling the carbon from the atmosphere. This global green machine is a crucial safeguard against runaway global warming from human-made carbon dioxide. But trees (along with plants and algae in the ocean) alone aren't enough to protect us from climate change, which will only be averted if we switch to carbon-free sources of energy.

THEY HAVE THEIR OWN INTERNET!

Plants connect to each other through the ultimate landline: their roots! Roots are tied into a vast underground network of fungal threads known as mycelium, which one famous fungus scientist called "Earth's natural Internet." Plants—even members of different species—use this "wood wide web" to share nutrients, boost each other's defenses against diseases, and even broadcast warnings of hungry insect invasions and other threats. It's a natural network right beneath your feet. Who knew plants were so busy!

Why don't trees scream when we cut them down?

Don't be so sure about that. Plants might not have pain-sensing nerves or brains like animals, but they're still living things trying to survive in a world filled with danger. Plants defend themselves and communicate with chemicals we often can't smell and even noises too high for our ears to detect. A bean plant under attack from hungry aphids, for instance, will squirt a smelly chemical that attracts wasps, which turn the munching bugs into lunch. These chemical clouds can also warn nearby plants of attack. When giraffes use their long necks to nibble on thorny acacia trees in Africa, the trees' leaves pump out a toxic chemical that all the neighboring trees detect, triggering them to release the chemical, too. The giraffes hate the chemical's taste and wander away before they can cause too much damage. Some trees during a drought emit high-pitched vibrations from their trunks, literally screaming for water. Forestry workers using sensitive microphones can detect these sounds and irrigate the trees before they die.

SAY WHAT?!

BY ONE ESTIMATE, THERE ARE AS MANY TREES IN THE AMAZON RAIN FOREST—ABOUT 390 BILLION—AS THERE ARE STARS IN OUR GALAXY!

WHY can't we control the WEATHER?

The sky darkens, thunder rumbles, the wind whips away your plate of potato salad, a sudden squall douses the grill—oh, no! Another barbecue busted by bad weather. Wouldn't it be nice if you could open a smartphone app and dial the weather from soggy to sunny? You're not the first person to wish you could wrangle the weather. Rainmaking dances and other weather-related rituals were part of life in the ancient cultures of China, Greece, North America, and elsewhere. Those rituals were rooted in religion and the power of positive thinking. Today, science has gotten into the weather-controlling business, usually with about the same results as the ancients and their rain dances. To understand why, you need a quick lesson on weather ...

So what is weather?

What we call weather is just the current mood of a monstrous beast: the atmosphere. Compared to the entire planet, the atmosphere isn't that big: just a thin skin of gases wrapping around the world. But to us living in it, breathing its air, and dealing with its many moods, the atmosphere is our entire world, extending about 6,200 miles (10,000 km) above us to space. And it's a complex system affected by many factors: gravity, the heat from the sun above, the types of terrain below, the ocean, the Earth's rotation, and even the tilt of the planet. These factors interact to determine the state of the atmosphere in any given location, which is what we call the weather. Trying to wrangle the weather is like trying to tame a seven-headed dragon by tempting it with a saltine: The dragon would hardly notice you or the cracker exist, and even if you attracted the attention of one dragon head, the others might attack in unexpected ways. The weather is no different. We have a hard enough time predicting it, let alone controlling it! That hasn't stopped scientists from contemplating—and in some cases trying—different ways to wrangle the weather ...

WIND BREAKERS

THREE WEATHER-TAMING technologies

CONTROLLING RAIN

WHAT CAUSES RAIN? Rainstorms form because the sun warms the planet's surface, where the air is at its thickest (thanks to gravity) and able to hold the most heat and moisture. Moisture in the ground or sea evaporates into the warm surface air as invisible water vapor, and as the air warms, it rises until it reaches cooler altitudes. Cool air can't hold as much moisture, which condenses from the air to form tiny droplets we see as clouds. In clouds that carry enough moisture, the droplets begin to pool together and freeze until they get heavy and fall as either snow or rain.

HOW CAN WE CONTROL IT? CLOUD SEEDING! Developed more than 70 years ago, this rainmaking process involves planes spraying the sky with tiny crystals that chemically bond with a cloud's ice crystals, artificially making them heavier so they'll fall.

DOES IT WORK? Seeding may kick-start a rainstorm in certain types of clouds under particular conditions, useful for either soaking an area caught in a drought or draining the rain from clouds to force a sunny forecast the next day. In the run-up to the 2008 Summer Olympics in Beijing, the Chinese government launched hundreds of rockets to seed clouds and trigger rain so that the opening ceremonies wouldn't get washed out. The games opened with a dry spell while it poured in a neighboring city.

CONTROLLING HURRICANES

WHAT CAUSES HURRICANES? These monstrous storms need the right combination of warm seas, moist air, and ocean winds to form. That's why they take shape over tropical oceans and coasts, where warm, wet air rises from the ocean's surface to create an area of low air pressure. The movement of air from areas of high pressure to low pressure is what creates wind. Bundles of thunderstorms form, fueled by the warm ocean temps and whipped into a swirling churn by Earth's rotation. When winds reach 74 miles an hour (119 km/h), the tropical storm is officially declared a hurricane and tracked by cautious coastal residents.

HOW CAN WE CONTROL THEM? BEAMS FROM SPACE! Satellites in orbit fire microwave beams to heat the ocean's surface around a forming hurricane, causing it to change direction. Using this method, scientists can "steer" hurricanes away from land.

DOES IT WORK? Only in computer simulations. But scientists think hurricanes are just too large—a 1979 storm grew bigger than half the contiguous United States!—and too powerful to control.

CONTROLLING LIGHTNING

WHAT CAUSES LIGHTNING? Drops of rain and bits of ice bump against each other in a storm cloud, charging it with static electricity and turning it into a big fluffy battery. Positively charged particles rise to the cloud's top while negatively charged particles sink to the lower levels. The difference between the positive and negative particles builds up a current and—ZZZZZT!—electricity arcs through the air as bolts of lightning.

HOW CAN WE CONTROL IT? LASERS! Powerful portable lasers fire pulses of energy into a storm cloud. The pulses tear up the air, creating a virtual lightning rod for big zaps to follow back to a designated impact spot on the ground.

DOES IT WORK? Scientists using lasers have managed to direct simulated lightning strikes in small lab experiments, but they have yet to replicate these results in the real world. If perfected, this technology might one day harness the incredible electrical power of lightning. One bolt can carry up to a billion volts of electricity—enough to power about 10 homes for a full day!

Extreme WEATHER SCHEMES

DESTROYING HURRICANES!

Scientists once proposed stopping hurricanes by obliterating them with nuclear bombs. But beyond doing more harm than good, nukes still wouldn't be able to defeat these monster storms, which release as much energy as one nuclear bomb every 20 minutes!

BLASTING HAILSTORMS!

Some farmers since the 18th century have declared war on hail, firing cannons into clouds to shatter these frozen shards of water before they can grow in size and riddle crops with holes. Although hail cannons don't work, they're still in use today.

INDOOR CITIES!

If you can't beat the heat, block it! That's the big, big, big idea behind the Mall of the World in Dubai, United Arab Emirates (the world's richest country). Scheduled for completion around 2020, this domed metropolis will be the world's largest indoor city (about 10 times larger than the world's biggest mall), complete with apartment buildings, hotels, its own transportation system, an amusement park, and air conditioning to combat the desert heat.

If we can't CONTROL THE WEATHER, then how are humans affecting THE CLIMATE?

Because weather and climate are two different things. Weather refers to the atmosphere's current conditions—its temperature, level of moisture, and so on—in a particular area over a short period of time. Climate is the average of those conditions over a much greater period of time. Earth's climate has undergone many natural changes—from snowy ice ages to worldwide heat waves—throughout history. But, according to an overwhelming majority of scientists, human activity has begun changing the climate. The planet's atmosphere has warmed 1.5°F (0.8°C), mostly since 1960. That's when humans began ramping up their burning of fossil fuels (coal, oil, and natural gas) to power cities, cars, planes, and factories. Burning these fuels produces carbon dioxide, a "greenhouse gas" that builds in the atmosphere and traps heat from the sun. At the rate humans are pumping out carbon, Earth's atmosphere could warm as much as 7.2°F (4°C) by the end of this century. Such a spike will result in rising sea levels, coastal flooding, and an increase in extreme weather like floods, hurricanes, and tornadoes.

How can we stop the climate from warming?

As long as we rely on fossil fuels, global temperatures will continue to climb. And these fuels won't run out anytime soon. The challenge is persuading oil, gas, and coal companies to leave the profitable fossil fuels in the ground and switch to renewable sources of energy (see sidebar), but that might require the outcry of millions of people and government intervention.

SAY WHAT?!

GAS-POWERED CARS AREN'T BOUND FOR THE JUNKYARD IN A GREEN-ENERGY WORLD. Their engines can be converted to burn a saltwater plant known as a halophyte, which can be grown cheaply and easily in lakes pumped from the oceans to the world's deserts. And raising crops of this "biofuel" will actually absorb the excess carbon dioxide that's now warming the Earth's atmosphere, making halophyte farming a win-win for the world.

UNLIMITED POWER

THREE CLEAN energy MACHINES

SOLAR POWER

When sunlight strikes a solar panel, it knocks off tiny particles called electrons, which are directed into an electrical current that travels through wiring to power appliances or feed into batteries for long-term storage. Vast banks of panels spread across plains and lakes can power entire towns. Scientists are also figuring out how to make skyscraper glass, roof tiles, and even street surfaces out of solar panels.

WIND POWER

When wind strikes the blades of a large fanlike machine called a turbine, it spins magnets around a coil of conducting wires—a system known as a generator—to create electrical current. "Wind farms" made of many giant turbines will capture constant breezes to power cities. New turbine-equipped kites may soon harness the jet streams: fast-moving rivers of air that course through the atmosphere at the altitudes planes fly.

SEA POWER

Just as wind turbines can turn trade winds into electricity, marine turbines can harness the motion of the ocean. Equipped with blades just like a wind turbine, these sturdy machines can either sit submerged on the ocean bottom to capture currents or hover at the surface to harness the energy of the tides. Researchers estimate that just one-thousandth of the energy of the Gulf Stream current would supply Florida with 35 percent of its electrical needs.

Q: tips

How YOU CAN HELP COOL OFF A WARMING PLANET ...

Climate change is a global problem that will take the cooperation of governments and corporations to solve, but you can still do little things that help—especially if enough people join you ...

- Get smart! Ask your parents to equip your house with "smart" technologies that rely on sensors to run lighting, air-conditioning, and heating systems more efficiently.
- Turn down the heat! For about eight hours a day each winter, turn down your house's thermostat by three degrees.
- Switch the lights! Start replacing old-fashioned incandescent lightbulbs in your house with energy-efficient LEDs.
- Eat slightly less! Raising cattle and transporting food requires a lot of energy. Reduce your diet by about 2 percent (around 48 calories). If you eat meat, try to trim about a pound each month from your menu.
- Ride your bike! If you can commute to your friends' houses or school safely by pedal power, hop on your bike (or consider public transportation) rather than asking Mom or Dad for a ride.
- Drive smart! The next time your parents replace the family car, float the idea of buying an energy-efficient vehicle (such as a hybrid) that gets at least 56 miles (90 km) to the gallon. Carbon emissions in the United States would fall by 10 percent if everyone drove such a vehicle.

GOING green

Renewable energy is beginning to take hold in the United States and more rapidly in other countries. Germany has plugged into the sun in a big way, receiving half of its electricity from solar power. Denmark is leading the world in wind power. Iceland gets much of its power from the heat of the planet, known as geothermal energy. The costs of these technologies are dropping but still high. The environmental costs of not switching to renewable energy are much higher.

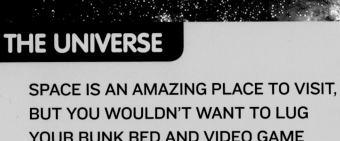

THE UNIVERSE

SPACE IS AN AMAZING PLACE TO VISIT, BUT YOU WOULDN'T WANT TO LUG YOUR BUNK BED AND VIDEO GAME CONSOLES UP THERE FOR A LONG STAY—at least using modern space travel technology. Why not? That's just one of the many far-out questions we'll answer in this chapter that explores the light and dark sides of the planets, stars, and galaxies that make up our seemingly endless universe. Strap in for blastoff. It's going to be a wild ride—and you just might meet a few alien life-forms along the way.

3 SPACING OUT

WHY doesn't THE SUN orbit the Earth?

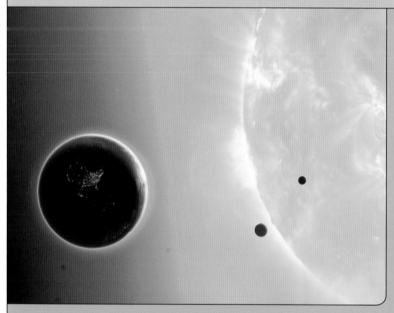

Gravity is a mysterious force—scientists know it's created by matter and yet they aren't sure why or how—but it does follow simple rules laid out by 17th-century English physicist Sir Isaac Newton. One of those rules: Lighter objects always orbit heavier ones because of the heavier object's stronger gravitational pull. The sun is by far the heaviest object in our solar system, accounting for 99.8 percent of every planet, moon, asteroid, comet, and grain of anything in the solar system. (More than a million Earths would fit inside the sun!) It has been the center of our solar system ever since it formed from a massive cloud of gas and dust about 4.6 billion years ago. That material shriveled under its gravity to become the sun, while smaller whirlpools around the gas cloud clumped together to form the planets, one of which you're sitting on right now.

Why isn't the sun red, white, or blue?

Actually, the sun is white when seen from space. It only appears yellow to us Earthlings because we're seeing it through the atmosphere. (Although you should never, ever look at the sun. Seriously, for real. It can cause irreversible damage to your delicate peepers.) Earth's atmosphere scatters sunlight tond makes the sun appear yellow when it's overhead and orange and red during sunrise or sunset (when sunlight travels through a thicker strip of atmosphere before reaching our eyes). But our sun is only one of billions of stars in the galaxy. Stars come in all types, sizes, and colors—including red and blue. Red stars aren't as hot as the sun (although they're still hot enough to theoretically support planets with life), whereas blue stars are hotter than the sun.

Sun DAZE

Nothing wrong with a little sun worship: We wouldn't have a solar system without our sun! But although the closest star to Earth is literally the star of our show, it's not really special in the grand scheme of the galaxy, home to 200 to 400 billion other stars, many like our own. Scientists call our sun a "G-type main-sequence star," which in simpler terms means it's on the cooler side compared with some of the hotter types, on the smaller-than-average size, and not the most common type of star but hardly rare. It's a "main-sequence star" because it's in the prime of its 10-billion-year-long life span, doing what most stars in the universe do: convert hydrogen to helium deep inside their cores. This main-sequence process, called nuclear fusion, creates energy that travels to the sun's surface (or photosphere) and is released as heat and light. The sun's core will run out of hydrogen gas eventually, which will put an end to our fun in the sun. (But we won't have to worry about that for another five billion years or so.)

SUNSPOTS

These cooler regions of the sun's surface can emit charged particles known as solar flares that disrupt electrical systems on Earth. Galileo Galilei (elsewhere on this page) was the first astronomer to notice sunspots.

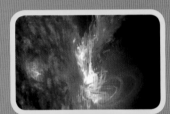

PROMINENCES

Occasionally, these ribbons of glowing gas—cooler than the surface but still scorchingly hot—erupt from the sun and hang suspended by our star's powerful magnetic field before collapsing back into the surface. Prominences are more than 10 times the size of Earth.

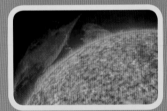

SUN DROPS

The sun might look like a perfect sphere, but closer inspection by special telescopes reveals imperfections ...

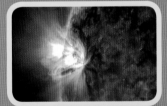

SILLY QUESTION, SERIOUS ANSWER

Because of the direction Earth spins, from west to east, the sun (and the moon and the stars) will always rise in the east and set in the west. But not all the worlds in the solar system rotate the same way. The gas giant Uranus spins on its side like a top that's tipped over, which makes for some oddball seasons and decades devoid of the sun's faint light. On Venus, which spins in the opposite direction, the sun rises in the west and sets in the east, although the planet's slow rotation means a day lasts longer than a year. Scientists suspect Venus and Uranus spin in odd directions compared with the rest of the solar system's planets because they collided with massive asteroids early in their formation.

PERSON OF INTEREST

WHO?
Galileo Galilei

WHAT is he famous for?
Being the father of modern science

WHEN?
1600s

WHERE?
Italy

WHY is he important?
Although people realized Earth was a sphere thousands of years ago, it took us a lot longer to accept that our planet orbits the sun and not the other way around. For centuries, the Roman Catholic Church preached that all the planets, moons, and stars in the heavens orbited Earth, which sat motionless at the center of all creation. In 1543, Polish mathematician Nicolaus Copernicus figured out that Earth and its fellow planets actually orbit the sun. Fearful of contradicting the church, he didn't publish his big idea until his final days. Then, in the late 16th century, an Italian scholar named Galileo Galilei peered through a telescope he helped perfect and saw that the church was wrong and that Copernicus was right. When Galileo spoke up about his findings, the church arrested him for his beliefs. But he continued to experiment, write, and study the heavens. He pioneered the process of testing theories through observations and experiments (known as the scientific method) and established the basis of modern physics. Albert Einstein called Galileo the father of modern science.

WHY doesn't THE MOON have a name?

Pretend you have the world's first pet cat. You've never seen a cat before, so you decide to call her a "cat" because that word seems to describe her somehow. Then one day, you discover more cats around the neighborhood. You call these animals "cats," because now you know that cats are a thing and "cat" was your original word for this thing. Your first cat is still called "cat" and all the new cats get nifty names to set them apart from your original cat. The moon's name—or seeming lack of one—has a similar story. Technically, the moon has a name: We call it the "moon" in English, based off the old English word "mona," which goes back to older words for "month." The moon is called the moon because ancient humans watched it follow a monthly pattern across the sky, and they needed to call it something long before we knew exactly what it was. When Galileo began peering at the heavens through one of the world's first telescopes in 1610, he saw that Jupiter had moons, too. Suddenly, the moon was no longer a single thing but a word to describe a whole class of things. The name "moon" stuck for our original moon in English, and all the new moons got cool or unusual names, often from Greek or Roman mythology. So far none of them has been named "Cat."

WHAT'S THE moon CALLED ...

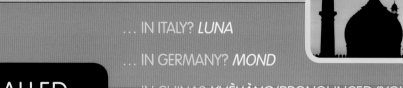

... IN ITALY? *LUNA*

... IN GERMANY? *MOND*

... IN CHINA? *YUÈLIÀNG* (PRONOUNCED "YOU-AY-LEE-ONG")

... IN INDIA? *CHAAND* (PRONOUNCED "CHOND")

Why isn't the moon always full?

The moon doesn't shine on its own; moonlight is actually sunlight reflected off the moon's surface. And just like here on Earth, the moon has a day side that points toward the sun and a night side that points away from the sun. The difference is that the moon takes nearly 30 days to rotate as it orbits Earth, which means a full day-and-night cycle on the moon takes nearly 30 days as well. A full moon seen from Earth represents high noon on the side of the moon facing us. A new moon, on the other hand, is like midnight for the side facing us. All the phases in between represent the various stages of morning, afternoon, and evening.

Why isn't the moon visible only at night?

The moon's monthly orbit and phases happen independently of Earth's daily rotation, which means the moon is as likely to rise during the day as it is at night. Sunlight reflecting off the moon's surface is bright enough for us to see the moon hanging in the blue skies of daylight hours.

MYTH MASHED
Why DOESN'T THE DARK SIDE OF THE MOON GET ANY LIGHT?

Actually, it does! The moon orbits Earth in such a way that it always shows the same side to us Earthlings. People mistakenly call the far side of the moon the "dark side" because it's a mysterious place, but it gets the same amount of sunlight—roughly 15 days—as the side locked toward us. The far side of the moon became much less mysterious when a probe provided our first glimpse in 1959. Since then, probes and astronauts orbiting the moon have captured much clearer photos, although no human has ever set foot on the far side. Because it's always pointed away from Earth and more exposed to asteroid and comet impacts, the far side of the moon is more rugged and pocked with more craters than the side facing us.

Why isn't
the surface of the Earth covered with craters like the moon?

Because unlike the moon, Earth has a thick atmosphere that protects its surface from all but the largest meteor impacts. When smaller meteors and other bits of space debris strike the atmosphere, they either skip off into space or melt to vapor from friction with the air. The moon's nearly airless surface, meanwhile, has come under constant bombardment over billions of years. The powdery lunar dust is pocked by craters and dented by dark basins people once thought were seas but are actually vast plains of lava that spread and cooled in the moon's earliest days.

THE MOON'S MANY faces

| NEW MOON | WAXING CRESCENT | FIRST QUARTER | WAXING GIBBOUS | FULL | WANING GIBBOUS | THIRD QUARTER | WANING CRESCENT |

WHY haven't humans COLONIZED the moon?

Only 11 other people have walked on the moon since astronaut Neil Armstrong took that one giant leap for mankind from the ladder of his lunar lander in 1969. Lunar explorers have conducted experiments on the moon's surface, kicked up lunar dust with their moon buggies, and even played a little golf, but they never lingered long enough to build habitats or lay the groundwork for future cities. The last moon mission headed for home in 1972, and humans haven't been back since—mostly because moon missions are so expensive. Today, space agency NASA's priorities have shifted away from the moon toward orbital launches with its fleet of space shuttles, exploring the solar system with probes, and planning a manned mission to Mars.

But some scientists argue that a moonbase would serve as a stepping-stone to the rest of the solar system. Colonists could mine rocket fuel and precious metals from the lunar soil to power ships bound for Mars or elsewhere. No moonbases are in the works yet, but NASA is planning to build a "Deep Space Gateway" near the moon, a space station that will test technologies and train astronauts for missions to Mars and beyond.

Why doesn't
Earth have more than one moon?

Actually, Earth is lucky to have any moons at all compared to the three other inner planets (Mercury, Venus, and Mars). Our moon formed from a cosmic accident around 4.5 billion years ago, when a roving rogue planet the size of Mars collided with our infant planet, blasting a cloud of debris into orbit. That cloud eventually scrunched down to form our moon. Mercury doesn't have a moon because of its weak gravity compared to the bullying pull of the nearby sun, which would yank free any potential Mercury satellites. Venus, similar in size and gravity to Earth, has no moons. (Scientists aren't certain why.) Mars has two, but they're relatively small and oddly shaped compared to our mighty moon. Meanwhile, the gas giants Saturn, Jupiter, Neptune, and Uranus rule over so many moons, they're like mini-solar systems (some astronomers consider them failed stars). Saturn and Jupiter each have more than 50 officially named moons, with hundreds more waiting to be identified.

THANKS, MOON!
FOUR ESSENTIAL
lunar SIDE EFFECTS

→ Our calendar month is based on the moon's monthly orbit around Earth.

→ Our daily cycles of high and low tides are caused by the gravitational pull of the moon (and to a much lesser extent, the sun) on the oceans and large lakes as the Earth spins.

→ Our day lasts 24 hours thanks to the moon's pull slowing our planet's rotation over billions of years.

→ Life on Earth may not have risen without the stabilizing effect of the moon's gravity, which keeps the Earth from wobbling wildly on its axis. A wild wobble would throw the seasons out of whack and cause rapidly changing climates.

SAY WHAT?!

JUST AS EARTH'S MOON HASN'T BEEN AROUND SINCE THE BEGINNING, IT WON'T HANG AROUND UNTIL THE END.

It's actually drifting away from Earth by a few centimeters every year. But don't bid goodbye to the moon just yet. It will remain a fixture in Earth's sky for billions of years—longer, even, than the sun will.

SILLY QUESTION, SERIOUS ANSWER

Why don't some people believe we really went to the moon?

Original moonwalkers Neil Armstrong and Buzz Aldrin made history when they became the first astronauts to stroll on the lunar surface in 1969, but some insist the landing was one giant lie instead of one giant leap for humankind. They claim that NASA secretly filmed the mission on a hidden Hollywood set to convince the Soviet Union that the United States had won the space race to the moon. Landing deniers point to NASA footage of Aldrin planting the American flag in lunar soil. A subtle wiggle in the flag fabric, they say, proves that it blew in the wind—which doesn't exist in the ultrafaint atmosphere of the moon. NASA claims the flag only wiggled because Aldrin was twisting it into the moon's surface. The astronauts also returned with souvenirs: rocks and soil samples verified of lunar origin.

WHY haven't we landed on MARS?

Even before humans walked on the moon, we've been dreaming about setting foot on the red planet. A German rocket scientist in the 1950s wrote a novel predicting we would reach Mars by 1985 using a fleet of 10 rockets carrying astronauts—along with a squad of commandos to protect them from any hostile Martians! But although the surface and orbit of Mars bustles with robotic vehicles and probes that are mining the planet for all sorts of info, no manned missions have landed on the planet despite more than 70 years of planning. Sending probes and robot landers to Mars is simpler—and less costly—than safely landing a team of astronauts, keeping them alive for months or years on the nearly airless surface, then returning them safely home. Mars might be our planetary neighbor, fourth rock from the sun after Earth, but it's an average of 200 times farther from Earth than the moon. The voyage to Mars would take about seven months, a long trip in a cramped spacecraft exposed to dangerous radiation that Earth's atmosphere and magnetic field shield us from. Launches and return trips must be timed for when the red planet's orbit brings it closest to Earth every two years. Meeting these technical challenges requires vast sums of money (one proposed mission plan costs three times as much as the 1969 trip to the moon) and time, spanning downturns in global economies and the terms of multiple U.S. presidents who must carry on their predecessors' commitment. So far, no Mars mission plan has overcome these hurdles. And yet the planning continues. NASA is researching options and technology to launch manned missions to Mars by the 2030s, using a proposed space station near the moon as a launching point.

Why can't
we visit Venus?

You'd expect a warm welcome on a planet considered Earth's twin, but the surface of Venus is so warm it might melt your space suit (with you in it)! This second planet from the sun is like Earth in reverse. A day here lasts longer than a Venusian year, the sun rises in the west and sets in the east, and—whew!—is it ever hot outside. Venus's average temperature is more than six times hotter than the hottest spot on Earth. That's hot enough to turn a slab of lead into a molten puddle. And sunset wouldn't bring relief from the scorching heat. Day or night, from its north pole to its south pole, every day of the year, Venus is locked in a perpetual heat wave. Blame the blanketing atmosphere of carbon dioxide, thick enough at the surface to crush a submarine! Visitors to Venus would need force-field technologies that right now exist only in science fiction to survive the crushing pressure, intense heat, and clouds of hull-melting sulfuric acid.

Why can't we land
on Jupiter, Saturn, Uranus, or Neptune?

Because there's no land to land on. Unlike Earth—a terrestrial planet made of rocks, metals, and other solid stuff—these four outer planets are gas giants, made of nothing but atmosphere. Looking for a landing pad here would be a very bad idea. As your craft dove deeper into Jupiter's atmosphere of ammonia and hydrogen, for instance, the pressure—and temperature—would keep increasing around you. Soon the air pressure would compress the atmosphere into a molten liquid, slowing your decent until the air thickened around your ship like boiling stew, squeezing and squeezing and squeezing, until the craft melted and became part of the stew around you.

Danger ZONES

Crushing air pressure isn't the only local danger for gas-giant visitors. Jupiter generates a field of radiation more than a thousand times the lethal dose. Saturn's atmosphere is home to electrical storms the size of the United States. Uranus has clouds of methane ice that could rip through a spaceship. Neptune has the windiest weather in the solar system, with gusts as fast as a fighter jet in storms that would engulf all of Earth.

Why doesn't
Earth have rings like Saturn?

Actually, three other planets in the solar system have rings along with Saturn—Jupiter, Uranus, and Neptune—all formed from bits of asteroids and comets that were captured by their powerful gravity. And believe it or not, Earth did have rings at one point, but they weren't like Saturn's famous icy rings, and no humans were around to spy them in the sky. In fact, life on Earth didn't even exist yet. About 4.5 billion years ago, a small planet smashed into Earth and blasted trillions of tons of debris into orbit that eventually bunched up to form our moon. But before that big crunch, the debris spread across the sky to create rings of brown rock around our world.

BEEN THERE, SEEN THAT:
POSTCARDS FROM THE SOLAR SYSTEM

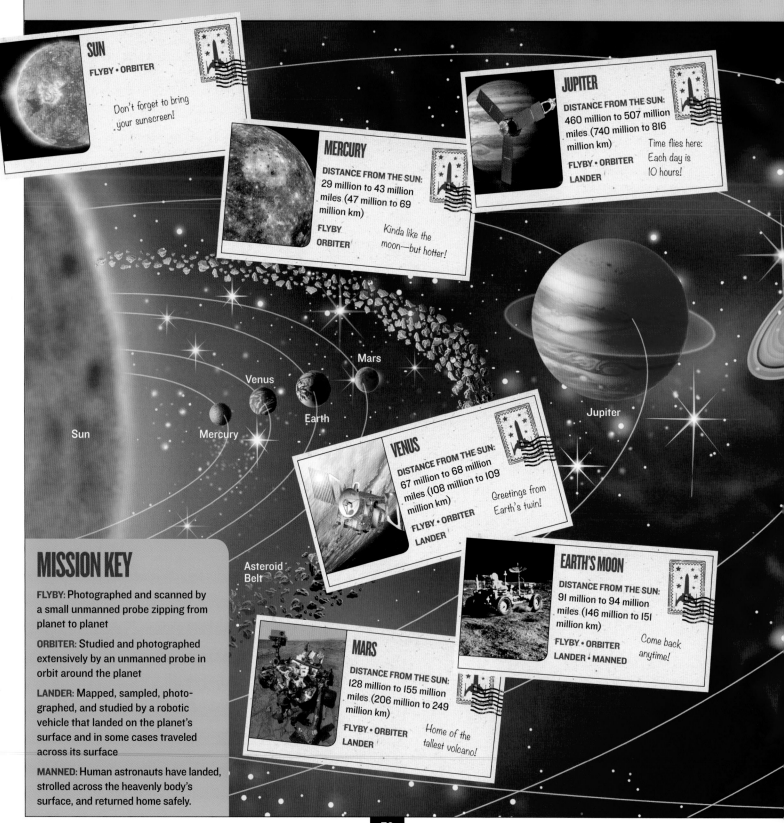

SUN
FLYBY • ORBITER

Don't forget to bring your sunscreen!

MERCURY
DISTANCE FROM THE SUN: 29 million to 43 million miles (47 million to 69 million km)
FLYBY
ORBITER
Kinda like the moon—but hotter!

JUPITER
DISTANCE FROM THE SUN: 460 million to 507 million miles (740 million to 816 million km)
FLYBY • ORBITER
LANDER
Time flies here: Each day is 10 hours!

VENUS
DISTANCE FROM THE SUN: 67 million to 68 million miles (108 million to 109 million km)
FLYBY • ORBITER
LANDER
Greetings from Earth's twin!

EARTH'S MOON
DISTANCE FROM THE SUN: 91 million to 94 million miles (146 million to 151 million km)
FLYBY • ORBITER
LANDER • MANNED
Come back anytime!

MARS
DISTANCE FROM THE SUN: 128 million to 155 million miles (206 million to 249 million km)
FLYBY • ORBITER
LANDER
Home of the tallest volcano!

Sun
Mercury
Venus
Earth
Mars
Jupiter
Asteroid Belt

MISSION KEY

FLYBY: Photographed and scanned by a small unmanned probe zipping from planet to planet

ORBITER: Studied and photographed extensively by an unmanned probe in orbit around the planet

LANDER: Mapped, sampled, photographed, and studied by a robotic vehicle that landed on the planet's surface and in some cases traveled across its surface

MANNED: Human astronauts have landed, strolled across the heavenly body's surface, and returned home safely.

If you think of our solar system as a neighborhood, Earthlings haven't ever gone farther than our own front porch. (The farthest we've journeyed from home is about 250,000 miles—402,000 km—during 1970's Apollo 13 mission to the moon.) But that hasn't stopped us from sending scouts: fleets of robotic probes and landers serving as our eyes and ears (and all sorts of other senses) across the solar system. Here's a checklist of where we've been, what we've seen, and some postcards from each planet ...

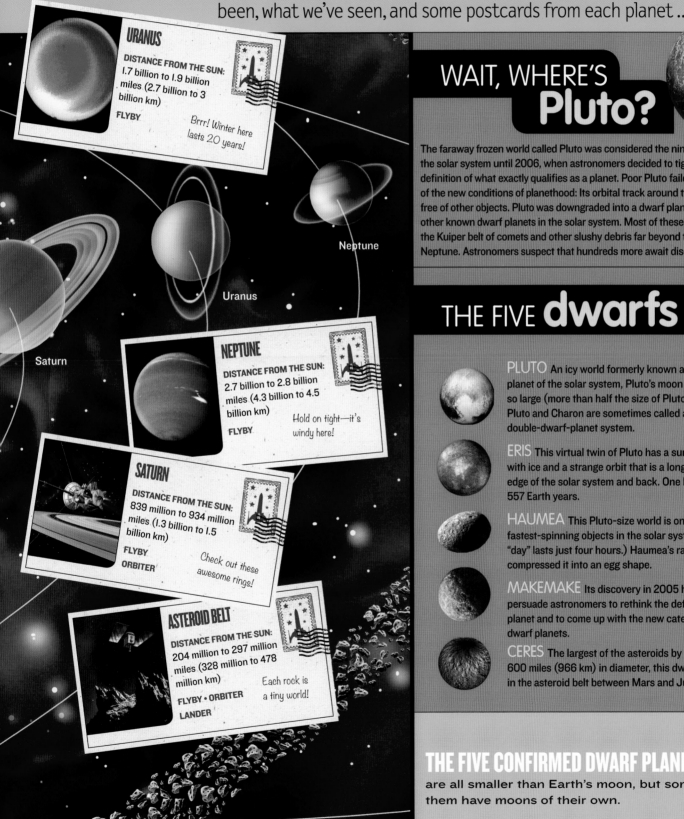

URANUS

DISTANCE FROM THE SUN:
1.7 billion to 1.9 billion miles (2.7 billion to 3 billion km)

FLYBY

Brrr! Winter here lasts 20 years!

Neptune

Uranus

Saturn

NEPTUNE

DISTANCE FROM THE SUN:
2.7 billion to 2.8 billion miles (4.3 billion to 4.5 billion km)

FLYBY

Hold on tight—it's windy here!

SATURN

DISTANCE FROM THE SUN:
839 million to 934 million miles (1.3 billion to 1.5 billion km)

FLYBY
ORBITER

Check out these awesome rings!

ASTEROID BELT

DISTANCE FROM THE SUN:
204 million to 297 million miles (328 million to 478 million km)

FLYBY • ORBITER
LANDER

Each rock is a tiny world!

WAIT, WHERE'S Pluto?

The faraway frozen world called Pluto was considered the ninth planet in the solar system until 2006, when astronomers decided to tighten up their definition of what exactly qualifies as a planet. Poor Pluto failed to meet one of the new conditions of planethood: Its orbital track around the sun isn't free of other objects. Pluto was downgraded into a dwarf planet, one of five other known dwarf planets in the solar system. Most of these join Pluto in the Kuiper belt of comets and other slushy debris far beyond the orbit of Neptune. Astronomers suspect that hundreds more await discovery.

THE FIVE dwarfs ...

PLUTO An icy world formerly known as the ninth planet of the solar system, Pluto's moon Charon is so large (more than half the size of Pluto), that Pluto and Charon are sometimes called a double-dwarf-planet system.

ERIS This virtual twin of Pluto has a surface glazed with ice and a strange orbit that is a long trip to the edge of the solar system and back. One Eris year is 557 Earth years.

HAUMEA This Pluto-size world is one of the fastest-spinning objects in the solar system. (Its "day" lasts just four hours.) Haumea's rapid spin has compressed it into an egg shape.

MAKEMAKE Its discovery in 2005 helped persuade astronomers to rethink the definition of a planet and to come up with the new category of dwarf planets.

CERES The largest of the asteroids by far at nearly 600 miles (966 km) in diameter, this dwarf planet lies in the asteroid belt between Mars and Jupiter.

SAY WHAT?!

THE FIVE CONFIRMED DWARF PLANETS
are all smaller than Earth's moon, but some of them have moons of their own.

WHY can't
we see all the stars and
GALAXIES
in the universe?

On the darkest of nights far from cities and streetlights, after you've let your eyeballs adjust to the darkness for about 30 minutes, you can peer up at the sky and take in as many as 5,000 stars (plus planets and even a few galaxies, depending on where you're watching from). It's an awe-inspiring sight, especially when you consider that each of those pinpricks is a star, probably with its own system of planets, and maybe one of those planets is home to an alien kid peering up in your direction. But 5,000 stars is a drop in the ocean compared with the total number of stars just in our own galaxy, the Milky Way, home to nearly 400 billion stars. Our universe may have as many as two trillion other galaxies, many with billions of stars of their own. (The Andromeda galaxy, our nearest neighboring galaxy, may have as many as a trillion stars.) Much of the universe is still unaccounted for when we peer into the heavens, even with powerful telescopes and other advanced sensors. Here's why ...

NEARSIGHTED

WHY ASTRONOMERS CAN'T see it all ...

NIGHT LIGHTS

It's no surprise the harsh glare from high-rise buildings and streetlights overpowers the relatively dim glow cast by stars that are dozens, hundreds, or even thousands of light-years away. (A light-year is how far light travels in a year.) Called light pollution, this blight of bright light is also the reason you don't see stars in the sky in photos from the moon, where the reflection of the sun on the lunar surface is just too overpowering.

MATTER SPLATTER

The universe is so immensely ... er, immense—and growing larger all the time—that it's easy to imagine it as a nearly empty void with galaxies and stars scattered far and wide. But there's still enough stuff—clouds of gas and dust known as nebulae, for instance—drifting around out there to obstruct our view of distant stars and newly formed galaxies, which are often shrouded in the stuff. In fact, we can't even see the core of our own galaxy through these clouds of star-making stuff.

LIGHTS OUT

Nothing—not even light—escapes the powerful gravitational pull of black holes, which form when large stars run out of fuel and collapse on themselves. Astronomers estimate that our galaxy may have as many as 10 million to a billion of these mighty matter munchers, which soak up all passing light and can hide distant stars from our eyes and sensors.

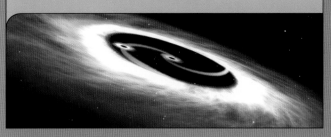

TIME AND SPACE

The number one reason so much of the universe remains hidden is simple: Many stars and galaxies are too young for their light to have reached us yet. When you peer up at the sky, you're looking at a window to the past. The sun we see now is actually how it looked more than eight minutes ago, because that's how long it took the sunlight—moving at the speed of light—to leave the sun and reach our eyeballs here on Earth. Stars in the constellation Orion, about a thousand light-years away, appear to us how they looked in the Middle Ages. If one of those stars had exploded, say, 500 years ago, we wouldn't see it until the light from its supernova reached us around the year 2500. Our own galaxy is about 100,000 light-years across, so the light from every stellar object in the Milky Way has had time to reach Earth within the span of our species' history. But light from galaxies that formed millions or billions of years ago—but are millions or billions of light-years away—hasn't reached our eyes yet. To us, these heavenly bodies remain invisible until their light finally reaches us. And here's where things get a little more complicated: All the matter and energy created by the "big bang" that formed the universe 13.7 billion years ago is still expanding outward. Galaxies new and old continue to hurl farther apart from one another, increasing the distances—and time—it takes for their light to reach us. Astronomers believe most of the stars and galaxies in the universe are still hidden from us by time and space.

SAY **WHAT?!**

BY ONE ESTIMATE, OUR UNIVERSE MAY HAVE MORE THAN A SEPTILLION STARS. THAT'S 1,000,000,000,000,000,000,000,000!

WHY can't I see colorful images like the one below through my TELESCOPE?

Backyard astronomy can fill your evenings with awe, offering a close-up view of heavenly bodies that are barely there to the unaided eye. But you'll never see an image quite like the one here—and for two reasons: Because of how telescopes take these types of photos, and more importantly *where* this photo was taken. The image was snapped by the Hubble Space Telescope, a bus-size satellite launched into Earth orbit in 1990. Its powers of observation come not from its size (the Hubble is actually a medium-size telescope) but from its extreme height advantage above Earth's atmosphere. All that air above us acts like a blurry filter—which is why stars appear to shimmer in the sky—for telescopes based here on the ground. In orbit, the Hubble is unobstructed by atmosphere for an eagle-eye view of the heavens.

But even if you spacewalked to the Hubble and peered through its lens, you wouldn't see an image nearly this dazzling. At the very best you'd see some shadowy shapes against even darker shadows. Like all "optical" telescopes—such as the one you might lug into your backyard—the Hubble's main job is to gather and focus light. When that light is faint and far away, such as the glow from distant stars and nebulae, the Hubble must gather and focus that light for weeks and weeks onto its imaging system to render images like the one you see here. Your own eyes just don't work that way.

HOW MANY stars CAN I SEE ...

... with the naked eye? About 5,000 under the right conditions.

... through a pair of binoculars? About 200,000.

... through a simple telescope? As many as 15 million (but good luck keeping count!).

... through the Hubble Space Telescope? Thousands of galaxies.

THE big PICTURE

Astronomers can learn only so much about the universe when they peek through optical telescopes that magnify visible light. To get a complete picture, they probe deeper with a wide array of specialized sensors that see what our eyes cannot. Ultraviolet telescopes peer through dust clouds to see what's on the other side. Infrared telescopes analyze the chemical compositions and temperatures of stars and even distant planets' atmospheres. Massive radio telescopes—with antenna dishes the size of stadiums—listen for the radiation given off by the universe's oddest objects, such as quasars and black holes. They can also detect the echoes of the universe's birth in the big bang 13.7 billion years ago.

STARGAZING

FIVE TYPES OF stars

YELLOW DWARFS

Our sun is this type, an average-size star that fuses its hydrogen fuel into helium over 10 billion years. Because they provide more heat than red dwarfs (below) and last much longer than larger, hotter supergiant stars, yellow dwarfs are more hospitable to life forming on their orbiting planets.

RED DWARFS

The most common stars in the universe, red dwarfs are cooler and smaller than our own sun. They consume their hydrogen fuel much more slowly than our sun and last much longer: up to 10 trillion years.

RED GIANTS

When stars like our sun run out of hydrogen fuel, their cores heat up and expand outward in a vibrant cloud known as a red giant, appearing as a beautiful nebula to distant star systems. We won't start to see the effects of our sun's demise for at least a billion years.

NEUTRON STARS

When stars at least twice the size of our sun run out of hydrogen fuel, they collapse into these bizarre star nuggets—just 12 miles (19.3 km) wide—but with the gravitational pull of their original size. (Only black holes, formed from even larger stars, have a more powerful gravitational field.)

SUPERGIANT STARS

Dozens of times larger than our sun, supergiants shine bright and hot but burn through their fuel much more quickly—in just a few million years. Then they go supernova, or explode into massive clouds of dust and gas known as nebulae. Because they live fast and die young, supergiants are considered less hospitable for the formation of life on any planets in their systems.

SAY WHAT?!

OUR SUN RULES THE SOLAR SYSTEM ON ITS OWN, BUT MANY STARS SHARE THEIR SYSTEMS WITH A SECOND OR THIRD STAR THAT ORBIT EACH OTHER.

WHY don't astronauts use the SPACE SHUTTLE to explore the solar system?

After 30 years of liftoffs and landings, NASA's fleet of space shuttles touched down for the last time in 2011 without ever having traveled farther than low Earth orbit, or 330 miles (531 km) into space. (A voyage to the moon, by comparison, is more than 700 times farther.) But that's hardly a failure on the shuttle's part. It was doing exactly what it had been designed to do: transport astronauts and cargo—such as satellites and space station parts—into Earth orbit, then return to repeat the mission over and over, more than 130 times. The shuttle carried just enough fuel and rocket power (in a detachable tank and reusable engines) to blast into orbit, then slow itself enough to achieve reentry, at which point it glided on wings to a runway for a landing. Those wings and an underbelly of heat-absorbing tiles—crucial to the craft's survival during reentry and landing—were dead weight in the airless void of space, where every pound counts in the fuel costs of accelerating and course corrections. The shuttle, excellent in its job as a reusable orbiter, made a lousy long-distance spaceship.

Why don't spacewalking astronauts worry about drifting away into space?

Because they're very careful. In fact, all astronauts who step out the International Space Station's air lock connect themselves to the station with a steel tether. And in the unlikely event this tether snaps, each astronaut wears a sort of life jacket for spacewalking: the SAFER jetpack. Short for "Simplified Aid for EVA Rescue," the SAFER has small thrusters that fire bursts of nitrogen to steer them back to the safety of the air lock.

Why don't spacecraft burn up when they reenter the atmosphere?

Take a deep breath and thank that thick blanket of atmosphere around you. It gives you air to breathe, and (bonus!) you won't catch on fire if you move through it at reasonable speeds. Scream through it at 16,000 miles an hour (25,750 km/h)—the speed of a space shuttle reentering the atmosphere from orbit—and friction with the air's particles creates such intense heat that the atmosphere bursts into flames. This isn't a bad thing. It's what keeps thousands of tons of meteorites from slamming into Earth's surface every day (all these small rocks burn up in the atmosphere as shooting stars). And for spacecraft reentering Earth's atmosphere, friction with air particles puts on the brakes, slowing them to safe landing speed. Spacecraft descend through the atmosphere at a specific angle—flat end first rather than knifing though nose down. This creates a shock wave that helps hold the heat slightly ahead of the vehicle. By combining this reentry technique with special heat-absorbing materials, spacecraft can withstand the intense temperatures—up to 3000°F (1649°C)—of reentry.

SILLY QUESTION, SERIOUS ANSWER

Why can't we climb a ladder to space?

A ladder makes a dangerous space-entry vehicle (it would snap in half under its own weight after a few hundred feet and topple easily in a stiff breeze, for starters), but engineers have proposed a similar concept that borrows a page from "Jack and the Beanstalk": a space elevator. The idea is simple. Elevator builders would launch a construction satellite into orbit above a fixed spot on the ground. The satellite would then lower a ribbon to the planet's surface, where workers would anchor it to a ground station. Robotic construction machines would scurry up and down this ribbon, reinforcing it with superstrong materials until it becomes tough enough to support the weight of elevator cars built to ferry cargo and, eventually, passengers from Earth all the way to space. The space elevator concept has undergone many engineering studies proving it could work, although it still faces one big hurdle: Scientists haven't figured out how to mass-produce the superstrong material needed for the cables.

WHY wouldn't you want to GROW UP in space?

Space is a hostile place, airless, lethally cold or hot (depending on whether you're in the sun or shade), and blasted by dangerous radiation (more on that in a minute). But space also lacks something as crucial to a growing body as your daily serving of veggies and a good night's sleep: gravity. Although Earth's gravitational field is only slightly weaker in orbit, astronauts feel weightless in space because they're in a constant state of falling around the planet. Without the weight of our world to work against, muscles begin to shrivel (as much as 5 percent each week) and bones become brittle. Weightlessness also changes the shape of the eyes and can hinder your vision. Scientists aren't sure what would happen to any kids growing up up there (the youngest astronaut was 25 years old and fully grown), but they suspect nothing good. Animals bred in weightlessness have a hard time readjusting to gravity. Astronauts who return from long stints in orbit often leave the reentry vehicle in a wheelchair, taking months to recover. If you spent too long growing up in space, your body might become too delicate from weightlessness and damaged from radiation to return to home.

Why is it so hard to create artificial gravity?

Sci-fi movies make turning on artificial gravity as easy as flicking a switch (probably because weightlessness is an expensive special effect), but in real life it's not so easy. The only thing that creates a true gravitational field is matter—aka stuff—and the more the matter, the greater the gravity. Because building an Earth-size spaceship to generate Earthlike gravity isn't exactly practical, rocket scientists must turn to other options to give spacefarers their daily serving of up and down on long space flights ...

GRAVITY GIZMOS: Astronauts in orbit have strapped themselves to treadmills, hefted special "weightless" weights, and sealed themselves in body-encasing vacuums to work their muscles and strengthen their bones.

SPEED TRAP: Ever notice how you sink into the car seat when Mom zooms away from a green light? That same sinking feeling would keep a space crew's feet pressed to the floor of their ship as long as they spent their voyage in a constant state of acceleration. Halfway through their trip, they would need to stop the engines (resulting in

temporary weightlessness), rotate the ship so its engines point in the other direction (toward their destination), then reengage the rockets to begin slowing the craft at a constant rate. As long as the craft continued its steady deceleration, that sinking feeling would resume and a sense of gravity would be restored.

SILLY QUESTION, SERIOUS ANSWER

How fast am I actually traveling right now on Earth?

Your speed here on Spaceship Earth varies depending on where you're sitting. Earth spins fastest at the Equator—the imaginary line halfway between the North and South Poles. That's where the Earth is widest along its axis, so any point along the Equator has a greater distance to travel during each daily rotation than any point closer to the poles. People at the Equator are traveling faster than a fighter jet: 1,070 miles an hour (1,722 km/h). The farther you move away from the Equator, the more slowly the planet spins. Anyone standing precisely on the North or South Pole is just turning in place. Meanwhile, Earth orbits the sun at an average speed of 67,000 miles an hour (107,826 km/h). And just as Earth orbits the sun, the sun orbits the center of our galaxy, once every 230 million years (known as a galactic year). No matter where you wander on Earth or in space, you're always on the move in relation to the universe around you.

This theoretical type of artificial gravity—not yet attempted in spaceflight—would require vast amounts of fuel or engines powered by renewable energy, such as sunlight or lasers beamed from the home and destination planets.

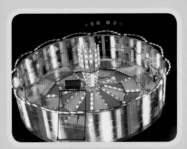

SPIN CYCLE: You can see this sort of artificial gravity in action right here on Earth in spinning amusement-park rides with cool names like Starship or the Gravitron. Around and around the riders go, faster and faster until the floor drops from their feet and they're pinned to the wall by the power of the spin. Now imagine this stomach-churning ride on a much larger scale, fitted out with living quarters and laboratories and sent spinning around an axle containing engines that drive the entire craft forward. Gravity could be increased or decreased by changing the speed of the spin until it matched Earth's own gravity, known as "one G." Such a wheel- or tube-shaped craft would need to be as wide as a football field or the astronauts inside would feel like they were living on a Gravitron ride.

spaceship EARTH

It's too bad we can't just pack up Earth and fly it across the universe. Our planet really is the perfect spaceship! Not only does it offer all the air, water, dinners, movie theaters, bathrooms (toilets are a big part of spaceship research!), and gravity we need to stay healthy and entertained, it has an invisible force field that spacecraft—and even many planets—lack. Earth's magnetic field protects us from two forms of dangerous space radiation: charged particles spit out by the sun during rare solar storms and cosmic rays cast off by dying stars in distant solar systems and other galaxies. Studies show that such radiation can cause cancer and lead to brain damage. Our planet's magnetic bubble deflects this radiation as far out as low Earth orbit, where astronauts can work worry free in the International Space Station, but any manned missions to the moon, Mars, and elsewhere will leave this force field behind. Mission planners are investigating technologies that can protect astronauts from cosmic rays and sudden solar storms. (Lunar astronauts narrowly missed one of these storms in 1972.) Some ideas on the drawing board: radiation bunkers deep inside the ship and even real-life force fields that block radiation just like Earth's magnetic field does.

SAY WHAT?!

IN JUST THE PAST FIVE MINUTES, THE EARTH MOVED ABOUT 5,000 MILES (8,047 KM) ON ITS ANNUAL TREK AROUND THE SUN.

WHY do most SCI-FI MOVIES

get almost everything wrong about space?

Space stations! Faraway planets! Asteroids! Orbital docking procedures! No one would ever say outer space is a boring place—certainly no astronaut who has ever blasted into orbit or bounded in the low gravity of the moon. But moviemakers often edit out dull mission procedures and rewrite laws of physics to add pizzazz to the humdrum routines of traveling between worlds. Does movie magic really make outer space more magical? Decide for yourself as we compare the real "out there" versus Hollywood's louder, flashier, faster-paced final frontier ...

In movies, space is loud. In real life, space is silent.

Vooooaaarrr! Sci-fi spaceships scream through the cosmos on roaring rocket engines while blasting asteroids and enemies with thundering laser cannons. *Pew! Pew! Pew!* But if directors stuck to the script of physics, every space movie would be a silent one. There's no sound in space. Here on Earth, we hear what we hear because noise needs something to travel through, such as air or water or even the ground beneath your feet. In fact, sound is nothing more than waves—or vibrations—carried through something. Outer space, unlike the atmosphere held around your face by Earth's gravity, is a vacuum, meaning it has no air to carry sound. Astronauts can chat inside a space station because it's pumped with air (which carries the sound and, conveniently, also keeps everyone alive). Two spacewalking astronauts can talk to each other via their space suit radios because radio waves—unlike sound waves—don't need air to travel. But if those same two astronauts shut off their radios and shouted at each other, even a few feet apart, they'd better be good at reading lips.

In movies, spaceships fly like fighter planes. In real life, spaceships fly like spaceships.

Starfighters in sci-fi movies bank through turns, pull into gut-churning loops, and corkscrew around asteroids. Real spacecraft never perform any of these daring maneuvers, which would require vast amounts of fuel and likely send the ships tumbling like wobbly tops. Unlike airplanes, spaceships zipping through the void of space aren't slowed by friction from the atmosphere around them. Without air to resist a ship's motion or strike control surfaces such as wings and rudders, spaceships can only change direction and speed with carefully timed bursts of their thrusters (routine course-correcting maneuvers with the exciting name "delta V"). Once a ship has undergone delta V, it will continue on its new course forever—until it changes direction again, fires retrorockets in the opposite direction to slow down, or is pulled into a planet or star's gravity.

In movies, distant spaceships communicate instantly. In real life, communication could take hours, days, or even years!

There's no such thing as instant messaging in deep space. Radio transmissions, like all forms of electromagnetic radiation, travel at the speed of light. That's zippy enough for chatter close to home—it took just under three seconds for astronauts on the moon to speak to mission control on Earth and hear a reply. Once astronauts land on Mars, it could take more than 20 minutes for their radio messages to reach us. This communication delay is why planetary probes and rovers are robotic, able to make decisions without constant input from Earth-based controllers. Imagine how frustrating it would be to drive a remote-control car that took 20 minutes to respond to your controls—and then you didn't even know if it responded for another 20 minutes!

IN SCI-FI MOVIES ... Asteroid belts are spaceship-smashing jumbles of rock.

IN REAL LIFE ... The average distance between rocks in our solar system's asteroid belt, between the orbits of Mars and Jupiter, is about 600,000 miles (966,000 km).

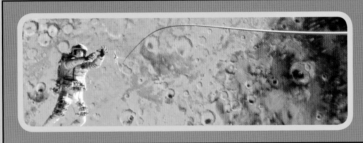

IN SCI-FI MOVIES ... Astronauts in zero gravity move in slow motion.

IN REAL LIFE ... Astronauts in zero gravity move at regular speed.

IN SCI-FI MOVIES ... Ships, asteroids, and space stations blow up in fiery explosions.

IN REAL LIFE ... Explosions need air—in particular, oxygen—to fuel their fire. Because there's no air in space, explosions flame out the instant they consume whatever air fueled them.

In movies, spaceships are fast. In real life, spaceships are fast, but not nearly fast enough.

In the Star Wars movies, daring starship pilots "make the jump to light speed" to travel between distant star systems in less time than it takes to watch a Star Wars film. In real life, nothing can reach the speed of light other than forms of energy. (Physicist Albert Einstein said it would require all the energy in the universe for something other than energy to reach the speed of light.) But even light speed—186,282 miles a second (299,792 km/s)—is kind of pokey for travel between the stars. At that speed, it would still take more than four years to reach our nearest neighboring star, Proxima Centauri, and at least a hundred thousand years to cross the galaxy. Most movies also ignore a time-tripping side effect of travel at high speeds: The faster you go, the more slowly time passes for you compared to anyone traveling at slower speeds. If space travel in the Star Wars movies portrayed this freaky phenomenon—known as time dilation—realistically, heroine Rey would take the Millennium Falcon for a three-hour trip between star systems only to find that friends at her destination had aged 10 years and the First Order had probably won years ago.

WHY is there NO PLACE LIKE HOME?

If you're looking no farther than your home solar system, then yeah, there really is no place like the ball of rock beneath your feet. Venus, often called Earth's twin because it's similar in size, lost its water long ago to the boiling temperatures of its cauldron-like atmosphere. The solar system's other planets are likewise too hot or too cold to support liquid water—a key ingredient for life to form—but Earth orbits the sun in the Goldilocks zone, a distance that's just right. Oceans cover nearly 70 percent of the planet's surface and are a source of the water vapor responsible for our climate. And, of course, Earth is home to something we've yet to find anywhere else in the universe: life.

But space is a big place, and though astronomers have ruled out finding a planet like ours among the planets and dwarf planets of our own solar system, they've only just begun the hunt for an Earthlike world among the exoplanets.

Exoplanets?
What are those?

These are any worlds that orbit stars outside our solar system. Remember, our own galaxy is home to billions of stars, and astronomers believe that each of these stars, like our own sun, has planets orbiting it—at least one and most likely several. Astronomers even think most of these planets are Earth-size and rocky rather than gas giants like our own solar system's outer planets (Jupiter, Saturn, Uranus, and Neptune). According to some estimates, a minimum of 1,500 exoplanets might lie within 50 light-years of Earth. Whether any of these worlds are like home is hard to tell. It's nearly impossible to see them.

SAY WHAT?!

AFTER CRUNCHING THE DATA FROM THE EXOPLANET-HUNTING KEPLER SPACE TELESCOPE, astronomers expect that there's at least one Earth-size planet capable of supporting life within 10 light-years of our solar system.

If we can't see exoplanets, how do we know they're there?

Wielding a variety of specialized Earth- and space-based telescopes, astronomers have many high-tech tricks for detecting exoplanets hundreds or even thousands of light-years away, including ...

CHASING SHADOWS

Just as the moon passing in front of the sun causes a solar eclipse here on Earth, exoplanets can eclipse their stars far, far away. Using special computer programs to monitor for these dips in star brightness, astronomers can detect when distant exoplanets pass, or transit, in front of their suns. Watching for these shadows is the easiest and most common way to detect exoplanets. Astronomers can even tell the size of an exoplanet and its distance from its sun by measuring how much of the star it blocks and how long its transit lasts.

EXOPLANETS FOUND: More than 2,000

WOBBLE WATCHING

Lighter objects (such as planets) always orbit heavier ones (such as stars). That's one of the rules of gravity you learned near the start of this chapter. But that doesn't mean the heavier objects just sit there while the smaller ones go around and around. Think of a planet and the star it orbits playing a game of tug-of-war, with gravity as a sort of invisible rope. Just as you might force your big brother or sister to lean back slightly during your own games of tug-of-war, a tiny planet is able to force the big star to shift its balance. Astronomers watch for this wobble in stars as a sure sign of orbiting exoplanets. The bigger the wobble, the larger the star-tugging planet.

EXOPLANETS FOUND: More than 600

ZOOMING IN

Physicist Albert Einstein theorized that gravity does a lot more than just keep our feet on the ground. The gravitational force of large objects actually bends any light passing by from more distant stars. Under the right conditions, this bending can steer the light in our direction and magnify it—a phenomenon known as gravitational microlensing. It doesn't quite provide a zoomed-in view of distant objects, but gravitational microlensing does cause telltale flashes in stars with exoplanets, and it's particularly useful in detecting exoplanets thousands of light-years away—out of range of the other methods. Astronomers never know when these microlensing events will happen. Robotic observatories scan large patches of the sky to look for them.

EXOPLANETS FOUND: More than 40

TAKING A LONG, HARD LOOK

Seeing an actual exoplanet from Earth is virtually impossible because these distant worlds are lost in the glare of light, heat, and other radiation of their stars. It's like trying to spot a needle in a haystack—while the haystack is on fire! But thanks to new advances in imaging technology and special light blockers that work like sunglasses for telescope imaging systems, astronomers are starting to find exoplanets just by looking for them directly.

EXOPLANETS FOUND: More than 40

WHY haven't we found any signs of ALIEN LIFE?

Have some patience. Scientists are working on it! For decades, the Search for Extraterrestrial Intelligence—or SETI project— has scanned the universe for radio signals from alien civilizations (no luck so far, but we're about to step up the search—see sidebar opposite). Closer to home, in our own solar system, astronomers are probing the planets and their moons for any hint of life, even itty-bitty microbes. Such a discovery would mark the start of a new era for humanity: an era in which we know we're no longer alone in the universe. Some astrobiologists—or scientists who look for life on other planets—predict we may find evidence of alien life by 2030.

HOT SPOTS

THE SOLAR SYSTEM'S MOST PROMISING PLACES TO FIND Extraterrestrial Life

MARS

The red planet was once home to seas and rivers, and astronomers have found evidence of trickles of salty pools still trickling on the surface today. Any life-forms found on Mars would likely be long dead and fossilized—yet still proof that life can form elsewhere besides Earth.

EUROPA

The frozen surface of this moon of Jupiter likely hides an ocean larger than all the seas on Earth—and perhaps with a similar chemical balance. Trapped beneath ice at least 10 miles (16 km) thick, Europa's pitch-black seas are cut off from the life-giving energies of the sun, but biologists have found organisms in similarly harsh environments—from Arctic ice to deep-sea volcanic vents—here on Earth.

ENCELADUS

This icy moon off the rings of Saturn is now the most exciting place in the solar system for astrobiologists. Like Europa, Enceladus hides a planet-spanning ocean beneath its frozen armor of ice. But recent flybys with the Cassini spacecraft discovered something interesting erupting from the icy crust: plumes of water vapor containing carbon dioxide, methane, and hydrogen. Why do these geysers have scientists in a tizzy? Those same chemicals and compounds are found around deep-ocean vents here on Earth, where microbes thrive. (The little life-forms actually snack on hydrogen like it's candy!) The oceans of Enceladus, like our own planet's deep seas, are like a healthy soup for the formation of life. Astrobiologists are hoping to test the waters sometime in the next decade or so.

THE ASTEROID BELT

Scientists estimate that more than a million asteroids—most of them little more than blobs of gravel—orbit the sun in the asteroid belt between Mars and Jupiter, likely remnants of a planet that never formed. Mining companies may one day deploy robots to extract gold and other precious minerals from the asteroid belt, but the discovery of life anywhere else in the solar system might make these roving rocks valuable for another reason: According to a theory called "panspermia," life may have successfully transferred from planet to planet by catching a ride on a meteor.

Why haven't
we heard from any aliens yet?

A physicist named Enrico Fermi took the universe's old age (13.7 billion years old) and its vast size and calculated that our Milky Way galaxy ought to be teeming with intelligent life. By that logic, Earth should be bathed in radio transmissions—interplanetary emails, ship-to-ship communications, otherworldly meme videos—from across the galaxy. And yet astronomers have failed to detect any signals from distant worlds. Called the "Fermi paradox," this radio silence from space has some scientists convinced that we are alone in the universe. Other scientists theorize that advanced alien civilizations communicate with technology that we can't detect, or that an advanced extraterrestrial culture would scan Earth and determine that it harbors no intelligent life.

SILLY QUESTION, SERIOUS ANSWER

Why don't we try saying hello to aliens?

Oh, we have, several times! In 1974, for instance, scientists broadcast a message including a stick-figure Earthling, various numbers and chemical formulas, and even a simple image of the telescope. The message was beamed into a cluster of stars 25,000 light-years away, which means any intelligent life-forms in that part of the galaxy won't receive our signal for 25,000 years. The Voyager 1 and 2 space probes launched in the late 1970s carry their own Earthling greeting, including images of our planet and the sounds of crashing surf, whales singing, and even "hellos" in 150 languages.

SAY WHAT?!

PHYSICIST STEPHEN HAWKING, A TRUE BELIEVER IN ALIEN LIFE, THINKS WE'D BETTER DO EVERYTHING WE CAN TO HIDE FROM EXTRATERRESTRIAL ASTRONAUTS. He fears that alien invaders would ransack Earth for its resources, colonize it, or perhaps spread a deadly plague of space germs.

WHY can't we tell if EXOPLANETS have life?

Well, it's not quite as simple as hopping in a rocket ship and dropping by to see if anyone is home, but we can look for signs. Using telescopes on Earth and in space, astronomers can analyze the size of each exoplanet, its distance from the sun (and whether it orbits in the Goldilocks zone), the length of its year, and, most important, the makeup of its atmosphere. The presence of water vapor, oxygen, carbon dioxide, and ozone (a gas that is both created by living things and protects them from space-based radiation) is a good sign that something might be alive out there. Future advances in telescope imaging and techniques such as gravitational microlensing might even provide photos with enough detail to reveal oceans and landmasses.

Why can't we send astronauts to explore exoplanets?

Because the trip would just be too long, too dangerous, and too boring. It would take at least 30,000 years for astronauts in a modern-day spacecraft to reach the nearest exoplanet to Earth, Proxima b, four light-years away. But although humans could never make the journey (at least until someone invents a faster-than-light warp drive), our machines can. A new project called Breakthrough Starshot is planning to send an itty-bitty "nanocraft"—about the size of a postage stamp—to peek at Proxima b and any other planets in the Alpha Centauri star system sometime in the next 25 years. Because it's so small and light, the sensor-studded nanocraft can accelerate and travel much faster than a full-size spacecraft—up to 20 percent the speed of light, about 100 million miles an hour (161 million km/h). At that speed, the nanocraft would reach Alpha Centauri in about 20 years. Any photos and data it sends back would take four years to reach Earth, so the odds are good you'll see snapshots of an alien world within your lifetime.

EXCITING **Exoplanets**

Astronomers have discovered more than 4,000 worlds beyond our solar system. Let's blast off to explore a few standouts ...

PROXIMA B

DISTANCE FROM EARTH:
Four light-years

This rocky Earth-size world orbits Proxima Centauri, which at four light-years away is the nearest star to our solar system. Scientists believe Proxima b orbits in the Goldilocks zone, meaning it's capable of supporting liquid water, but they're unsure if it has an atmosphere or a magnetic field to protect any life-forms from the intense radiation of its star.

LHS 1140B

DISTANCE FROM EARTH: 39 light-years

Astrophysicists once believed it was impossible for giant Earthlike planets—known as super-Earths—to form. Their intense gravity attracted gas, scientists believed, ballooning these worlds into gas giants similar to Jupiter. Then in 2014, astronomers found a real monster orbiting 39 light-years away in the constellation Cetus. This rocky world is about 40 percent larger than our own, is rocky like Earth, and lies in its star's habitable zone where liquid water can form. Any super-Earthlings would need to be superstrong to thrive in their planet's intense gravity.

TRAPPIST-1

DISTANCE FROM EARTH: 40 light-years

Astronomers studying TRAPPIST-1, a dwarf star cooler and smaller than our sun in the constellation Aquarius, found a bonanza of Earth-size exoplanets, at least seven in total—three of which orbit within the star's Goldilocks zone and may have oceans on their surface. The discovery made TRAPPIST-1 a top contender for life outside our solar system. But life on any of these worlds would be weird compared to conditions here. Because TRAPPIST-1 is smaller and dimmer than our sun, its planets orbit closer in and faster. All seven planets are likely tidally locked, meaning they always show the same face to the sun while the opposite side is locked in a perpetual night. A year on any of these fast-orbiting worlds is as short as just a few Earth days, and neighboring planets would hang even larger than the moon in our sky. Scores of Earth- and space-based telescopes are now trained on the TRAPPIST-1 system, the focus of scientific scrutiny for decades.

SILLY QUESTION, SERIOUS ANSWER

Why can't we use black holes as shortcuts through space?

Hey, that's not such a silly question! Astrophysicists (and sci-fi writers) theorize that black holes might lead somewhere else—to the other side of the galaxy, another galaxy altogether, or even alternate dimensions (through exits known as white holes)—or they might lead somewhen else, to a different point in time. Astronomers have never seen a black hole (they're invisible because their powerful gravity sucks in all light), but they suspect these mighty munchers of matter exist because they can observe their effects. The most common types form when large stars—those about 20 times bigger than our own sun—run out of fuel and go supernova, or explode. The dying star's core collapses under its own gravity until it scrunches into a tightly packed point known as a singularity. The gravity around a singularity is so powerful that any approaching spaceship would be stretched into a noodle of its tiniest bits and destroyed. So it's just as likely that—instead of serving as wormhole shortcuts through space—black holes would lead nowhere, the equivalent to jumping into a planet-smashing trash compactor.

HISTORY

HISTORY MIGHT BE SET IN STONE, BUT THAT DOESN'T MEAN WE CAN'T SECOND-GUESS THE PAST. Why didn't the *Titanic* steer clear of that iceberg? Why didn't dinosaurs survive that meteor impact? Why didn't explorers just stop and ask for directions? History is filled with no shortage of mysteries. Get ready to solve scores of them as we mine the ages for answers.

SAY WHEN

4

WHY aren't there any DINOSAURS alive today?

Around 65 million years ago, an asteroid or comet the size of a small city slammed into the seabed off the Yucatán Peninsula (in modern-day Mexico) at 45,000 miles an hour (72,420 km/h). It was curtains for *Tyrannosaurus rex* and his kind. The impact hurled dust and vapor to the edge of Earth's atmosphere. A global heat wave was followed by a planetwide chill. Over the next few thousand years, roughly 75 percent of all species went extinct, including most of the dinosaurs. But not all of them. In fact, you can probably see a few survivors perched outside your window today: They're called birds.

Wait, birds are dinosaurs?

Chickens, parakeets, penguins, ostriches—every bird you see today is a dinosaur. (Seriously!) The earliest birds first appeared around 150 million years ago as small, feathered, winged dinosaurs that probably couldn't fly but could glide like a chicken. They belonged to the same group of larger two-legged, meat-eating dinosaurs that includes *Tyrannosaurus rex* and the velociraptors. These bigger beasts, with their bottomless appetites, couldn't adapt to the catastrophic climate changes triggered by the meteor impact. But the avian (bird) dinosaurs were smaller, quicker to adapt, and able to scavenge for food in a changing world. Although their larger cousins died out, early birds continued to evolve quickly to fill habitats and explode in diversity. Today more than 10,000 species of these living dinosaurs thrive from the tropics to the Antarctic, on land, in the sea, and in the air.

ALL BIRDS ARE DINOSAURS, but not all dinosaurs were birds. In fact, the pterosaurs—the first vertebrates (or animals with a backbone) able to fly—are not dinosaurs at all but members of a different group. That means today's birds are closer cousins of the *Tyrannosaurus rex* than the soaring pterodactyl.

Why can't scientists bring extinct dinosaurs back to life?

Don't believe everything you saw in those Jurassic Park movies. Unlike with more recently extinct species such as the woolly mammoth, scientists just don't have enough genetic material to clone dinosaurs back into existence. The closest scientists have come is creating dino-faced baby chickens by manipulating the genes that control beak development. The scientists' goal wasn't to resurrect a toothy creature from the past but rather to study the evolution of beaks in birds. In any case, you don't need to worry about dino-chickens breaking loose from some lab and going on a Jurassic Park–style rampage. The experimental dino-faced chicks were never hatched from their eggs.

MASHED

MYTH

Why ARE CROCODILES CONSIDERED LIVING DINOSAURS?

They're not. Although the ancestors of crocodiles (and their relatives, such as alligators) lived during the time of the dinosaurs—and even hunted dinosaurs—they're not considered members of that group of fearsome reptiles. Crocodiles, alligators, dinosaurs (and their modern descendants, birds), all share common reptile ancestors: the archosaurs. But the archosaurs' family tree split around 250 million years ago, with crocodiles and their relatives going in one direction and dinosaurs, pterosaurs, and birds going another. All the nonavian (that is, nonbird) dinosaurs perished in the aftermath of that meteor impact 65 million years ago. Hunkered down in the sea and swamps, crocodiles were able to ride out the worst of the catastrophe's effects and continue to evolve.

WHAT'S WRONG (OR RIGHT) WITH THIS

Paleontologists, or scientists who study dinosaurs, have uncovered a trove of info about their subject in the past 30 years that makes this image of the fearsome reptile either obsolete or accurate.

Still Life

Humans fleeing from the *T. rex* in the movie *Jurassic Park* dodge his jaws by standing still, believing that this king of the reptiles can't see you if you don't move. But paleontologists are pretty sure playing "red light/green light" wouldn't save you from becoming a *T. rex* snack in real life. They think this fearsome predator had keen eyesight and a sense of smell that could track prey even if it made like a statue.

Arm Charm

It's funny because it's true: *Tyrannosaurus rex* had ridiculously stubby arms. Paleontologists have debated the reasons for the king of the dinosaurs' meager forelimbs for decades. Some suggest *T. rex* used its little arms to hold prey in place or grapple with mates. Others think the arms were stronger than they look, able to lift at least 400 pounds (181 kg). More and more paleontologists are coming to the conclusion that the arms were useless, leftovers from one of *T. rex*'s evolutionary ancestors.

How do paleontologists know what dinosaurs looked like?

They don't for sure, but they can make educated guesses from all the evidence left behind. And no dino clue is too small or too gross! Fossils of dinosaur bones bear the imprints of feathers or grooves in the bone where the feathers fit. Analysis of some feather fossils gives glimmers of stripes, hinting at colorful plumage. Study of fossilized dinosaur poop—called coprolite—reveals the dino diet. They ate fruit, meat, and even wood covered with fungus.

PICTURE OF A *TYRANNOSAURUS REX?*

Why couldn't dinosaurs fly if they had feathers?

As any ostrich, penguin, or other flightless bird will show you, feathers are handy for more than just flight. Feathers appeared on the fossil record even before the first birds, on many different dinosaur species—none of which could fly. Light and strong, feathers serve a hundred and one functions: They kept dinosaurs (and their nests) warm and dry, protected their skin from the sun, acted as camouflage, and helped communicate through displays. Some paleontologists suspect dinosaurs performed elaborate mating dances just like many modern birds, such as peacocks and ostriches. The fearsome feathery *T. rex* may have danced its own version of the chicken dance.

Tall Tail

People once thought dinosaurs such as the *Tyrannosaurus rex* pictured here lumbered through their environment, dragging their tails kind of like the monsters from a Godzilla movie. Now paleontologists believe many dinosaurs were nimble. How would anyone know? Scientists attached an artificial tail to *T. rex*'s modern relative, the chicken, and watched it walk! Paleontologists believe *T. rex* likely carried its tail in the air like a chicken to balance the weight of its enormous, toothy skull and to help it run up to 25 miles an hour (40 km/h), slightly slower than a horse at full gallop.

Ruffled Feathers

Those scaly reptiles that scared audiences in the Jurassic Park films need a wardrobe change. The more paleontologists learn about dinosaurs, the more they become convinced that many of these fearsome reptiles—not just the ones that evolved into birds—sported some type of feathers, from fuzzy downlike "protofeathers" to thick piles of plumage rivaling a peacock's. Whether *T. rex* was covered in feathers or scales is a topic of debate. Fossils of its smaller relatives show evidence of shaggy feathers. But paleontologists believe a hefty meat-eating animal like the titanic *T. rex*—40 feet (12 m) long, 20 feet (6 m) tall—would overheat under a blanket of feathers, just as an elephant would become miserably hot if it were covered with fur. So, much like an elephant's patchy scruff, *T. rex*'s feathers were probably short and sparse.

CROC-A-DOODLE-DOO! By creating models of dinosaur skulls and comparing them with birds and crocodiles (modern-day dinosaur relatives), paleontologists are trying to figure out not only what dinosaurs looked like but also what they sounded like, too! One theory: Instead of throaty roars, dinosaurs may have made cooing sounds more like a dove or turkey.

WHY aren't there any NEANDERTHALS still around today?

Good question! After all, our species and theirs also coexisted—traded, chatted, fought, and possibly even interbred with each other—tens of thousands of years ago. And Neanderthals, which split from our common ancestors only 400,000 years ago, shared many similarities with modern humans. Scientists suspect they wore clothes, wielded sophisticated tools, harnessed fire for cooking and warmth, buried their dead, chatted using simple language, and perhaps even expressed their creative sides by carving images into cave walls. Despite this, Neanderthals died out around 40,000 years ago.

Although the reasons for this extinction are largely a mystery, competition and conflict with modern humans was likely a major factor. We *Homo sapiens* survived because of our ability to adapt to new situations and environments. Neanderthals, meanwhile, mainly specialized in one activity: hunting hulking Ice Age animals. Even as our *Homo sapiens* ancestors invented nets and other tools to catch small animals, Neanderthals stuck to stalking big game—which may have sealed their fate as these animals perished from climate change.

Human REUNION

Neanderthals weren't the only early humans that shared time and space with *Homo sapiens*, aka modern humans. At least three other separate *Homo* species interacted, cooperated, chatted, and even fought with us (an experience that must have been a little like living alongside an alien intelligence) during our earliest years, including ...

HOMO ERECTUS

WHEN DID THEY LIVE? 1.9 million to 140,000 years ago

The oldest humans in our particular branch of the human family tree, *Homo erectus* were humanity's trailblazers. They developed stone axes, discovered how to control fire, and possibly cared for their old and sick. Their arms and legs were of similar proportions to our own, indicating that they had adapted to life on the ground and could cover long distances. They were the first humans to leave Africa.

HOMO FLORESIENSIS

WHEN DID THEY LIVE? 95,000 to 13,000 years ago

These tiny humans lived on the Indonesian island of Flores alongside pygmy elephants and Komodo dragons until relatively recently. Members of this species—unknown to science until 2003—didn't grow much taller than a modern three-year-old child. Archaeologists dubbed them "hobbits" because of their itty-bitty stature.

HOMO HEIDELBERGENSIS

WHEN DID THEY LIVE? 700,000 to 200,000 years ago

This species of early humans may have given rise to our own in Africa (which is perhaps one reason why they have little overlap with *Homo sapiens*). And we certainly could have learned much from *Homo heidelbergensis*: They were the first early humans to reach Europe, hunt with wooden spears, and build shelters.

SILLY QUESTION, SERIOUS ANSWER

What if you transported a Neanderthal through time to the modern world?

Things could get ... awkward. They would certainly stand out, physically and socially. Neanderthals had prominent brows above large eyes, football-shaped skulls, stocky bodies, stumpy fingers, small chins, and fat noses. A Neanderthal time-warped to, say, the mall or your school cafeteria (after a crash course in modern language and technology) would probably be the strong, silent type. Neanderthals likely lacked our knack for sophisticated communication and abstract thinking—to imagine the future and talk about the past. But even early modern humans would have trouble processing the modern world if we time-warped one from 200,000 years ago. Some scientists believe that, like the Neanderthals, early modern humans lacked abstract thinking skills until about 70,000 years ago, when changes in diet and some genetic mutations boosted our budding brainpower.

MYTH MASHED

Why CAN'T WE FIND THE "MISSING LINK" BETWEEN APES AND HUMANS?

This question is often posed by people who oppose the theory of evolution, which naturalist Charles Darwin proposed in 1889 to explain how all plants and animals—including humans—slowly change over time, developing into new species to improve their chances of survival. If humans evolved from apes, skeptics claim, then why haven't scientists found bones of the species linking us to our common ancestor? But this argument is built on a faulty idea: that evolution follows a neat line from one species to species, with one species dying and its next evolutionary descendant taking its place. Instead of a straight chain, evolution's path splits and splits and splits again, like the branches in a bush, with new species breaking off from the original group. That means scientists will never find a single "missing link" connecting us to the ancestors of chimpanzees, because there are actually dozens of species, all branching off the human family tree over the past six million years. And scientists have actually identified nearly 20 species in four major groups leading to the branch occupied by *Homo sapiens*.

WHY don't we know who invented FIRE?

Thomas Edison invented the lightbulb. Johannes Gutenberg invented the printing press. Rodney Spinsalot invented the wheel. Great inventions not only change the world—they turn their inventors into household names (which is why one of those names sounds off; we made up Mr. Spinsalot!). So why don't we know the name of whoever came up with the greatest invention of all time: fire? This discovery happened long before there were smartphone cameras or books or even modern humans (aka *Homo sapiens*) around to record it. Fire was likely discovered by *Homo erectus*, an earlier human, possibly as far back as 1.5 million years ago.

How did early humans figure out fire?

Of course, fire isn't really something that can be invented. It's a chemical reaction, flaring to life when sufficient heat, oxygen, and a combustible (or burnable) material such as wood combine, begin to smoke, and then—poof. Fire! Early humans didn't need to know how to start fires. They saw it happen naturally: trees or brush set ablaze by lightning strikes or meteor impacts. Our ancestors realized fire was a precious thing—a resource and a luxury, capable of improving life in so many ways (see sidebar). *Homo erectus* first learned how to control natural fires, preserving the flames in stuff that could smolder: chips of dense wood or animal doo-doo. They carried these embers, shielded them during the cold and wet seasons, and used them to kindle new fires around hearths built from stone. Still later, perhaps around 800,000 years ago, early humans learned how to start their own fires using friction between pieces of wood or by banging special rocks to create sparks. We'll never know the name of the early human who figured this out, but he or she probably had one. Researchers suspect that our evolutionary ancestors began inventing words to describe tools and fire-making techniques—and probably each other—as far back as a million years.

Why is fire SUCH A BIG DEAL?

Naturalist Charles Darwin considered our harnessing fire one of our greatest achievements, right up there with the invention of language. Mastery of fire, in fact, led to a chain reaction of human achievements, including ...

NIGHT LIGHTS

The roaring campfires of our human ancestors acted as predator repellents, frightening away dangerous creatures in the night.

COLD COMFORT

Our ancestors didn't have sleeping bags and wool socks to hold the cold at bay. Fires kept them toasty and allowed them to travel to chillier climates.

HUNTING HELP

Forest fires today are terrible; in prehistoric times, they offered an easy way to barbecue game without breaking a sweat (or risking injury from dangerous hunts). Our hunter-gatherer ancestors would set large fires, then scour the ashes for meat to eat or use the flames to chase animals into traps.

SOCIAL NETWORKING

The seeds of civilization were planted around campfire hearths. To tribes of early humans, fires were gathering places to socialize, practice and develop early language, and trade hunting and gathering techniques.

FOOD FOR THOUGHT

The brains of early humans began to boom in size around 1.8 million years ago, giving our ancestors a boost in their ability to think on their feet, adapt to new environments, communicate with each other, and invent tools. Scientists think it's no coincidence this mental growth spurt coincided with two changes in our ancestor's lifestyles: They began eating lots of meat, and they started barbecuing everything they ate. A big noggin needs a lot of energy—about a fifth of what you put in your mouth fuels your melon. Our ancestors couldn't microwave a burrito or pop a waffle in the toaster, but they hunted for foods even richer in calories: fatty cuts of mammoth flanks and woolly rhino steaks. Barbecuing meat tenderizes it and makes it easier to digest its protein. Roasting fruits and vegetables in some ways "predigests" the food, softening it up for our guts and breaking down the energy-rich starches so they're easier for the body to absorb. By some estimates, cooked food provides 30 percent more energy than raw veggies and meats. Roasted meat and veggies gave us more fuel for our brain development. Early humans evolved with larger, smarter brains.

WHY don't people live in this NIFTY CITY anymore?

Archaeologists may never know the true purpose of Machu Picchu, a city among the clouds perched atop the eastern slopes of the Andes Mountains in modern Peru. Before it was rediscovered and revealed to the world in 1911, this sky-high city was certainly... something significant in the Inca Empire, the dominant civilization of South America in the 15th and 16th centuries. But whatever its purpose, Machu Picchu became a ghost town about a century after it was built, around the time conquistadores from Spain started raiding the Inca civilization for gold. Meanwhile, an outbreak of a deadly disease called smallpox—also likely caused by the Spanish invaders—ravaged the Inca. Imagine if your own house was attacked by invaders or became a dangerous place to live for one reason or another: Your family would leave, too! Which is why so many once great cities in prime locations—from the Maya Caribbean port of Tulum to the ancient Egyptian city of Thonis—have floated in and out of history, lost and then found.

Why haven't
we found the lost city of Atlantis?

Because this mighty city—which the Greek philosopher Plato described as an island civilization that sunk into the Atlantic Ocean long ago—is most likely mythical. When divers discovered the strange undersea rock formation known as Bimini Road in the Bahamas, they wondered if they'd found Atlantis. Geologists say no, and Atlantis remains an alluring legend.

Why haven't we found
the golden city of El Dorado?

When Spanish conquistadores explored South America in the early 16th century, they heard tantalizing tales of a gilded city founded by a king coated in gold dust. They called the chief "El Dorado," or "the gilded one," and they believed his city was the source of all the gold in the New World. The conquistadores

thought they were closing in on El Dorado when they found gold at the bottom of Colombia's Lake Guatavita in 1545, but the trail ended there. Tales of this fabled "city of gold" have since lured many explorers to risk their lives for a mythical prize.

Why didn't
Egyptians live in pyramids?

Despite their impressive size—the largest was built from more than 2.3 million limestone blocks and was the world's tallest building for nearly 4,000 years—the pyramids of ancient Egypt would've made lousy houses. They had only a few passages and chambers; everything else was solid block. But they were never meant to serve as houses or apartment buildings. The pyramids are tombs for Egypt's kings and queens.

Why don't we know what
happened to Roanoke's "Lost Colony"?

Thirty-three years before the pilgrims landed at Plymouth Rock, a group of English colonists arrived on Roanoke Island on the coast of what is now North Carolina for a fresh start in the New World. Supply ships arriving in 1590 found the settlement abandoned, with few clues to the colonists' whereabouts. The fate of this Lost Colony has baffled historians.

Pretty Big Deals
MILESTONES IN HUMAN HISTORY

6 MILLION YEARS AGO: DOWN TO EARTH
The common ancestor of modern humans and chimpanzees (our closest living relative today) climbs down from the trees and begins walking on two legs. Not long after, hominids appear and branch off from the lineage that gives rise to chimps. Hominids include modern humans (us), our immediate ancestors (such as *Homo erectus*), and our close relatives the Neanderthals.

2.6 MILLION YEARS AGO: TOOL TIME

Early humans living in East Africa make the first "tool kits" of handy rocks, including hammering stones for tenderizing meat and sharpened flakes of rock to butcher animals. The Stone Age begins.

1.5 MILLION TO 800,000 YEARS AGO: ALL FIRED UP
Early humans begin figuring out how to control fire.

1 MILLION YEARS AGO: LANGUAGE ARTS
Early humans begin inventing words to describe tools, fire-making techniques, animals, and other hot topics of prehistory. Language is born. Suddenly, our ancestors can share, compare, and pass down survival strategies.

200,000 YEARS AGO: MODERN HUMAN BEGINNINGS
Our species, *Homo sapiens* (which means "wise humans"), arrives on the fossil record in eastern Africa. Also known as modern humans, they look identical to people living today but share their world with several other early human species.

60,000 YEARS AGO: MOVING OUT
In tribes of hunters and gatherers, modern humans depart the mother continent, eventually spreading to every corner of the globe.

12,000 YEARS AGO: SETTLING DOWN
Modern humans learn how to raise animals, grow crops, and store grains and other food. Suddenly, every human doesn't need to know every survival skill to survive in a changing world. With the free time and brain space to learn new skills, humans begin to specialize in specific jobs (building shelters, storing food, and so on), and cooperate with other members of their tribe or village.

5,500 YEARS AGO: RODNEY SPINSALOT INVENTS THE WHEEL

Kidding! Just like with fire, we'll never know who invented the wheel—but archaeologists think it happens around this time in prehistory.

5,000 YEARS AGO: GETTING CIVILIZED
The first large settlements—the earliest civilizations—form in southwest Asia and Africa. They begin trading and sharing culture and keeping records of their lives, marking the start of recorded history. New civilizations rise and flourish. Others fall or are conquered. Information is shared at a more rapid pace than ever, leading to a boom in innovation.

WHY didn't explorers get LOST

in the days before global positioning systems?

Oh, they got lost. All the time. Some of the most momentous events in history happened because explorers made wrong turns or misjudged distances. Italian explorer Christopher Columbus only stumbled upon the Americas in 1492 because he mistook a Caribbean island for Asia after underestimating the circumference of Earth. Spanish conquistador Ponce de León, according to legend, stumbled on Florida while seeking the island of Bimini and its legendary "fountain of youth." Exploration during the "age of discovery," from the 15th to 18th centuries, was a matter of trial and error. (Mostly error.)

How did
early navigators navigate?

With a lot of luck and "dead reckoning," a mistake-prone process in which explorers would set a course from a known spot, then head toward some distant destination while keeping track of their speed, direction, and the time spent traveling at that speed. Dead reckoning worked for short distances across land or when sailors could update their progress with known landmarks and the few well-charted coastlines. But the farther explorers traveled from the known into the unknown, the more likely they were to misjudge their speed or travel time, which would send them drifting off course and increase their chances for getting hopelessly lost. (Remember, this was before Google Maps.) Despite its massive margins of error, dead reckoning was the main method of navigation for Columbus and other pre-18th-century mariners.

Tricks and Technologies
OF ANCIENT NAVIGATORS

LATITUDE ADJUSTERS

Explorers as far back as ancient Greece knew how to determine their latitude—or distance north or south of the Equator—by measuring the angle of the sun and stars in the sky at certain times of the day.

PAYING ATTENTION

Long before Columbus and the age of discovery, daring mariners such as the Vikings from Scandinavia and the Polynesians of the Pacific relied on simple yet powerful navigation tools: their powers of observation. They navigated treacherous uncharted seas and spread their cultures by watching the sun and stars for compass headings, studying patterns of wind and the tides, and recognizing the behaviors of birds and fish for clues when land was just over the horizon.

EXPERT HELP

Many of history's most famous explorers would've gotten hopelessly lost without the help of unsung experts. The Lewis and Clark expedition charged with charting the middle of the United States in the early 1800s, for instance, relied on Sacagawea, the teenage daughter of a Native American chief, to guide them through the trails of her childhood, translate when talking to other tribes, and point out which plants could serve as food and medicine.

TIMEKEEPERS

Latitude offers just half the picture explorers needed to plot their position. The other half of the equation is longitude, or distance east or west around the world. Determining longitude is trickier than finding latitude. It requires an accurate clock—called a chronometer—that can keep time while far from land on a tossing ocean. The first seaworthy chronometers weren't invented until the 19th century, when mariners could finally rely less on dead reckoning and draw accurate maps of coastlines and oceans.

EYES IN THE sky

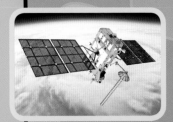

Explorers studied the stars to help them find their way; today's travelers navigate using a different kind of heavenly body: global positioning satellites. Launched into orbit in the late 1970s, these satellites use radio signals to locate traveler positions anywhere on Earth while GPS software offers turn-by-turn directions to just about any destination you can think of (although remote corners of the world remain uncharted even today). Such technology would seem like a miracle in the era of dead reckoning.

Why didn't
explorers run out of food?

Charting the world was no picnic before roadside rest stops and fast-food restaurants. Explorers traveling over land ate on the go, hunting for meat, foraging for edible plants, and drinking from streams. Sailors, however, had to stow all their food and water in barrels. Chickens and livestock provided fresh eggs and meat—and a smelly zoolike atmosphere belowdecks—until all these animals were eaten fairly early in the journey. Then, crew and captain alike survived off salted pork and rock-hard bread. Water was spiked with rum—a mixture called grog—to kill harmful bacteria. But although they rarely starved, many sailors living at sea for months at a time would become feverish and weak from an illness known as scurvy. The culprit: a dull diet lacking in vitamin C—a crucial nutritional need that the body doesn't store. It's found in citrus fruits such as oranges and limes, as well as some vegetables. Scurvy wasn't cured until the end of the 18th century, when crews began adding lime juice to their grog.

SAY WHAT?!

MUCH OF THE EARTH'S SURFACE wasn't accurately charted until the 18th century and even later. California, the third largest U.S. state, was drawn as an island on maps for more than 200 years! The mistake started when a Spanish sailor named Fortún Ximénez landed on the southern tip of Baja in 1533. He mistook the peninsula for an island and decided to name it the island of California, after a fictional paradise from a Spanish novel. The fiction was taken for fact, and the island of California appeared on many maps until the 18th century.

WHY didn't the *TITANIC* dodge that iceberg?

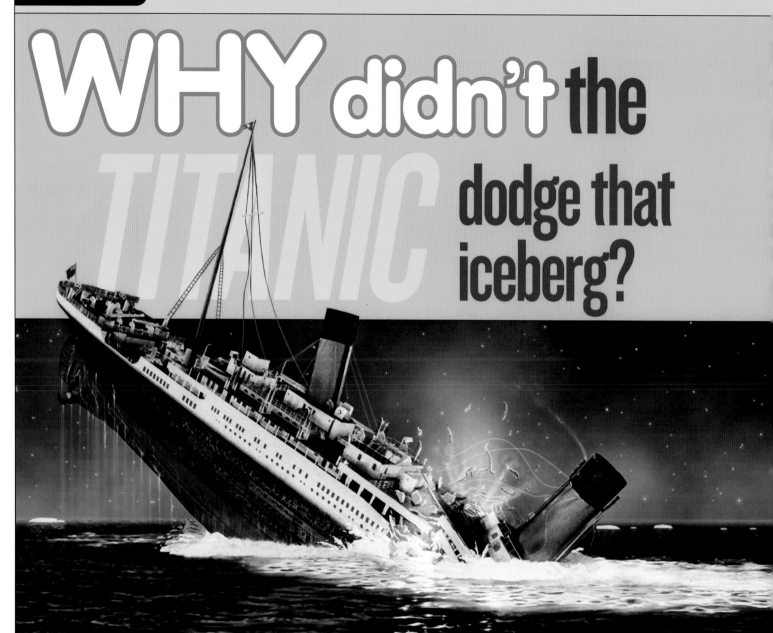

The *Titanic*'s first voyage would be its last. On the night of April 14, 1912, the unsinkable ship (complete with a heated swimming pool, two barber shops, four elevators, and 15 separate watertight compartments designed to keep it afloat in any circumstance) struck an iceberg about 400 miles (644 km) southeast of Newfoundland, in Canada. The ice slashed the ship's side under the waterline, flooding five of the watertight compartments. Within three hours, the *Titanic* sank to the bottom of the North Atlantic.

The ship had been traveling too quickly through icy waters in the days before danger-detecting radar. Analysis of the ship's construction showed that the rivets holding it together were weak, causing the hull to shear away easily at the moment of impact. The watertight compartments were built to withstand a head-on collision rather than a long sideways gash.

No single mistake led to the *Titanic*'s demise. It was a combination of faulty technology and errors in judgment that sank the "unsinkable" ship.

SOS THREE DISASTERS AT SEA

THE *VASA*

WHEN: 1626

WHERE: Stockholm, Sweden

WHAT SUNK IT: Gravity

Constructed under the orders of Sweden's king in 1626, the *Vasa* was a four-deck warship loaded with bronze cannons and gilded sculptures to demonstrate the country's maritime might and majesty. But the one thing it didn't demonstrate was good shipbuilding! All those cannons made the *Vasa* top-heavy. It toppled over and sunk less than 300 feet (91 m) from shore on its maiden voyage. The ship was salvaged in 1961 and is now a popular museum in Stockholm, Sweden.

THE SPANISH FLEET

WHEN: 1715

WHERE: Florida coast

WHAT SUNK IT: Hurricane

Riding low in the water, their holds laden with gold and silver worth $300 million in today's U.S. dollars, the Spanish treasure ships set sail for home from Cuba in the summer of 1715. The galleons were part of the world's most powerful navy, heavily armed against the pirates prowling the Caribbean. But cannons were useless against the monster that bore down on the treasure fleet a week later off the coast of Florida. Furious gales ripped apart the rigging. Two-story waves smashed the hulls to splinters. One by one, the galleons succumbed to a storm that seemed endless. Of the 11 ships that set out, only one made it home; more than a thousand sailors lost their lives. Sunken treasure littered beaches across the Atlantic coast of Florida. It's no wonder the Spanish called the storm that sank their fleet a *huracán,* the Maya word for an evil weather god.

THE *ESSEX*

WHEN: 1820

WHERE: Pacific Ocean

WHAT SUNK IT: Sperm whale

Whale hunters aboard this 19th-century whaling ship became the hunted when an 85-foot (26-m) sperm whale—twice their normal size—rammed the hull twice, piercing it on the second pass and sending the *Essex* to the bottom of the Pacific. The crew abandoned ship in three whaling boats, drifted for 80 days to the coast of South America, and was rescued by a passing ship. Only 8 sailors out of a crew of 21 survived. The fate of the *Essex* inspired the classic American novel *Moby-Dick.*

WHY didn't FOOD SPOIL BEFORE REFRIGERATORS?

Cold cuts, last night's lasagna, broccoli in the crisper drawer, spicy mustard and relish on the door—foods stay fresh in your fridge because its low temperatures make molds and bacteria lazy, slowing the spoilage process. But the household refrigerator is a recent invention—less than a century old. How did people keep their supper from turning stinky and green before the 20th century?

Fridges might be relatively new, but the idea of chilling food to keep it fresh is not The ancient Greeks and Romans stuffed ice and snow into pits to keep meat and milk from going bad. People throughout history lashed airtight jars filled with perishable food to the banks of icy springs and rivers. In tropical climates where ice and chilly water were unheard of, cultures came up with ingenious techniques for preserving food from rot: They dried meat, veggies, and fruits in the sun or baked them in special ovens, creating a kind of jerky that lasted for months. They pickled perishable food in vinegar or cured it with salt, then packed it into jars and barrels. Fruits were mixed into jams along with honey. Grains were fermented into a nutritious beer that even kids drank. Some historians even think the discovery of fermentation is what coaxed human hunters into becoming farmers about 12,000 years ago.

Why didn't people die of boredom before TV and the Internet?

We humans have been around for about 200,000 years. TV and the Internet, Pokémon and Xbox, smartphones and even electric lights have existed for less than .001 percent of that time. That doesn't mean human beings spent most of history twiddling their thumbs and watching the grass grow. We were too busy staying alive! Before humans learned how to grow crops and raise animals, about 12 millennia ago, we spent our waking hours chasing three things: food, shelter, and security from all the dangers of the world (wild animals, other humans, and even human cousins such as Neanderthals). Life on the farm—tending to crops and wrangling animals—didn't leave room for much leisure time. Farmers moving to cities during the industrial revolution of the 18th century traded long hours in the fields for long hours in factories.

But that doesn't mean life before modern entertainment was all work and no play. People entertained themselves by peering into the night sky and connecting the stars to create pictures—called constellations—of animals, objects, and legendary heroes. During the Middle Ages, servants and peasants were given time off to attend feasts and dances. Long before professional sports leagues, people organized tournaments of skill and played ancient versions of soccer or football using solid-rubber balls or inflated pieces of pig anatomy: the bladder (which is where we get the term "pigskin" for a football). The pursuit of food, shelter, and security became much easier as we moved into the 20th century. Leisure time increased greatly, along with the diversions—such as TV shows and the Internet—to fill it.

SILLY QUESTION, SERIOUS ANSWER

Why isn't a day 23 hours or 25 hours instead of 24?

Measuring time by days, months, and years makes sense; all three units of time are based on planetary clockwork that we can see with our own eyes. (A full day follows one rotation of the Earth, months are based on the 12 annual cycles of the moon, and a year is the time it takes for the Earth to complete one orbit of the sun.) But why is a day broken down into 24 hours? Did some ancient timekeeper just pull that number out of a hat? Not quite. We can thank the ancient Egyptians for our system of measuring daily time. Around 1500 B.C., they invented a sundial: a T-shaped stick stuck vertically into the ground that casts a moving shadow as the sun wheels overhead. The Egyptians used the length and direction of this shadow to divide the sunlit hours into 12 units, which later became known as hours. Twelve held special significance because it's tied to the number of months in the year, and months were important to a civilization that depended on the seasonal flooding of the Nile River to irrigate farmlands and grow food. After sundown, the ancient Egyptians used a system of counting stars to divide the night into 12 units, laying the groundwork for the 24-hour clock we use today. Hours were later broken down into minutes and seconds with the invention of more accurate timekeeping devices.

WHY didn't people feel GROSS before indoor baths?

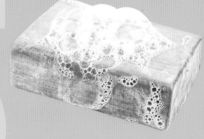

Movies and TV shows portray people of the past as impeccably styled and freshly showered, but the real picture of historical hygiene isn't so rosy (and it probably didn't smell all that rosy, either). Soap and indoor plumbing were expensive luxuries before the mid-19th century. Consider the hassle of a hot bath in the Middle Ages: Water had to be hauled from the castle's well or a nearby river and then heated by special servants called ewerers charged with preparing the bathtub for the lord and lady. But even nobles snubbed a daily scrub-a-dub-dub because they feared that cleaning their skin might invite evil into their bodies. (England's Queen Elizabeth I boasted that she bathed once a month, "whether she needed it or not.") It's not that people of the past didn't take pride in their appearance or look after basic hygiene needs. Archaeologists studying the body of an Irish king, preserved in a peat bog for 2,000 years, found that he styled his hair using a gel made of oil and tree sap imported from France. In drought-prone corners of Africa and other places without access to running water, people still took time to scour their bodies clean with scraping tools, clumps of ash, and even smoke baths that washed the skin with sweat without raising a stink.

History's STINK STOPPERS

PERFUME

To cover their stench, ancient Egyptians wore wigs scented with sweet-smelling wax and deodorants mixed from incense, lettuce, fruit, and myrrh.

MINT TOOTHPASTE

Medieval peasants took care of their teeth and fought bad breath using a finger or twig dipped in a crude toothpaste made from salt, wine, and mint.

NOSEGAYS

North America's 18th-century colonists buried their noses in scented kerchiefs to block the sweaty stench of their unwashed neighbors.

Why didn't people just go to the bathroom anywhere they wanted before toilets?

Indoor plumbing, steaming-hot showers, fridge ice makers—these are all newish luxuries; toilets have been around in one form or another for thousands of years. And for good reason! Thousands of years ago, in the earliest of settlements, people went potty outside of village limits—no closer than arrow-launching distance, according to legend—because nothing can ruin the mood of a budding civilization quite like pools of human poop. Not only is sewage stinky, it carries bacteria that can make people sick. As settlements grew in size, even arrow-shooting distance was too close for comfort (and health). Tinkerers invented ways to answer nature's call in comfort while not jeopardizing the neighbor's health. Behold the evolution of the best seat in the house ...

SILLY QUESTION, SERIOUS ANSWER

Why don't toilets stink today?

Fair question, considering all the stinky stuff we flush and where it winds up: in underground sewage pipes that carry waste away to treatment facilities. And although toilet technology has come a long way since the first in-home commodes were developed 5,000 years ago, the top stink-stopping innovation was developed in 1775 by a Scottish watchmaker named Alexander Cumming. He came up with an S-shaped drain pipe that traps a barrier of water between your nose and the sewer, blocking any stinking smells. Most toilets today still use Cumming's invention.

KISS YOUR COMMODE EVERY NOVEMBER 19, AKA WORLD TOILET DAY!

That's when the World Toilet Organization calls attention to the 2.6 billion people across the globe who lack access to such a crucial convenience.

Momentous
MOMENTS IN COMMODE HISTORY

3000 B.C. The first in-home toilets are developed in Skara Brae, a small settlement on a chilly Scottish island. Holes in each stone hut lead to poop-stained drains that carry the waste away.

1700 B.C. The Palace of Knossos on the Greek island of Crete is home to history's first known flush toilet. Built for the queen, it has a wooden seat set over a drain flushed with water poured through earthenware pipes.

A.D. 200 Roman citizens do their business side by side on benchlike toilets that empty into an elaborate sewer system. They even share a sponge-tipped stick for wiping! But toilet technology goes down the drain after the fall of the Roman Empire. For the next 1,700 years, most people poop and pee in chamber pots they empty out the window.

A.D. 1596 Englishman Sir John Harington invents a new type of flushable "water closet" for his powerful godmother, Queen Elizabeth I, but Harington's invention goes unnoticed for 200 years until Alexander Cumming invents his odor-blocking pipe. (More in the sidebar at left).

A.D. 1884 English plumber Thomas Crapper perfects flush-toilet technology at a time when indoor plumbing becomes more common in Europe and the United States. Crapper's improvements bring toilets into the mainstream. Toilet paper also comes into popular use around this time.

TODAY After remaining stagnant for more than 200 years, toilet technology is finally getting an overhaul for the roughly 2.6 billion people in the world who don't have access to sewer systems and sufficient water to waste on every flush. Funded by billionaire software developer Bill Gates, scores of engineering teams are racing to invent the toilet 2.0: self-sufficient commodes that will contain their own mini-treatment plants that zap the stinky stuff from waste while using less water and space to dispose of it.

WHY shouldn't you take your FAMILY DOCTOR for granted?

If you had a migraine in ancient Peru, your doctor would have drilled a hole in your head to relieve the pressure (and free the evil spirits). In a medieval castle—where your barber doubled as your surgeon—a typical treatment would have involved being bled to the point of dizziness (possibly using leeches!). And European doctors in the 16th century would have crafted you potions from ground-up mummies. It's tough to tell what was worse in the days before modern medicine: getting sick or getting healed. Modern doctors know that what we can't see (germs) can make us sick (by causing infections and spreading diseases). But before the 19th century, nobody knew how diseases spread. Healers in various times and places thought sickness was a punishment from the heavens or caused by icky odors in the air. With no knowledge of the causes of disease, physicians could only guess at the cures. Treatments for an outbreak of a deadly plague—known as the Black Death—in the 14th century ranged from dangerous to ridiculous. Victims ate ground-up emeralds or washed themselves in urine or rubbed their plague blisters with a chicken's plucked rear end. The only surefire way to avoid the plague was to avoid its victims. That meant Europeans had better luck if they just stayed away from the doctor to begin with.

Bad Medicine

Most modern medications go through intense testing to make sure they heal instead of harm you. That wasn't the case in the early 1900s, when more than 30,000 snake oil concoctions were made and sold in the United States to cure toothaches, migraines, joint pain, bug bites, scuffed knees—"whatever ails you," their inventors claimed. The active ingredient, fluids wrung from snakes, possessed healing powers, according to Chinese and Native American lore, and slick-talking salespeople peddled these potions at fairs and sold them to drugstores. Modern studies of snake fats show that these oils do pack some health-boosting properties, but the snake oils of the past lacked medicinal value for a big reason: They didn't contain any snake oil! When government officials analyzed one particularly famous liniment, they discovered it was mostly mineral oil, with a dab of beef fat and some nasty turpentine to make it smell like medicine. Which, of course, it wasn't. Authorities soon cracked down on the sale of other snake oils—a term that has come to cover all useless concoctions marketed as cure-alls.

Did healers of the past actually, you know, heal anybody?

Of course! In fact, many of the medicines doctors prescribe today are based on remedies uncovered in the ancient past. The ancient Egyptians were especially good at healing the sick and treating the injured. Priests cast spells and pre-scribed charmed amulets and other trinkets, but they mixed this hocus-pocus with actual medicine: herbs pounded into potions that fought infection and boosted immunity. Egyptian healers understood that the heart was a vital organ connected to the body's pulse. They could mend broken bones and perform minor surgeries with scalpels made of razor-sharp rock. The men and women who treated the sick and injured were usually part-time scribes or priests who went to medical school at the temples and learned a specialty. "The country is full of physicians," said the Greek historian Herodotus when he visited ancient Egypt. "Some treat the eye, some the teeth, some of what belongs to the abdomen, and others internal diseases." Rulers of foreign countries requested house calls from these desert docs for their unrivaled expertise. Even if some of the cures—pig teeth to settle upset stomachs and whole mice to cure coughs—relied on the power of magic and positive thinking.

PERSON OF INTEREST

WHO?
Hippocrates

WHAT is he famous for?
Establishing the lifesaving rules of modern medicine

WHEN?
400 B.C.

WHERE?
Ancient Greece

WHY is he important?

If you were to pick any doctor of the ancient world to summon through time for a house call, you'd want this guy, Hippocrates, widely considered the father of modern medicine. It's not that this teacher of physicians in ancient Greece under-stood everything about the body. (Hippocrates was under the mistaken impression that good health depended on keeping four fictional flu-ids—called humors—in balance.) But he tried to take the hocus-pocus out of healing by teaching that the environment, exercise, and other factors can affect a person's health. He was careful to observe his patients and refrain from any treatments that might do more harm than good. In fact, before practicing medicine, all new doctors today take the Hippocratic oath to do no harm.

WHY doesn't the U.S.A.

have, say, 49 states or 51 states instead of 50?

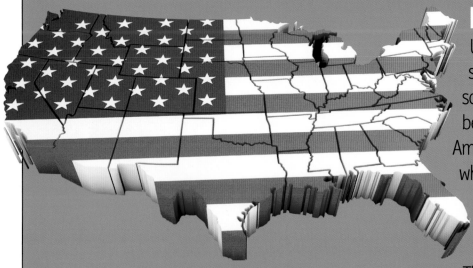

Fifty is a nifty number, but the U.S.A.'s size, shape, and number of states wasn't part of some grand scheme planned out from the very beginning. The United States of America has come a long way since 1776, when its original 13 colonies declared their independence from England. Those 13 colonies, arrayed along the eastern seaboard, became 13 states. Those 13 grew to 20, then 30, then 48 as the country expanded westward across the middle of the North American continent, finally topping off at 50 with the additions of far-flung Alaska and Hawaii in 1959. But the United States wouldn't be even half of its size today if not for the Louisiana Purchase of 1803, when the U.S. government bought the Louisiana Territory—all 828,000 square miles (2.1 million sq km) of it—from France for the price of $15 million, or about four cents an acre. This big deal extended the nation's territory west of the Mississippi River to the Rocky Mountains and north from the Gulf of Mexico to Canada. At least parts or all of 15 states were eventually formed from the Louisiana Territory. If the deal had collapsed, those born west of the Mississippi today might be citizens of France, Spain, or Mexico, speaking French or Spanish as their native language. California, Nevada, Washington, and all the other territory west of the Louisiana Territory would never have become part of the United States (although Alaska and Hawaii still might've joined the Union).

Why can't
U.S. presidents serve as many terms as they can get elected to?

Because America's first president set a good example. The original U.S. Constitution—the government's instruction manual—didn't establish a limit on how long someone could serve as president. But George Washington, hero of the American Revolution and a model first president, could easily have won a third term after serving his first two (eight years total). He refused. Washington didn't want to reign for life like a king or queen of England, from which America had just fought for its independence. All presidents to come followed Washington's example until Franklin D. Roosevelt, who led the country through the Great Depression of the 1930s and World War II. After Roosevelt's death, in his fourth term, the U.S. Congress ratified an amendment to the Constitution limiting a president to just two terms.

Why isn't
Washington, D.C., a state?

It was never meant to be one. The Constitution gave Congress (the U.S. lawmaking body) the authority to create a seat of government free from the influence of any particular state. The result was the District of Columbia, which to this day remains under the jurisdiction of the federal government. But Washington, D.C., wasn't always the capital. The unofficial capital had been Philadelphia, Pennsylvania, where the Declaration of Independence from England was written in 1776. The capital was moved to its current location 140 miles (225 km) southwest in 1800 for a variety of reasons, including threats from U.S. soldiers angry at not getting paid, a breakout of deadly fever in Philadelphia the year before, and a compromise between the northern and southern states. (Washington, D.C., is more centrally located than Philadelphia.)

Why isn't
the American flag red, white, and green?

Politicians and history buffs have assigned special significance to the stars and stripes over the past two centuries: The red stripes represent the sacrifice of patriots in battle! White stands for our nation's pure intentions! Blue stands for justice! But these interpretations all came after the flag was designed in 1776. Historians don't know the reasons for the flag's colors—or even who designed the original flag. (The story that it was sewn by upholsterer Betsy Ross based on a drawing by George Washington is a disputed legend.) When the Second Continental Congress adopted the flag in 1777, its resolution offered no clues about the meaning of its colors. "Resolved, that the flag of the United States be thirteen stripes," it said, "alternate red and white; that the union be thirteen stars, white in a blue field, representing a new constellation." We know the stars represent America's states, and the 13 stripes represent the original 13 colonies. The colors themselves—red, white, and blue—were most likely taken from the Union Jack of England, our mother country's original flag. Beyond that, the star-spangled banner's colors are wide open to interpretation.

Why isn't U.S.
money red, white, or blue?

Paper currency—also known as notes or bills—comes in a rainbow of colors in countries around the world, but U.S. money is so famous for its green color that "green" is another word for money. But American "green" wasn't always green. From the early 19th century to the Civil War, notes came in a jumble of sizes, designs, and dominations. Bills printed in black and white were vulnerable to counterfeiters who could photograph them and print their own funny money. So the backsides of bills were printed with green ink to foil the black-and-white cameras of the time. These bills became known as greenbacks, which were available in a variety of sizes until the government standardized bills in 1929. The U.S. mint stuck with the green theme front and back because the ink was plentiful and resisted damage from chemicals and rough handling (green also symbolizes growth and prosperity, which is a good color to associate with a nation's economy). Cash has been green ever since, although the mint began adding splashes of color in 2004.

WHY can't you eat FRIED CHICKEN WITH A FORK in Gainesville, Georgia, U.S.A.?

Because it's against a law passed in 1961. In fact, a Louisiana woman named Ginny Dietrick was arrested for breaking this law in 2009, when the Gainesville police chief caught her eating chicken with a fork in a restaurant. Fortunately for Dietrick, her "arrest" was just a practical joke arranged by a friend (and the mayor quickly pardoned her for the crime). The 1961 law itself was a publicity stunt to promote Gainesville as the poultry capital of the world. But this finger-licking prohibition against utensils is hardly the zaniest law. Cities and states across the world have statutes (or laws) that might seem silly and useless today but were necessary when they were passed in the past. A law against tripping horses in the state of Oklahoma, for instance, might seem ridiculous in the 21st century, but it was a necessary rule before the invention of the car, when horse and carriages were the main method of getting around town. Changing or repealing laws is a time-consuming and expensive undertaking, so many of these silly old laws are still in the books but no longer enforced, including ...

Odd Laws
FROM AROUND THE WORLD

You can't wear high heels in Carmel-by-the-Sea, California, U.S.A.

Origin of the law: To prevent lawsuits from people tripping over sidewalk bumps or tree roots. Greece has a similar law to protect the stone foundations around its ancient monuments from damage from spiky heels. Wearing them is literally a crime of fashion!

A chicken **can't** cross the road in Quitman, Georgia, U.S.A.

Origin of the law: So that ranchers will keep their fowl from running wild and fowl-ing up traffic.

You can't play pinball in Beacon, New Jersey, U.S.A.

Origin of the law: Many cities in the 1970s outlawed pinball because they mistakenly thought it was a form of gambling linked to the mob and other criminal activities.

You can't roller-skate across the street in Canton, Ohio, U.S.A.

Origin of the law: To stop skating in the streets. You're still allowed to roller-skate across the street at a crosswalk, though—just don't dillydally!

You can't wear a suit of armor in the British Parliament.

Origin of the law: Passed more than 700 years ago when such laws were necessary, this statute prevents members of the British House of Commons from disrupting lawmaking debates by brandishing their armor and swords, which are also forbidden. Parliament members were once provided with a hook to hang their swords in the cloakroom.

You can't chew gum in Singapore without a doctor's permission.

Origin of the law: Singapore, a famously neat nation, banned chewing gum in 1992 after vandals began cramming chewed-up wads into subway doors and mailbox locks. In 2004, gum company Wrigley worked up the gumption to convince Singapore's government to allow the sale of special gum for medical purposes, but everything else is off-limits.

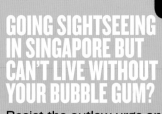

Astronauts **can't** vote in space unless they're from Texas.

Origin of the law: Because that's where most astronauts live—at least when they're not orbiting Earth in the International Space Station. Thanks to legislation passed in Texas, U.S.A., in 1997, any astronauts with mailing addresses in Texas can vote in any election electronically from the International Space Station, which granted its crew personal access to the Internet in 2010. Astronauts simply fill out an online ballot in orbit and email it to a clerk on the ground, who then inputs their selections on a paper ballot. This way astronauts working in space can still make their vote count here on Earth.

Parents **can't** give their kids silly names in Denmark.

Origin of the law: To protect the youngest of Denmark's citizens from potentially embarrassing names. Denmark is actually one of many countries that provide a list of approved names for newborns. Any names not on the list must be green-lit by Danish authorities.

You can't pay with more than 25 pennies in Canada.

Origin of the law: To limit the use of pennies, which the Canadian mint began to phase out of circulation in 2012.

YOUR BODY

HUMAN BEINGS HAVE SURVIVED FALLS FROM MILES IN THE SKY, dove hundreds of feet deep into the ocean on a single breath, walked on the surface of another world, and crammed nearly a hundred hot dogs into their bellies in one sitting. Yep, we can accomplish amazing things when we put our minds (and bodies) to it. In this chapter, you'll discover why your body works the way it works, why it sometimes doesn't work the way you wish it would, and even how you can use your mind to achieve your body's full potential. It's time you got to know the real you!

WHY don't I have a DOPPELGÄNGER?

You mean an exact replica, wandering somewhere out in the world? Don't bother hunting for one—because you're special. Like seriously super-duper extra special. In fact, no two humans alive today—or who have ever lived—are exactly the same. Even identical twins appear slightly different if you eyeball them up close. What makes you you is mostly a mix of your mom and dad, who are in turn a mix of their parents, and so on going back at least 200,000 years to the earliest days of the human species (and even before that). Maybe you've been told that you have your dad's eyes or your grandma's nose? That's because you inherited these features. Actually, you inherited the genes that gave you Grandma's nose or your dad's eyes.

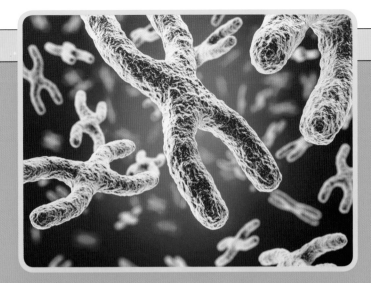

Genes, huh? **What** are those?

You probably guessed they're not your favorite pair of ratty pants (although the word is pronounced the same, and some people who stay remarkably thin claim they have "skinny genes"). Genes are itty-bitty strips of chemicals called DNA, found in every cell of your body. Don't worry too much about that technical stuff; what's important is their purpose. Genes are like the pages of an instruction manual for each cell, telling it how to create specific proteins to build your body and make sure it runs just right. All your cells contain the same genes—roughly 20,000 of them, in fact—but these genes provide the coded instructions for making different proteins depending on where they are in your body. Cells in your skin, for instance, produce proteins that build and maintain sweat glands. Cells in an organ called the pancreas produce proteins that create a crucial hormone called insulin, which regulates the levels of sugar in your bloodstream.

Your genes determine almost everything you see in the mirror, from your height to your hair color to less obvious traits such as whether you have perfect vision or the ability to wiggle your ears. And genes come in pairs: one from Mom and one from Dad in a process called "heredity." That's why you might resemble one or both of your parents, or your siblings—who also got their genes from Mom and Dad just like you.

But **what** if I don't look like either Mom or Dad?

Don't worry—you're still their kid! Much about heredity remains mysterious. (Scientists understand the purpose of only about 3 percent of our DNA.) Many of your physical characteristics aren't determined by just one gene but by combinations of them, which can lead to unpredictable physical traits or features that lurk in the family background for several generations. One example is hair color, which is why two brown-haired parents can have a redheaded kid. Some genes—called dominant genes—are more influential on your appearance than others. But your genes determine your appearance only to a certain point. The rest is affected by your environment, diet, social life, level of exercise, and many other factors not controlled by those coded instructions in your cells. That's one of the reasons identical twins—even though they share 100 percent of the same genetic makeup—don't look exactly the same.

SILLY QUESTION, SERIOUS ANSWER

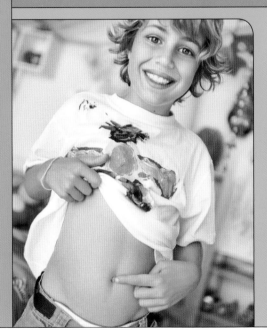

Why is my outie not an innie (or vice versa)?

When it comes to the disposition of your belly button, your genes don't matter much at all. To understand why, you first need to know why you have that little lint collector in your lower abdomen. All "placental mammals," or animals nourished inside their mothers before birth, have belly buttons (even dolphins, whose navels are more of a slash shape). Before you were born, when you were still developing in the womb, you were hooked up to your life-support system through a special cord that plugged into your navel. Through this "umbilical cord," you received food and oxygen and passed waste. The day you were born, you let out a cry and began breathing on your own. That let the doctor know she could cut the umbilical cord—which is the moment that defined your belly button's standing. Any leftover nub of cord eventually dried out and fell off. Longer leftover nubs are more likely to result in outies, which are less common than innies.

Whichever type you have is perfectly normal—just another thing that makes you special.

WHY wasn't
I born with the
ABILITY
to sing or paint or dance or [insert cool talent here]?

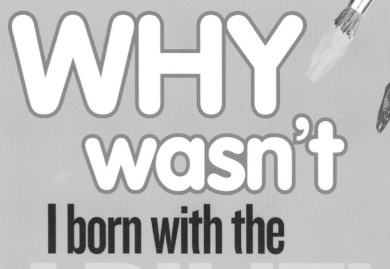

You just learned that your physical appearance is affected by both internal (genetic) and external (environmental) factors. But what about the traits inside your brain: your ability to write an exciting story or ace geometry problems or sink a three-pointer in basketball? You're about to step into one of the great debates in science: Are humans the product of our genes or our experiences and environment? Scientists call this debate "nature versus nurture." The answer: a bit of both.

Only prodigies—children under 10 who display professional abilities—may be born with a leg up in a particular skill. Famous composer Wolfgang Amadeus Mozart was performing before audiences when he was five! But these supernaturally talented kids are supremely rare—maybe one in 10 million. For everyone not born with a rare gift, studies show that practice is more important at building skills than genetic makeup. We can see how by looking at a very simple (and possibly silly) ability: tongue rolling.

What does tongue rolling have to do with my abilities?

Quick, stick your tongue out in the mirror and see if you can roll the edges up like a taco shell? If you can do it, you're part of the 81 percent of people who can roll their tongues. Scientists once thought that tongue twisting was determined purely by genes—in other words, that only people born with the gene for tongue rolling could pull it off. But studies of identical twins revealed cases in which one twin could roll their tongue while the other twin could not, despite being born with identical genes. Still other studies showed that some—but not all—non–tongue rollers eventually figured out how to roll their tongue by practicing in the mirror. The point: Tongue-rolling ability is a mix of both genetic factors (such as genes for a wider tongue, longer tongue muscles, and so on) and practice. Some people are natural-born tongue rollers, while others can learn on their own.

These studies go to show that genetics are only part of the equation that makes you who you are. Just as there's no single gene or even a group of genes for tongue rolling, there's no gene combination that lets you paint like Leonardo da Vinci or dunk a basketball like LeBron James. Talent takes practice to cultivate. The trick is to find activities that feel both natural and fun. If you think time flies when you play the piano, for instance, then you'll have no problem logging the 10,000 hours of practice that experts believe you need to achieve greatness.

What are the chances of someone looking just like me?

Ah, yes, back to the hunt for your doppelgänger. If you want an exact replica that could fool even your own mother, you would need an astronomical amount of luck. A 2015 study that examined eight facial traits (such as the shape of the head and the distance between the eyes) determined that the likelihood of two people sharing the same measurements for all eight traits was supremely slim: one in 100 trillion. (That's more than 14,000 times the population of the planet!)

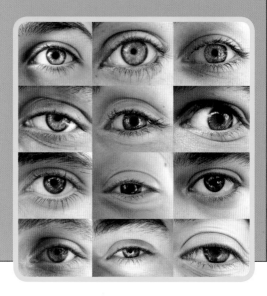

Okay, but what about someone who looks close enough?

If you were willing to accept a doppelgänger with a few little differences—such as a narrower nose or bushier eyebrows—you'd have a little more luck, especially if you search closer to your ancestors' point of origin. "Individuals with shared ancestry—or are more related to one another—are going to have a higher chance of looking similar," says Charlyn G. Partridge, a professor who teaches genetics at Grand Valley State University in Michigan. "While only about 8 percent of the world's population has blue eyes, for instance, in Finland it is closer to 75 percent." If your family hails from Finland, in other words, you're more likely to find someone who shares similar physical traits with you.

But let's say you don't have the time (or the airfare) to trek to your ancestors' point of origin. What are the chances of finding your doppelgänger in an ethnically diverse country like the United States? "Let's assume we're looking for three physical traits that come together to make up a person's face," Partridge says. "Each trait is still influenced by four genes and each gene has five variants." Crunching those numbers, Partridge comes up with a figure: around one in 244 million. "This is still a low chance," she says, "but not impossible." Considering the United States has a population of around 320 million, your doppelgänger is probably out there. Keep those eyes peeled.

WHAT DETERMINES my...

... skin color? Your genes and environment! You are the color you are because your genes determine the amount of melanin your body produces. Melanin is a special chemical pigment that protects your skin from the dangerous ultraviolet rays of the sun. Originally, all humans had dark skin to shield us from powerful solar rays in tropical Africa, point of origin for the human species. As humans spread to less sunny places, their bodies made less melanin so that their skin could absorb more sun to produce vitamin D, an essential vitamin for building strong bones. Over many generations, they developed fairer skin in the process. Today, people whose ancestors came from less sunny places have fairer skin while those whose ancestors came from sunnier places are born with more melanin and have darker skin. When people are out in the sun often, their bodies produce more melanin and they get darker and tanner (melanin will also create freckles in fair-skinned people). But too much sun exposure can cause dangerous skin cancers—particularly in fair-skinned people—so be sure to lather on sunblock before you head out for fun in the sun.

... eye color?
Your genes!

Those genes you inherited from your parents determine how much melanin you have in each iris, the colorful part of your eye. The more melanin you have, the darker your eyes. Less melanin makes for lighter eyes, which is why fair-skinned people often have light blue or gray eyes. Several genes are involved in determining the color of your eyes, which is why two parents with blue eyes can have a child with brown eyes.

... hair's appearance?
Your genes, environment, and personal style!

The hair on your head (and all over your body, in fact) grows from tiny tubes called follicles. Your genes determine the shape of those follicles. Flat follicles result in curly hair. Round follicles make straight hair. Bigger follicles result in thicker hair. Exposure to sunlight will lighten your hair. And of course, you can dye and style your hair in different ways, too!

... dimples (or lack thereof)?
Your genes!

Those little dents in cheeks (or chin, which is known as a cleft) might be associated with cuteness, but they're actually the result of a genetically inherited defect in the facial muscles that control smiling. Researchers aren't sure why humans evolved dimples or why some people find them attractive. One theory is we associate these little cheek divots with babies, and evolution has wired our brains to think babies are cute (so that we feel an urge to take care of them). Dimples are therefore a desirable physical trait that gets passed on to offspring.

... height?
Your genes and your environment!

If you want to know how tall you'll grow, look at your mom and dad (and your aunts and uncles). Your final height is in many ways determined by your genes. (Which means you'll probably reach a height somewhere in between your parents, although not always. Shorter parents can have tall children and the other way around.) Diet, exercise, and how much sleep you get can also affect how much you grow. (Want to grow taller? Get lots of sleep!)

Where did all these different traits come from?

Mutations! The first members of the human species all looked fairly similar to one another when they appeared on the fossil record around 200,000 years ago. But as humanity began to spread to different environments—sunny, snowy, soggy, sweltering—people began to adapt to their parts of the world. And these adaptations started with mutations. Occasionally an organism is born with a mutation, or an alteration to its genetic structure. Successful mutations—those that help an organism survive—are passed along to offspring. One famous example is something called the epicanthic fold: a small flap of skin that covers the inner corner of the eye. It helps protect eyes from harmful ultraviolet radiation in sunny regions, so it spread across these regions as a helpful adaptation. Today it's common in people of Asian descent. But not all mutations are something you can see. About 12,000 years ago, for example, a mutation allowed humans to chug cow milk without getting sick. This ability was enormously beneficial to our survival—not to mention welcome when you have a plate of chocolate chip cookies.

WHY don't I keep GROWING throughout my life?

Gosh, how tall do you want to get? During your growing years, plates in your bones expand little by little, adding to your height. The average growth rate (not including growth spurts) for boys and girls is about 2.5 inches (6.4 cm) a year. When you reach the end of puberty, these plates fuse and you stop sprouting like a bean stalk. Now, if you were to continue to grow past your teens until you reached the ripe old age of 79 (the average life expectancy in the United States), you'd eventually grow slightly taller than a two-story house!

SAY WHAT?!

ADD UP ALL THE HAIRS ON YOUR BODY AND YOU'D REACH A TOTAL OF ABOUT FIVE MILLION.

That's not far off from the amount of hair on chimpanzees, but their body hair is thicker than ours, making us look naked by comparison. (Bigger hair follicles grow thicker hairs.)

Why don't my eyelashes and eyebrows keep growing like the hair on my head?

Those artfully styled (or carelessly tussled) tresses atop your noggin are more than just a fashion statement. They mark you as a mammal. All mammals—even ocean-dwelling marine mammals such as manatees and dolphins—have hair. And although we evolved with sparser "fur" across our bodies compared with our ape ancestors and other mammals, humans still have hair everywhere except the palms of our hands, the soles of our feet, and our lips. Our hair serves different functions depending on where it appears on our bodies. Eyelashes and eyebrows protect our eyes (see sidebar), but imagine how useless they'd be if they just kept growing and growing like your mop up top? You'd have a shaggy mess blocking your view!

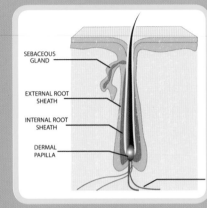

SEBACEOUS GLAND

EXTERNAL ROOT SHEATH

INTERNAL ROOT SHEATH

DERMAL PAPILLA

All the hair on your body, including the fine hairs on your forearms, sprout from tiny tubes in your skin called follicles, which go through the phases of growing and resting. The hairs on your head spend years at a time in the growing phase, while the hairs on the rest of your body—including your eyelashes and eyebrows—spend most of their time in the resting phase. While in this phase, the hair has stopped growing and the follicles shrink, which makes the hairs break and shed more easily. These hairs tend to stay short because they shed long before they have a chance to grow long, which is why you'll never need to ask your barber to take a few inches off your eyelashes.

Why don't I keep my baby teeth?

You were born flapping your gums without a pearly white in sight (sometimes babies are born with a tooth or two in place, but it's rare). Within six months, your first teeth began to sprout from your gums. (Doctors call these "deciduous" teeth—kind of like our practice set for chewing food.) As you'd expect, an infant's skull is too small to hold a full set of grown-up choppers, so our first set of 20 acts as placeholders. As your jaw grows, your permanent teeth begin

to grow in the oral cavity behind each baby tooth. Once a child reaches six or so, those baby teeth loosen and get the heave-ho by the pushy permanent teeth growing in from behind. As our jaws continue to grow, we sprout an additional 12 molars for a total of 32 permanent pearly whites.

HAIR EVERYWHERE

THE FUNCTIONS OF OUR "fur" FROM HEAD TO TOE

HEAD HAIR

The 100,000 or so hairs on your head help retain your body heat.

BODY HAIR

These thinner, shorter hairs across your body wick away sweat, keeping you cool.

UNDERARM HAIR

Around the time humans hit puberty, thicker clumps of hair sprout in our armpits and other places to trap substances we produce called "pheromones" (these fragrant chemicals play a greater role in the animal world—not so much in the human world).

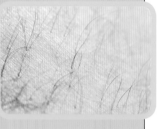

EYELASHES

Those bristly hairs around your peepers are their first line of defense, shielding them from dust and dirt.

EYEBROWS

The strips of fur above your eyes act like natural sweatbands, keeping rain and sweat from running down and clouding your vision.

MYTH MASHED

Why DON'T I KEEP ALL THE BONES I'M BORN WITH?

Human babies are adorable little bags of bones: as many as 350 of them. But x-rays of adults show only 206 bones. Where did all those baby bones go? Nowhere! They simply fused together to make fewer, bigger bones. A baby's skull, for instance, is made of three bones that later fuse into one tough helmet of calcium and other minerals that protect our brains. Some baby bones are made of a softer tissue called cartilage, which is more flexible and makes the birthing process easier for Mom. These cartilaginous bones join and harden to form our adult skeleton.

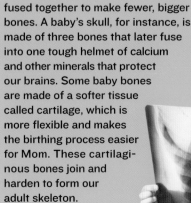

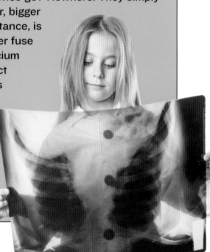

WHY isn't my HEART

shaped like a heart from a Valentine's Day card?

Our hearts were medically linked to our emotions for thousands of years and as recently as the 17th century, most likely because strong emotions such as fear and excitement can make our hearts go pitter-patter. Today, we know it's the brain that processes joy, sadness, and all other emotions, but the link between our heart and feelings of romantic love still sticks. No one is quite sure why the traditional symbol for the heart—that double-humped pointy-bottomed shape of Valentine's Day candies and boxes of chocolates—doesn't look more like the lumpier real thing beating away in your chest. It's not as if the heart's true appearance is some recent discovery; scholars have known what our heart looks like since ancient times. The traditional heart shape, however, goes back to ancient Egypt, where merchants traded in a now extinct plant with a heart-shaped seed. That plant had many uses, one of them linked to love, so perhaps the association carried on through the centuries. But the truth might be even more straightforward. Although the human heart is an amazing blood-pumping machine powered by electricity generated inside your body, it's not something you'd want to see on a Valentine's Day card. Take a look for yourself as we examine the heart's parts ...

SAY WHAT?!

YOUR CIRCULATORY SYSTEM IS MADE OF 60,000 MILES (96,561 KM) OF BLOOD VESSELS.

That's long enough to wrap around the Earth nearly two and a half times!

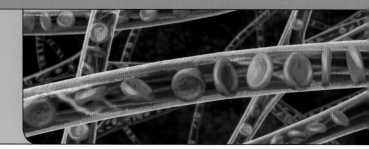

GETTING YOUR
blood pumping

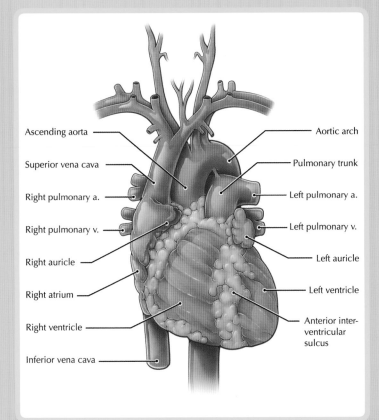

Ascending aorta

Superior vena cava

Right pulmonary a.

Right pulmonary v.

Right auricle

Right atrium

Right ventricle

Inferior vena cava

Aortic arch

Pulmonary trunk

Left pulmonary a.

Left pulmonary v.

Left auricle

Left ventricle

Anterior inter-ventricular sulcus

YOUR HEART IS A TOUGH MUSCLE, about the size of your fist, tucked between your lungs slightly to the left of center in your chest. It's not what you'd call pretty—unless you think a red slab of extra-rare beef is a thing of beauty—but it is a workhorse, beating an average of 100,000 times a day as it pumps blood to every cell in your body through an electric-powered system of chambers and valves. If your brain is the control center of your body, then the heart is its engine. And it's always running ...

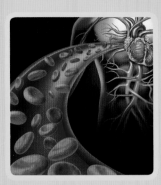

YOUR HEART IS MADE OF FOUR CHAMBERS—two on the top and two on the bottom— that all work together to pump blood throughout your body's "circulatory system" of blood vessels. Think of this system as a delivery company that relies on blood instead of a fleet of trucks. Your blood delivers all the good stuff (oxygen, vita-mins, minerals, infection fight-ers, and chemicals called hormones) to every cell in your body and then trucks away all the bad stuff (carbon dioxide and other wastes) for disposal. Without the heart to keep the blood flowing, this delivery sys-tem would jam up. Your cells wouldn't get their supplies and your body would close up shop.

THE CHAMBERS ON THE TOP OF YOUR HEART ARE CALLED ATRIA (each chamber is an "atrium"), and they form the first stage of your heart's blood-pumping process. The two chambers on the bottom are called ventricles, which make up the second stage. The left and right halves of your heart are separated by a strip of muscle called the septum. This dividing wall is important because each side of the heart acts as a separate pump with its own important task. On the left side, the left atrium fills with blood that has passed through your lungs, where the blood is filled with oxygen. That blood passes through the mitral valve to the left ventricle, one of the two lower chambers that form the second stage of your heart's blood-pumping process. An electrical impulse triggers your heart muscle to squeeze and—lub-dub!—your heart beats, squirting oxygen-rich blood in the left ventricle through the aortic valve into the network of blood vessels (called arteries) to all the cells in your body.

YOUR RIGHT SIDE OF THE HEART HANDLES THE DELIVERY SYSTEM'S RETURN TRIP: all the waste material for disposal, which follows its own network of blood vessels (called veins) back to the heart. Waste-filled blood enters the right atrium, passes through the tricuspid valve to the right ventricle, and then—lub-dub!—squirts out the pulmonary valve to your lungs. Here, the blood drops off its carbon diox-ide waste (which you exhale), is recharged with oxygen, and is pumped back to the left atrium, where the delivery process starts all over again. This entire chain of events—oxygen-rich blood moved through the left two chambers and waste-filled blood through the right—happens simultaneously with each beat of the heart, more than 2.5 billion times throughout the average life. Your heart is such a powerful pumping engine, in fact, that it takes only about 10 seconds for your blood to make a round-trip to your big toe. Not bad for a red slab of extra-rare beef.

 Q: tips

How TO KEEP YOUR HEART HEALTHY

Don't pig out

Unhealthy foods like fatty steaks, sugary snacks, and fried anything can make you gain weight or clog your blood vessels with junk, which makes your heart work harder.

Eat well

Substitute sugary sodas with sweet fruits, and eat the vegetables Dad puts on your plate. Eating healthy foods is smart for your heart.

Keep moving

Like any muscle, your heart needs exercise to stay healthy and strong. Your heart responds well to any exercise that leaves you out of breath, such as playing soccer or dancing.

WHY can't I TICKLE myself?

Tickle attack! You can't hold back giggles when a pal or a parent wiggles their fingers under your arms or along your sides—prime ticklish territory on humans—but try to tickle those same spots on yourself and you'll go "meh" instead of "heeheehee!" It's a mystery that has stumped scholars for centuries. (Yes, tickling has been the subject of study going back 2,000 years!) Recently, a group of scientists in Germany made a breakthrough in tickle science by wiggling their fingers against the backs and feet of rats. Turns out these rodents, along with many animals, are ticklish. Rats even emit a sort of high-pitched laughter when they're tickled! The researchers determined that tickling triggers the same parts of a rat's brain that reacts to playtime with other rats, which leads scientists to believe that social animals such as rats—and humans—evolved the tickle response to promote social interaction and contact with other members of their species. That's why you can't tickle yourself; it only works when you're at play with someone else.

SAY WHAT?!

YOU PROBABLY KNEW THAT YAWNING, which humans do to pump air into their sinuses to cool their brains, is contagious between people (it's so contagious that even reading about yawning can make you yawn). But did you know that it's contagious across species, too? Experiments show that dogs catch yawns from watching people!

Why can't I hold back the tears during a sad movie?

Your body actually produces three types of tears. The first kind, basal tears, flow constantly to keep your eyes from drying out. The second type, reflex tears, protect your eyes from irritants like dust and smoke. But it's the

third type, emotional tears, that flow during those tearjerker flicks. When directors and actors portray tragic and sad moments in their movies, they're toying with your body's chemicals. Feelings of sadness or stress trigger your brain to release hormones that turn on the waterworks. Some scientists believe that emotional tears help rid our bodies of bad chemicals that build up during stress—which is why you feel better after "having a good cry."

Why can't I stop a case of the hiccups?

Hiccups just happen. They're involuntary, meaning you can't stop them anymore than you can control your heartbeat or will yourself not to sweat at high noon under the Florida sun in August. The culprit is a sheetlike muscle called the diaphragm in your chest cavity. Normally it helps you suck air into your lungs, but sometimes after eating too much or too quickly or when you get nervous, it can go rogue. The diaphragm spasms, jerking air into your throat to make the familiar *hic-up* sound. Hiccup remedies range from holding your breath for 10 seconds to chugging a glass of cold water, but the only surefire cure is to let them run their course.

Why can't I control my heartbeat?

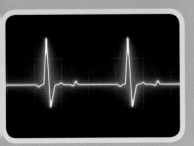

Your heart rate, along with your breathing and blood pressure, is an automatic function controlled by your brain stem, where you brain meets your spinal cord. Your heart rate does speed up when you exercise, because your body suddenly becomes more active and your cells need more oxygen. Likewise, it slows down when you plop on the couch and relax.

IT'S ALL IN THE reflexes!

EVERY TIME YOU SNEEZE, COUGH, GAG ON FOOD, BLINK, OR YANK YOUR HAND FROM A HOT STOVE, your body seems like it has a mind of its own. Each of these actions is a reflex—an automatic response that doesn't require a second thought (or any thought at all). Some reflexes are controlled by your brain stem, while others are triggered by your spinal cord. None of them require any action on your part. You didn't even have to learn them; you were born with reflexes! These fast, involuntary reactions help you respond to harmful situations as quickly as possible, side-stepping your own decision-making process.

WITHOUT A THOUGHT

FOUR FAMOUS reflexes

GAG REFLEX

WHAT'S THE POINT? To prevent you from choking when you're not trying to swallow

WHAT TRIGGERS IT? Something touching the back of your mouth

WITHDRAWAL REFLEX

WHAT'S THE POINT? To save your skin from severe burns

WHAT TRIGGERS IT? Touching something that's dangerously hot

KNEE-JERK REFLEX

WHAT'S THE POINT? To help keep you from losing your balance when your knees suddenly bend

WHAT TRIGGERS IT? A sudden bend in your knee (or a light blow with a rubber mallet from your doctor) causes your lower leg to kick out and straighten.

PALMER GRASP REFLEX

WHAT'S THE POINT? A holdover from our ape ancestors, this gripping reflex helped babies hold on to their mamas as they moved around or climbed in trees.

WHAT TRIGGERS IT? Placing an object in a baby's hand and stroking the palm will cause the hand to close in a sturdy grip. You don't have this reflex (unless you're still a baby); it goes away at around six months.

WHY can't I USE my left hand as well as my right one (or the other way around)?

About nine out of ten of you reading this book will turn its pages with your right hand— the same hand you use to write a note, wiggle your computer's mouse, chuck a fastball, and maybe pick your nose when no one's watching. About 90 percent of humans are right-handed— aka righties—meaning their right hand is their "dominant" hand. The other 10 percent are left-handed, also known as lefties or southpaws. Activities that feel natural with the dominant hand are awkward (or frustratingly difficult) with the other one. Ever try to sign your name with your nondominant hand? A chicken might scratch a neater signature.

Hand dominance is not a new development in human evolution. Cave paintings going back more than 5,000 years show humans favoring their right or left hands according to the same nine-to-one ratio we see today. Studies of the stone tools of our evolutionary ancestors show a similar dominance of the right hand as far back as 1.5 million years, long before the human species, *Homo sapiens*, appeared on the fossil record.

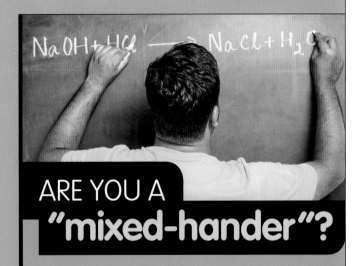

So **why** is one hand dominant?

You're born that way. Scientists have discovered a sequence of genes linked to hand dominance, making it a trait that's passed along to children just like hair color or dimples. These traits determine how our brains are wired. That wrinkly mass of tissue between your ears is amazingly complicated, and in some ways it's like two brains in one. Your noodle is split into two symmetrical (or mirror-image) halves known as hemispheres, with tasks split between them. In about 90 percent of people, the left side of the brain processes our language skills. These people are typically right-handed. People born with genes for left-handedness—about 10 percent of the population—typically have brains that process speech and emotions on the right side.

In other words, whichever side of the brain controls speech usually corresponds with a dominant hand on the opposite side. Because the left side of the brain controls the right side of the body and vice versa, scientists suspect that the evolution of our dominant hand is somehow connected to the development of our language capabilities, which are the most advanced in the animal kingdom. Hands aren't the only parts of the body that express dominance, either. Most people also have a dominant eye, a dominant ear, and even a dominant foot! Scientists are still trying to figure out why certain parts of the body are dominant, but that's just one of many reasons the human brain has been called the most complex object in the universe.

ARE YOU A "mixed-hander"?

LEFT-HANDED PEOPLE ARE SPECIAL in that some lefties can also use their right hands nearly as well. Scientists don't like using the term "ambidextrous," which implies neither hand is dominant. Instead, people who can use their nondominant hand almost as well as their dominant one are called "mixed-handers." About one percent of people can even write just fine with their nondominant hand. Are you one of these elite leftie/righties? Grab a piece of scratch paper and find out!

super SOUTHPAWS

BEING A SOUTHPAW IS NO PICNIC, what with everything from doorknobs to school desks to computer mice made for righties. Left-handers are slightly more accident-prone simply because they live in a world designed for righties. As recently as the 17th century, left-handedness was even seen as a sign of evil, an affront to the natural order of things. In fact, the term "sinister" comes from the Latin word for "left." But left-handers have some advantages. They tend to do better at some sports because their movements are less predictable to right-handed opponents. Recent studies have shown that left-handed people are more artistic while righties are more outgoing and chatty, although scientists say there's not enough evidence to back up these claims. But although lefties might be a rare breed, you're probably already familiar with quite a few of them, including ...

President Barack Obama

Media Mogul Oprah Winfrey

Microsoft Founder Bill Gates

Singer-Songwriter Lady Gaga

15th-Century Scholar Leonardo da Vinci

JUST AS HUMANS HAVE A DOMINANT HAND, elephants seem to favor either the left or right tusk for daily duties such as digging holes or stripping the bark from trees. The dominant tusk is typically worn down from work. Imagine if your dominant arm was a few inches shorter!

SAY WHAT?!

WHY don't I have

CLAWS

instead of fingernails?

Like our fellow "higher primates" (including apes, chimpanzees, gorillas, and orangutans), we evolved with flattened fingernails instead of the thicker, sharper claws found on most mammals. Researchers think that fingernails and toenails helped our ancestors climb trees, peel fruit, and use simple tools. But don't knock those neat little nails of yours. They come in handy! Their condition offers clues about your overall health. A little nail polish turns them into fashion accessories. And fingernails are the perfect tool for peeling an orange or scratching an itch.

Why doesn't
it hurt to cut
my fingernails?

For the same reason it doesn't hurt to cut your hair or peel off a patch of dead skin: It's not alive. In fact, that armor plating at the tips of your fingers is made of the same stuff as your hair and skin, a protein called keratin, which is also in the hooves and horns of animals.

SHOW OF hands

Your hands are amazing, but they're not particularly special. The evolution of hands started at least 380 million years ago with the fins of an ancestor of modern lungfish. Bulky bones in that fish's fins resembled the bones in today's arms, and over millions of years those bones evolved into smaller ones that gradually became wrists and then fingers. Today, scientists studying the evolution of hands find them across the animal kingdom—more evidence that we all evolved from a common ancestor.

TARSIERS

It should come as no surprise that higher primates closely related to humans have five-fingered hands, but so do monkeys and even the smallest primates such as tarsiers.

BATS

Beneath the leathery skin of its wing, this flying mammal has five long fingers and even a wrist that connects to the same long arm bones that we have.

KOALAS

These marsupials have four claws and thumb-like digits that help them grip plants. Look closely at a koala's paws and you'll even find fingerprints. (Koalas are the only animals aside from humans and other higher primates with fingerprints.)

DOLPHINS

The bone structure beneath a dolphin's fin skin is surprisingly hand-like, complete with shortened finger, wrist, and arm bones.

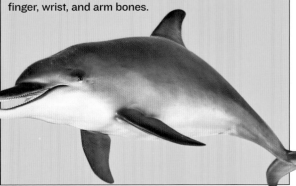

Why can't I grip things with my feet like I can with my hand?

The human hand is the world's greatest gripping machine, capable of tasks as finely tuned as performing microsurgery on the human brain or as brutish as carving a canoe from a tree trunk. The secret to our superior handiness is our pair of "opposable" thumbs, named for their ability to close tip to tip against other fingers. But humans have thumbs only on our hands, while all the higher primates have them on their feet as well, allowing them to grip objects with all four appendages. You might be able to snag a sock on the floor by flexing your little piggies, but that foot feat's nothing compared to the gripping abilities of a gorilla's grabby feet fingers. So why do our toes just wriggle instead of wrap around? We inherited our opposable thumbs from our primate ancestors around two to five million years ago. These ancient relatives needed handier hands to help grip simple tools, which in turn prompted our ancestors into standing upright. Their feet became less hand-like, making it easier to run. Long before the invention of the wheel, our ancestors traveled by jogging vast distances. They were the ultimate endurance athletes. Long, flexible toes like those of chimpanzees, our closest living relatives, make for clumsy running. So our upright ancestors evolved with shorter toes until our species arrived on the fossil record about 200,000 years ago with stubby feet built for speed. Our feet might make a mess of peeling a banana, but they helped our ancestors spread to new lands and outrun the occasional predator, so let's call it a fair trade.

Why don't identical twins have identical fingerprints?

No one living in the world today—or who has ever lived going back to the dawn of humanity—shares the same pattern of swirls and whirls, loops and arches that you see if you look closely at your fingertips. These faint ridges on your fingers (and toes, in case you didn't know) form before you're even born and remain unchanged throughout your entire life. Fluids in the womb put pressure on your developing digits, which combined with your rate of growth and genetic makeup create one-of-a-kind designs. Which is why identical twins, or siblings who share the same genetic makeup, have fingerprints that, although similar, are still subtly different from one another.

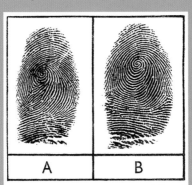

A   B

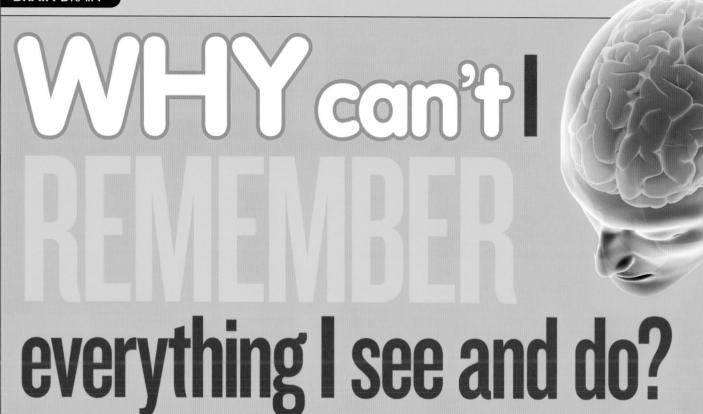

WHY can't I REMEMBER everything I see and do?

Because total recall isn't in your brain's job description. That three-pound (1.4-kg) mass of fat and protein in your noggin isn't a computer, although in some ways your brain is similar. It's made of more than a hundred billion nerve cells (called neurons) that process sensory input, control your body's functions, and store and create information. Computers contain billions of tiny switches called transistors that, like neurons, also process input, control various functions (called programs), and store and create information. But that's where the comparison stops. Computer memory forgets nothing unless you wipe it or reformat the hard drive; human memory glosses over fine details and retains only the key experiences, such as the thrill of sinking a game-winning basketball rather than the precise number of people watching in the stands. It's not that you don't have sufficient storage space in that hard drive between our ears. By some accounts, your melon can store about 2,560 terabytes of long-term memories—enough space to hold 300 million hours of TV shows. But although computer memory was designed for flawless recall, human memory gives priority to some experiences over others.

So **what** makes some memories stronger than others?

Every time you experience something new—meet a new classmate, try a new ice cream topping, watch a new movie—electrical charges fire through your brain, creating chemical links that form a network of pathways out of neurons. These connected neurons are what store your memories, and the details you retain and your ability to recall them depend on several factors. Repeated exposure to the same experience will boost your recall of it. Practicing a foreign language, for instance, fires the same neural networks again and again, strengthening your memory of the language and making it easier to recall. Powerful emotions and significant sensory input (such as strong odors) also make for richer memories that are easier to recall. But scientists suspect that the most powerful memory motivator is novelty. First-time experiences take priority over routine ones, which is why you probably have vivid memories of the day you got your pet pooch but can't recall the 20th time you took your pup for a walk around the block. And not all your memories are formed from what you see, hear, touch, smell, or taste. You can create your own memories from scratch inside your own head, in the form of dreams, daydreams, and brainstorms (or plans to deal with specific situations). Brainstorming is a valuable skill, one scientists believe plays a key role in the survival of our species.

So **how** does our memory help us survive?

Whenever we encounter a new situation, our brain automatically scans our memories to prepare us for anything that might happen. This way we can predict any dangers or threats based on similar experiences in the past. We don't need total recall of every little detail of our memories to brainstorm scenarios for our current predicament; we only need to recall the most crucial details. It's how our ancestors knew that predators might hide in trees or that waves crashing on the beach might contain dangerous rip currents—because they survived similar situations and could brainstorm how to deal with them.

ALL IN YOUR HEAD
TWO STAGES OF **memory**

STAGE 1: SHORT-TERM MEMORY

Whenever you encounter a new sensory input (or even internal inputs like dreams and big ideas), that experience is filed in your short-term memory. This part of your memory is like your brain's notepad, meant to store information—such as the showtime of a movie you want to see or a phone number until you can write it down—that you won't need to recall during your golden years.

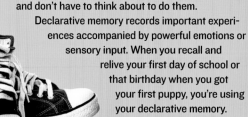

STAGE 2: LONG-TERM MEMORY

Short-term memories fade fast unless they're moved to long-term memory, which itself is made up of two storage systems. Procedural memory is your repository of know-how: skills that you learn through frequent repetition (such as memorizing flash cards, riding a bike, or tying your shoelaces) and don't have to think about to do them. Declarative memory records important experiences accompanied by powerful emotions or sensory input. When you recall and relive your first day of school or that birthday when you got your first puppy, you're using your declarative memory.

SAY **WHAT?!**

HOW'D YOU LIKE TO BE ABLE TO RECALL EVERY DETAIL of every day just by "Googling" the date in your head? You'd never need to study for a test because you had complete recall of everything your teacher ever taught you! A handful of people worldwide have this form of supermemory, called hyperthymesia. Mention a date and they can recall everything that happened that day, from the clothes they wore to what their friends said. Scientists aren't sure how hyperthymesia works because there are so few people to study.

WHY don't I perform AT MY BEST

when I'm under pressure?

It can make whiz kids think their brains turned to mush and athletes feel like they never practiced a day in their lives. You probably know the feeling: When the stakes are high or someone is watching your every move, simple tasks become extra tough. You mess up the math problem on the chalkboard or miss the pop fly in the outfield. You forget your lines in the school play or mangle an easy word in a spelling bee. Uh-oh! You just "choked" under pressure.

Experiments on athletes and students revealed several reasons why we choke. A fear of failure can play tricks on your short-term memory, causing you to momentarily forget long-practiced skills and simply blunder ahead. The most common cause of self-sabotage is simple: You think too much about what you're doing. When the pressure's on, your autopilot turns off. You begin to ponder the process step-by-step instead of just doing it as you've practiced. Facts are forgotten. Tasks that usually feel natural when the pressure's off suddenly become difficult. Sometimes, when the heat is on, we choke.

How TO AVOID CHOKING UNDER PRESSURE

Mental choking is just as real—and heavily studied—as choking on your food. And just as you can avoid choking on a chicken drumstick just by taking smaller bites and not chuckling at your siblings' antics, you can overcome mental choking hazards by following these simple techniques ...

Distract yourself from distraction

Sinking a short golf putt or catching a pop fly are automatic processes for experienced athletes, but such simple tasks become complicated when you stop to overanalyze things. The solution: distraction! Humming a tune, whistling, or focusing on some bland detail like the color of an opponent's uniform are often all it takes to put athletic skills back on automatic.

Write away the willies

In her book *Choke,* psychologist Sian Beilock suggests that quiet time before a big test is actually the enemy of success (it can lead to worries and doubts about the outcome). She suggests instead you should spend at least 10 minutes before each test writing about something, such as your thoughts or feelings or some recent emotional event.

Have faith in yourself

Don't underestimate the power of positive thinking when it comes to unblocking mental blocks. Instead of focusing on the particulars of the task at hand—such as giving a speech before the class or scoring a free throw—just calmly remind yourself that you've studied, practiced, and are otherwise fully prepared. Your autopilot will switch back on and take care of the rest.

Why can't I give a speech in front of a large group without nearly passing out?

For some people, appearing in front of other people—whether as a speaker or actor in a play—can be the scariest thing ever! According to at least one poll, people are more afraid of public speaking than of being buried alive. It can be that terrifying! Public speaking makes people nervous for a variety of reasons. Appearance is a big part of it; speakers don't want to look nervous or silly or unprepared. We're all concerned about what other people think of us, and speaking in front of a group is a prime opportunity to make a lasting impression on a lot of people. Having all those eyes on you makes it easy to forget lines or stumble like a total klutz. To overcome this particularly choking hazard, start by practicing in similar conditions. Assemble your own audience of friends and family, then rehearse your speech or acting scenes in front of them.

SILLY QUESTION, SERIOUS ANSWER

Why can't I stop nibbling my nails when I get nervous?

Because you suffer from onychophagy, or a compulsion to feast on your fingernails. It's a common habit among kids and rarely causes any long-term harm—except for some nasty-looking chewed-up fingertips. Most kids grow out of it or get treatment (such as a bitter type of nail polish) to unlearn the habit.

WHY can't I LOOK DOWN

from way up high without getting wobbly?

It's all about the drive to survive! Instincts kick in when we're up high—tumbles from trees and cliff faces are hazardous to human health, after all—and these instincts force us to overanalyze otherwise natural tasks such as walking or even standing still, which is why we feel a little unsteady on our feet while taking in the scenery from high up.

Our vision is another part of the equation. Our brains maintain our equilibrium—or state of balance—by processing a variety of inputs, including special motion-sensing organs in our ears. Our eyes contribute by focusing on objects within 30 feet (9 m) of us, which gives our balance-keeping system a reference point. We lose these reference points when we're peeking out of an airplane window or peering from the roof of a tall building. That's why you might clutch for the guardrail when you stand on the observation deck of a skyscraper.

Why don't some people, like mountain climbers and skydivers, seem to fear heights?

It's no coincidence that most action sports athletes have excellent equilibrium, or sense of balance. The same balancing skills that help them soar off a half-pipe on a skateboard or shimmy along a narrow mountain ledge make them feel more comfortable than most people when they peer down from extreme heights. These athletes also typically take up their sport when they're young and practice constantly, which conditions them to literally living on the edge. It's what psychologists call "exposure therapy," a treatment for extreme phobias that can help patients by exposing them slowly over time to the object, animal, or situation that frightens them. People with an extreme fear of spiders, for instance, can overcome it by first looking at photos of spiders, then watching them behind glass, before finally letting one creep within touching distance. (And if that sounds scary to you, you might have arachnophobia: fear of spiders.)

FUNKY phobias

As many as 5 percent of people have "acrophobia," a fear of heights that causes extreme reactions such as dizziness and sweating. It's the second most common phobia after the fear of public speaking (glossophobia), and it's a lot less obscure than these odd—but very real—fear factors …

Ablutophobia (AH-BLUE-TOW-FOE-BE-AH): fear of bathing

Coulrophobia (CALL-RO-FOE-BE-AH): fear of clowns

Omphalophobia (OMM-FAL-OH-FOE-BE-AH): fear of belly buttons

Anthophobia (ANTH-OH-FOE-BE-AH): fear of flowers

Pupaphobia (PUP-AH-FOE-BE-AH): fear of puppets

Heliophobia (HEEL-EE-OH-FOE-BE-AH): fear of sunshine

Lutraphobia (LOO-TRA-FOE-BE-AH): fear of otters

LEAN AND scream

Makers of shocking drop towers and other thrill rides capitalize on our unease around heights to deliver thrills and chills. The Tilt! experience at Chicago's Willis Tower, one of the tallest skyscrapers in the world, doesn't even go anywhere, but it can make guests' stomachs lurch! Visitors lean against the windows on the observation deck, grasp the handrails, and hold onto their lunches as each window slowly tilts out and over the city streets more than 1,000 feet (305 m) below.

WHY do I get SLEEPY at night?

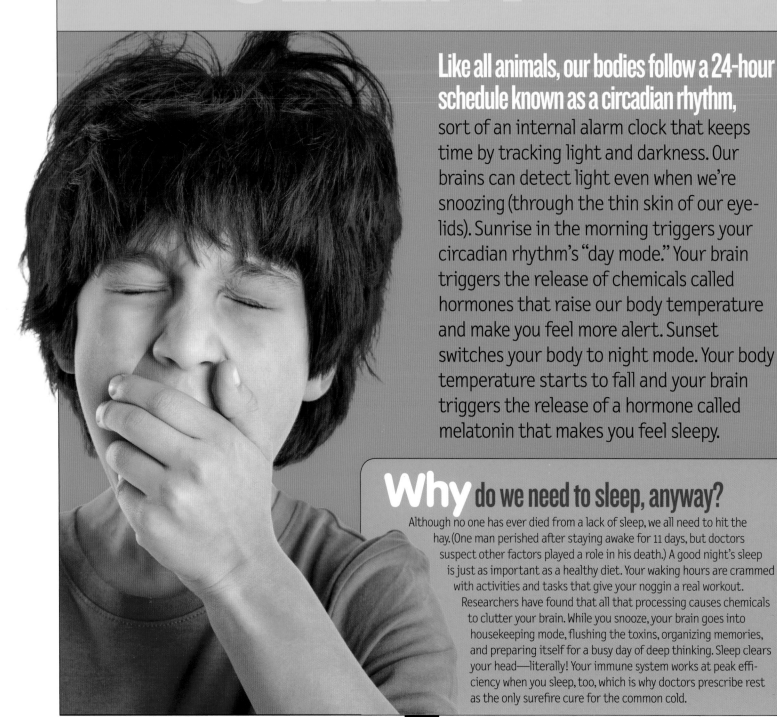

Like all animals, our bodies follow a 24-hour schedule known as a circadian rhythm, sort of an internal alarm clock that keeps time by tracking light and darkness. Our brains can detect light even when we're snoozing (through the thin skin of our eyelids). Sunrise in the morning triggers your circadian rhythm's "day mode." Your brain triggers the release of chemicals called hormones that raise our body temperature and make you feel more alert. Sunset switches your body to night mode. Your body temperature starts to fall and your brain triggers the release of a hormone called melatonin that makes you feel sleepy.

Why do we need to sleep, anyway?

Although no one has ever died from a lack of sleep, we all need to hit the hay. (One man perished after staying awake for 11 days, but doctors suspect other factors played a role in his death.) A good night's sleep is just as important as a healthy diet. Your waking hours are crammed with activities and tasks that give your noggin a real workout. Researchers have found that all that processing causes chemicals to clutter your brain. While you snooze, your brain goes into housekeeping mode, flushing the toxins, organizing memories, and preparing itself for a busy day of deep thinking. Sleep clears your head—literally! Your immune system works at peak efficiency when you sleep, too, which is why doctors prescribe rest as the only surefire cure for the common cold.

Why aren't I nocturnal?

From bats to rats, wolves to wombats, more than half of all mammals are indeed nocturnal, or more active at night. So why do people feel pooped when the sun goes down, but rise refreshed when sunshine peeks through the curtains? Scientists assume we evolved to be "diurnal," or more active during the day, because it helped us survive in our environment, but they're not quite sure why. Nocturnal creatures stay up all night because this lifestyle is crucial to their survival. (What, did you think they were party animals?) Desert animals like snakes and coyotes, for instance, sleep in burrows hidden away from the scorching sun during the day and emerge in the cool of the night. Tiny primates like the creepy aye-aye and rodents such as mice evolved their nocturnal lifestyles because it's easier to hide from predators in the darkness. But many predators such as bobcats and badgers followed suit, evolving with keen night vision and a powerful sense of smell to hunt in the darkness, which triggered more adaptations in their nocturnal prey. Skunks evolved with a stinky spray to deter predators and throw them off the scent in the darkness. Of course, humans have a much more flexible lifestyle than your average skunk or bobcat, and people sometimes choose to reverse their sleep schedules to, say, work a night shift or just party until the sun comes up.

animal ACTIVITY TIMES

DAY SHIFT ("DIURNAL" ANIMALS)			DAWN/DUSK SHIFTS ("CREPUSCULAR" ANIMALS)			NIGHT SHIFT ("NOCTURNAL" ANIMALS)		

Humans	Gorillas	Chickens	House cats	African wild dogs	Fireflies	Aye-ayes	Bats	Owls

SILLY QUESTION, SERIOUS ANSWER

Why can't I see the inside of my eyelids?

For the same reason you can't see in the pitch-black dark. Muscles in your eyeball's iris (the colorful part of your eye) control the pupil (the black hole in the center) to allow light into your eye, where it's focused by a lens onto cells at the back of the eye that register light and color. Closing your eyes blocks the light and stops the process, although you can still detect brightness and shadows if the outside light is strong enough to penetrate the thin skin of your eyelids. In fact, one important job of your eyelids is to block the ultraviolet (or UV) light given off by the bright sunlight, which can sunburn the surface of your eyes and damage the structures within (never, ever look at the sun). But even when you can detect bright light behind your eyelids, the insides of your lids are much too close for your eyes to focus on them. They're not much to look at, anyway: just a vein-laced patch of skin.

SAY WHAT?!

SCIENTISTS THINK ALL ANIMALS— EVEN INSECTS— NEED SLEEP IN ONE FORM OR ANOTHER.

Giraffes take power naps, dozing less than two hours a day. Dolphins and whales sleep with their brains half awake and one eye open.

WHY can't I fall ASLEEP sometimes?

Few things are more frustrating than tossing and turning in bed, counting sheep but never falling asleep—especially when you're already tired and have a big test tomorrow. Doctors have a word for the inability to fall asleep or stay asleep through the night—insomnia—and it can lead to problems beyond just a cranky next day. A lack of sleep over long periods can make your body more vulnerable to high blood pressure, heart disease, and other illnesses. Worrying about these problems is enough to keep you awake at night. Actually, worrying— or anxiety—is one of the main causes of insomnia. As you lie in bed and begin to drift off to sleep, you have less control over your thoughts, and those thoughts can quickly drift to some issue in your life, such as an argument with a friend or an upcoming book report you've been ignoring, that causes anxiety. Worrying quickly snaps you awake, and the whole process of falling asleep starts over again and again.

Why can't
I have only sweet dreams?

You might think the only good thing about a nightmare is your sense of relief when you wake up and realize it was all just a bad dream. But all dreams—even the scary ones—are good for you. Studies suggest they might make us smarter and more creative during our daylight hours. Nightmares arise from stress or particular problems we're facing during the day. They can often be triggered by big changes happening in your life. And although they might be scary when they strike in the night, nightmares can help us process our feelings and work though our problems.

Why can't
I remember all my dreams?

Research has shown that some people are better at recalling their dreams than others, although scientists aren't quite sure why. You don't start dreaming until you reach a deep sleep state called REM (or rapid eye movement) sleep, roughly an hour after your head hits the pillow. Although you dream during this state, your brain isn't in a mode for making new memories; you need to awaken to remember the dream you just had. Sleepers who awaken more easily—for instance, they're more likely to be awoken by noises in the night—remember more of their dreams. Sleepers who can snooze through anything typically remember fewer.

Why don't
people wake up from their own snoring?

You might think your big brother is blissfully sawing logs while his snores rattle the rafters, but that's probably not the case—at least during his loudest snoring fits. People snore because air isn't moving freely through the passages between their noses and mouths (maybe they have a sinus infection or bad sleep posture). Whatever the reason, snoring can get noisy. Loud snorers can break 100 decibels—louder than a fire alarm—and these super snores can actually rouse the snorer for a few seconds. That's not enough time to wake up fully, and snorers will typically settle back to sleep without remembering their noisy fits the next morning, but rest assured they're not snoozing as blissfully as you think.

Why won't my pillow stay cool when I sleep?

It's a maddening bedtime ritual that can keep you awake at night. You lay your head on your cool pillow and begin the sheep countdown until sleep when—yikes!—your head feels like it's stuck in a sauna. You flip your pillow to the cool side and begin the process all over again, hoping to fall asleep before your head heat makes you hot under the collar. What's happening here? Your head radiates heat just like any other part of your body. Your pillow absorbs that heat and traps it under your head until you flip the pillow over against the cooler surface of your bed. This becomes a problem during hot times of the year, when that heat buildup can rob you of sleep (humans catch more z's in a cool environment). Your most comfortable alternative is to buy a "breathable" pillow made of latex foam or microbeads— materials that take longer to absorb all that head heat. By the time they do, you'll (hopefully!) be fast asleep.

How TO KICK INSOMNIA

- **GO DARK:** Remember: We evolved to sleep in total darkness. Our sleeping brain can detect even dim lights—such as our TV or flashing notifications on our smartphone—which can trigger our day mode.

- **TAKE A WAKE BREAK:** If you're lying awake because of worry, hop out of bed and head to another room for a minute. You want to wake up fully, harness that stress, and set it aside. After a few minutes, your mind should clear up and you'll be ready to return to bed.

- **SETTLE YOUR STOMACH:** Don't hit the hay with a grumbling stomach. Hunger will keep you up, but you also don't want to scarf down an entire pizza within two hours of bedtime. An apple before you brush your teeth for bed should hit the spot if you're a little hungry.

- **UNPLUG:** It's not a smart idea to sleep with a smartphone or tablet on the nightstand. The urge to surf social media might be too great if you happen to wake in the night, while the notification might snap you out of a deep sleep.

- **STICK TO A SCHEDULE:** People sleep better when they go to bed and wake up at about the same time every day, so keep a regular sleep routine.

MASHED MYTH

Why DO I LOSE MORE HEAT THROUGH MY HEAD?

You don't! Recent experiments show that while you do lose heat through your head, it's no more or less than other exposed skin throughout your body. That means your head accounts for about 10 percent of your body's heat loss when you're out in the cold. Your ears are as sensitive to low temperatures as your fingers and toes, so you should still wear a hat to keep those ear tips toasty!

WHY can't I eat CUPCAKES for dinner?

Cake frosting instead of cauliflower? Cookies and cream instead of creamed spinach? Dessert for dinner (and breakfast and lunch) sounds like a miracle meal plan, but anyone who orders exclusively from the end of the menu would soon get a hankering for something a little more substantial. Like any high-performance machine, your body requires gas to go, and that fuel comes in the form of nutrients—vitamins, minerals, carbohydrates (found in breads and starchy foods like potatoes), fat, and minerals—in your food. Through the process of digestion, your body turns carbohydrates into energy and proteins into building blocks to help you grow taller; build muscle; prevent illness; and have healthy hair, teeth, and skin.

A balanced diet of healthy foods offers the best fuel. Ice cream, cakes, cookies, and candies don't pack sufficient protein to rebuild muscles and important vitamins that your body doesn't store. Eat nothing but sugary treats and you'll wreck your engine in a few months.

Sweets also lack something your body will miss in a matter of days: dietary fiber. Also known as roughage, it's the indigestible stuff in fruits, veggies, and grains. In the long term, roughage helps prevent heart disease, diabetes, and other illnesses. In the short term, fiber keeps you on a regular bathroom schedule.

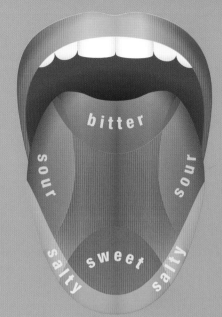

Why can't I get everything I need from a single food?

No single food group—such as dairy (milk, cheese), meat, fruits, and vegetables—offers all the vitamins, proteins, carbohydrates, and minerals your body needs to operate at peak efficiency. You've already learned that humans should chow down on a variety of foods—a so-called "balanced diet"—to not only thrive but also survive. Modern food science has reached the point where the laziest diners could probably get by day after day on a single food group as long as they gulped nutritional supplements. But our own body has other ideas, driven by the cravings of our hunter-gatherer ancestors. Eat your favorite food—even pepperoni pizza or fried chicken—for too long and your taste buds will tell you to switch it up. "Humans hate monotony," says nutritionist Jo Ann Hattner, registered dietician and author of the book *Gut Insight*. "We were really meant to eat a variety of food."

Why don't I like the same foods as my friends?

Your best pal might prefer her pizza piled with every topping (including—yuck!—anchovies), while you think anything more than pepperoni ruins the perfect pie. Why are you so picky? Maybe you're a supertaster! That's what scientists call the 25 to 30 percent of people with relatively more taste buds than others. These tiny bumps on your tongue are loaded with chemical receptors that interpret flavors—sweet, salty, bitter, sour, savory—and transmit that information to your brain. Because supertasters can sense more flavors, they're typically finicky eaters with strong opinions about different foods. (Broccoli can seem bitter, for instance, or cheesecake far too sweet.) To them, less is more, and a pizza with everything represents flavor overload. On the flip side, people with relatively fewer taste buds are called "non-tasters." This 25 to 30 percent of people can stomach a wider variety of foods because flavors make less of an impact. Non-tasters are more likely to pile on the spices and toppings to jazz up otherwise ho-hum meals. In the middle of both groups—about 40 to 50 percent of people—are the "average tasters" with the average amount of taste buds. They're less finicky than super-tasters but pickier than non-tasters. Bottom line: Anchovies are gross (unless you're a non-taster).

MYTH MASHED

Why CAN'T I TASTE WATER?

Wait, are you sure about that? Water might seem flavorless when it splashes across your taste buds, but scientists debate whether we can taste it. Studies show that water can trigger a sort of opposite aftertaste in our mouths right after eating something with a strong flavor. Take a drink of pure water after snacking on a salty chip, for instance, and you may detect a hint of bitter taste, the opposite of salty.

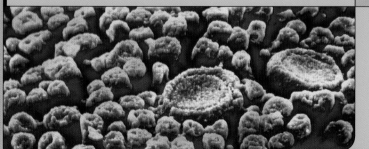

SAY WHAT?!

NOT ALL OF YOUR TASTE BUDS ARE ON YOUR TONGUE. About a tenth of your tiny flavor sensors line your cheeks and the back of your throat.

WHY doesn't healthy food TASTE better than junk food?

Human tongues are tuned to detect strong flavors—such as sweet, salty, and fatty flavors—rather than the subtler tastes of veggies, whole grains, beans, and other good-for-you foods. That might seem like a disadvantage given that wholesome foods help us live longer, healthier lives, but our hankering for bold flavors was once crucial to human survival. Sweet fruits and fatty meats pack a lot of energy, which was essential to our ancestors in the age before snack machines and fast-food restaurants. Food companies today are well aware of our preference for sweets, salts, and fats, so they tailor the flavors of cereals, candy bars, sodas, and other junk food to satisfy our cravings.

Why can't I eat just one potato chip (or pretzel, or pork rind, or ...)?

It's not the potato in the chip or the bread in the pretzel that makes your mouth water—it's their salty flavor. Like sweet fruits and fatty meats, salt was crucial to the survival of your ancestors, and it still is today! Salt helps your tissues stay hydrated and serves other vital functions. Too much of a good thing can be a bad thing, however; eating too much salt can lead to heart disease and other health risks.

Why CAN'T I EAT SOMETHING I DROPPED ON THE FLOOR AFTER FIVE SECONDS?

No one sets out to eat off the floor, but what choice do you have when you get a case of the butterfingers while munching on a Butterfinger? Fortunately, you have five seconds to scoop it up before the germs have a chance to hop aboard, right? Sorry, *bzzzzzt!* Scientists who study germs think the five-second rule should be renamed the no-second rule. Bacteria on the floor cling to fallen food immediately, and your gut reaction to rescue toppled treats might lead to some unfortunate reactions in your gut if you happen to ingest the wrong kind of germs. The lesson here: You should scoop up that candy bar, but chuck it in the trash instead of popping it into your mouth.

Why can't I eat something spicy without torturing my tongue?

Every time you scoop a spoonful of spicy chili into your mouth, you're picking a fight with a food that evolved to defend itself. Chili peppers—typically the ingredient that gives spicy food its four-alarm flavor—contain capsaicin (pronounced cap-SAY-uh-sin), a substance that triggers the sensations of pain and heat when it touches your tongue. In fact, the hottest type of pepper (the ghost pepper) is so hot that it will burn your skin unless you wear gloves. Pepper plants likely evolved this compound to keep away nibbling animals. Spicy food connoisseurs build up a resistance to capsaicin by gradually eating progressively hotter peppers until they can nibble thermonuclear meals while working up only a mild sweat.

Why can't I hear someone eating without getting annoyed?

Nobody likes sitting within spittle distance of someone chomping on chow with their mouth open. But for a small percentage of people, that racket of smacking lips, crunching chips, and soda sips makes their blood boil. This enraging condition even has a name: misophonia. It's a strong negative reaction to specific sounds, such as loud breathing, whistling, booming subwoofers, and noisy eating. Scientists studying this rare condition think people with misophonia are just born with it. Their brains are wired in a particular way that associates particular sounds with angry feelings and anxiety.

WHY can't I eat
peanuts or pet a fluffy dog without
FEELING ICKY?

Sounds like you have an allergy, and you're not alone! As many as 30 percent of grown-ups and 40 percent of kids suffer from allergies. Allergic reactions can take many forms—itching, sneezing, coughing, a runny nose, upchucking, rashes, shortness of breath—triggered by anything from food to bee stings to particular medicines. Allergic reactions happen when your body's immune system—which normally fights germs—treats something harmless like it's a dangerous invader. Once it detects an allergen, your immune system goes into red alert and creates antibodies to repel the intruder. This causes the tissues around the allergen to become inflamed or swollen, which is why you might have trouble breathing if you swallow a peanut. Extreme reactions can even result in a potentially deadly full-body response known as anaphylactic shock.

Why do we have allergies?

Stories of allergies go back to ancient Egypt, yet their causes remain largely a mystery. Not everyone has allergies. Some form in childhood. Some happen later in life. And sometimes they go away as you get older. You may inherit a likelihood of having allergies from your parents but usually not their particular allergies. Scientists suspect humans evolved with these extreme and mysterious immune reactions to combat genuinely deadly threats, such as parasitic worms or other toxins. And though doctors are doubtful they can ever cure allergies, they've come up with many ways to test for them and provide medications that treat the symptoms.

Why can't I work out without feeling sore the next day?

The word "ripped" is more appropriate than most fitness fanatics might think. When you exercise in a new and strenuous way—such as hitting the slopes at the start of snowboarding season or lifting weights for the first time in weeks—you're literally ripping your muscles. Microscopic tears appear in the muscle fibers, which triggers your body into repairing and rebuilding the damage with proteins. Muscles grow bigger and stronger in the process, but those gains come with pain: soreness and stiffness in the affected muscles, usually the day after a workout. Doctors call it "delayed-onset muscle soreness." These dull, deep aches are caused by the repair process, your body's way of telling you to lay off the heavy stuff. You can cut down on this pain by ending each workout with a 10-minute cooldown (such as a slow jog and some light stretches). This helps circulate blood around those tiny muscle tears, helping them rebuild more quickly. You should also give sore muscles at least a day or so to recover and grow bigger, one step closer to getting ripped!

AWFUL allergens

PEANUTS
One of the most common food allergens, along with shellfish

PET DANDER
Tiny flakes of shed fur and feathers can make your eyes water and your nose go *ahh-choo!*

DUST MITES

Millions of these microscopic arachnids live in your house, feasting on your dead skin cells. Cleaning stirs up clouds of mite shells and their micro-poop.

PENICILLIN

Antibiotics like penicillin kill bacteria that make us sick, but they can do more harm than good for patients allergic to them.

POLLEN

Plants project this fine powdery substance into the breeze to fertilize other plants. It can irritate the nasal passages of allergy sufferers, causing sneezing and watery eyes—a condition commonly called "hay fever."

Why can't I switch off sensations of pain?

You might think life would be more fun if you never felt any pain—no stubbed toes, burned tongues, or sore throats. But the opposite is actually true: Your life would be in great danger! Pain is your body's warning system, a key to your survival. Your brain perceives pain through an electrical system of nerves—part of your "nervous system"—stretching throughout your body. Special receptors on your skin and in your bones can detect tears and punctures, which your brain interprets as injuries. Without these sensors, you wouldn't know you were smashing your hand in a door or strolling through prickly rosebushes. Pain from these minor wounds protects you from much more serious, life-threatening injuries.

Why can't I feel my brain (or other organs inside my body)?

Only a few of your organs have nerve receptors like those on your skin, muscles, and bones. This is why you can't feel your heart beating (unless you put your hand over your chest) or sense your blood flowing through your veins (without checking your pulse with a finger). But our nervous system can still detect problems inside our bodies in the form of aches, pressure, and tender spots. Like all pain, these feelings serve as a warning that something inside might be amiss.

But aren't headaches just pain in my brain?

No, but that's a tough fact to swallow when it feels like your brain is about to bust out of your skull during a particularly pounding headache. Like many of your internal organs, your brain can't feel pain. The "ache" in a headache is actually from nerves around your head and neck, which are sensing some snafu inside the brain. One problem might be too much bloodflow caused by a change in diet. Stress can bind muscles in the head and neck, leading to tension headaches. Straining your eyes by reading in low light or focusing on faraway objects without your glasses can also lead to brain pain.

WHY haven't we CURED CANCER?

Despite more than a century of dedicated research, doctors are still unable to cure cancer: a scary disease in which the cells in certain parts of your body grow abnormally and out of control. Cancer is the number two killer in the United States after heart disease. But finding a cure is difficult because cancer isn't just a single disease—it's the catchall name for more than a hundred diseases that attack different parts of your body and have many different causes, from smoking cigarettes to radiation exposure to specific germs. Cancers are also difficult to treat because of the very nature of the dis-

ease: Each cancer cell is unlike any other, making it hard to target with specific medicines. It's similar to how medical science hasn't found a cure for the common cold, which is caused by more than 200 evolving viruses that all produce the same symptoms.

But the situation is far from hopeless. Cancer research has made great strides in 50 years, and cancers that once killed 95 percent of their victims have a survival rate of 95 percent today. Researchers are also coming up with new treatments that eliminate certain cancer cells and keep them from coming back, which is a problem with many types of cancer. Perhaps just as important, doctors have figured out how to detect some cancers early—in some cases, just by analyzing a patient's breath. Early detection vastly improves a patient's chances of surviving the disease. Meanwhile, the risks of many cancers can be reduced by making simple lifestyle choices, such as not smoking, avoiding too much red meat, and protecting your skin with sunblock.

Why can't we just kill all the germs?

Fair question. After all, the term "germ" encompasses all the microscopic terrors—viruses, fungi, parasites, and bacteria—that can sneak into their victims and cause all sorts of illnesses, from colds to flus to cancer! Unfortunately, any mighty germ killer would also wipe out all the viruses and bacteria that are actually good for you. Your body is built of trillions of itty-bitty living blobs, called cells, that work together to make you you. But for every cell you call your own, 10 foreign bacteria cluster around or near them. Scientists call these communities of foreign bacteria your body's "flora," and no two people host the same mix of microorganisms. Most of your body's microbes are essential for good health. In fact, scientists are beginning to think of your flora as just another organ. The good bacteria in our bodies boost our immune system to fight sickness and help extract nutrients and vitamins from our food. Eliminating all the germs would cause more harm than good!

SILLY QUESTION, SERIOUS ANSWER

Why can't I be frozen if I get an incurable disease and thawed when they find a cure?

The good news is this technology is available. The bad news is you can't be frozen until after you're dead. Low temperatures do slow down the body's processes, allowing the cells and the brain to survive for a longer amount of time without oxygen. This is why doctors can sometimes revive people who've fallen into icy water more than an hour after they've stopped breathing. But no one can be revived after they've frozen completely. At temperatures below freezing, all the water in the human body forms ice crystals that damage surrounding tissue.

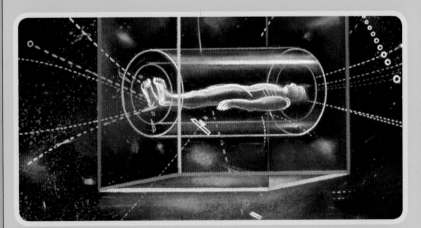

Yet believers in a form of preservation called "cryonics" claim the recently deceased can be frozen for centuries until medical science figures out how to both revive the dead patients and cure what killed them in the first place. It's the longest of long shots, with a process as complex as the mummification of the dead in ancient Egypt. Scientists believe such cold storage damages the human brain beyond repair. In the meantime they've begun experimenting with a technique that cools the body to 50°F (10°C), which slows down the body's processes and gives doctors more time to treat serious injuries. It's not the "suspended animation" of sci-fi movies, but it's a start.

PERSON OF INTEREST

WHO?
Karl Landsteiner

WHAT is he famous for?
Saving more than a billion lives

WHEN?
Early 1900s

WHERE?
Austria

WHY is he important?
Everyone's blood contains the same basic stuff, but mixed in with that stuff are "antigens"—special proteins that act like an ID tag for a person's blood, letting his or her body know the blood is theirs and not a foreign invader. In 1901, scientist Karl Landsteiner discovered that people had these different blood types and that only certain types are compatible with others. This discovery paved the way for safe transfusions—or transfers of blood—from healthy donors to compatible patients. Today, transfusions are the most common type of hospital procedure. Nearly 16 million blood donations are made each year, and the Red Cross estimates that just one donation can save up to three lives.

WHY don't my toots SMELL as bad as other people's toots?

OH NO!

That's what you think! Everyone breaks wind, and not every toot raises a big stink. Some of that gas from your backside is simply swallowed air that squeaked through your digestive system without getting expelled first as a burp. These tiny toots are not typically stink bombs. But the bulk of your flatulence (the scientific word for toots) is produced by billions of bacteria that have made a home inside your gut. These microorganisms mine vitamins from harder-to-digest foods such as potatoes, red meats, and fiber-rich veggies like broccoli that don't get fully processed in your stomach. As they munch on your meals, these bacteria produce skatole (the source of poop's particular odor) and sulfides that imbue our toots with that icky rotten-egg aroma.

Stinky? Sure! But your own toots are familiar to you, and the makeup of bacteria that creates this gas is as unique as your fingerprint. Humans are less disgusted by things associated with our own bodies, which is why you would swear your own toots smell better than the gas passed by passersby. We've also evolved to detest and recoil from stinky things such as rotting food and piles of poop because they can pass disease. Toots from strangers trigger that sense of revulsion while your own familiar toots do not.

Why can't I just quit bathing?

Singing practice isn't the only thing you'll miss if you start skipping showers. Your friends and family will probably start keeping their distance, too (or at least stand upwind). Why? Because *pee-yew*, you'll stink! More than 2.5 million glands in your skin ooze sweat to cool your body and flush out waste. All of that liquid is odorless when it's first secreted, but these secretions are a banquet for bacteria. Millions of microscopic life-forms munch on your sweat and produce stinky micro-poop—hence, B.O.—until you scrub them away in the shower.

SILLY QUESTION, SERIOUS ANSWER

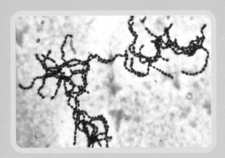

Why can't I eat my own boogers?

Surveys show that up to 90 percent of adults have picked their nose at least once, and 10 percent of those nose pickers have tried eating their boogers. But what's the big deal? You're already eating boogers—or at least the stuff that makes it! Boogers are built from snot, which is the unscientific term for mucus. Snot performs all sorts of essential functions, from guarding your lungs from germs to protecting stomach lining from its own digestive acids. Your body produces nearly two gallons (7.6 L) of mucus each week. You usually swallow all that snot without giving it a second thought. Boogers are simply dried snot in your nose, so when you swallow mucus you're just eating boogers in their raw form. Now, boogers also contain any dust, germs, and pollen particles that have been pushed from your nasal passages and deposited in your nose for easy disposal. Your body is trying to get rid of this stuff, so eating it undoes all the good work your snot is doing. A couple of doctors have suggested that eating snot can toughen up our immune systems, but no studies have confirmed these claims. So it's best to just settle for the snot you're swallowing already instead of digging deep for a nasty snack.

SIDE EFFECTS OF shower skipping

RASH ACTION

Microscopic molds, yeasts, and other plantlike pathogens thrive in wet, warm places like our armpits, belly buttons, and the dank spaces between our toes. They feed on our sweat and dead tissues and produce wastes that not only stink (which is why sweaty feet don't smell sweet)—they irritate your skin. Soon you'll have itchy rashes!

STINK STAINS

In addition to your "eccrine" sweat glands that secrete salty sweat to cool your skin, your body has special "apocrine" glands in your hairiest parts that produce a yellowish liquid. Without your daily shower, the job of sopping up this nasty stuff will fall to your attire. Soon, every T-shirt you own will have matching pit stains.

ZIT FITS

Millions of hair follicles cover your body and produce protective oils, and it takes just one clog to create a zit, aka a pimple, an adolescent's enemy number one. Without regular baths to keep those pores open, bacteria and oil will combine into a repulsive pus that erupts when you give your new pimple a squeeze.

INFECTION RISKS

If you happen to scratch your filthy skin or those itchy rashes too hard and accidentally draw blood, you can introduce surface germs into your bloodstream, which can lead to a dangerous infection. Next stop: the hospital, where the doctor will prescribe germ-killing antibiotics—and probably a nice long shower!

Why don't people say "bless you" when I burp?

It's rude not to say "bless you" after someone goes *ahhhhh-chooo!* That tradition goes back to before the Middle Ages, when people feared sneezing might signal the onset of a deadly plague. But sneezes are an accident—an involuntary reaction in which your chest, stomach, throat, and face muscles work together when the mucous membranes in your nose detect intruders, such as dust, dead skin, microbes, and other stuff you don't want in your lungs. Burps—particularly loud burps—on the other hand, are voluntary. Burps are a release of all the air you accidentally gulp every time you eat, drink, talk, chew gum, or yawn. When your belly balloons to its maximum capacity, it releases the bubbles back up your food tube—aka your esophagus—and out your mouth and nose, resulting in a belch. But you can usually hold back a burp, or at least release it without announcing it to the world. And just as it's rude to not say "bless you" after someone sneezes, there's no excuse for not saying "excuse me" after you unleash a belch.

TECHNOLOGY

SMARTPHONES, SMART CARS, SMART DISHWASHERS THAT ALERT US WHEN THEY SPRING A LEAK: Technology that would've been astounding yesterday is almost humdrum today! But that doesn't mean modern machines aren't mysterious. How exactly do cell phones communicate? Why aren't computers as smart as humans? Will they ever be? And, hey: Aren't we supposed to be zipping around with jetpacks by now? Gear up for a trek through the world of tech as you discover what was positively pioneering in the past, what makes today's gadgets tick, and why the future seems to be running a little late.

MYSTERY MACHINES

6

WHY don't we ride these funny-looking BICYCLES anymore?

Take a guess at what the inventor of this old-fashioned bicycle named it when he unleashed it on the streets of Paris and England in the late 1800s. The "titanic-tire bike," maybe? Or the "mile-high machine"? Actually, he called it the "ordinary bicycle" to set it apart from other early bike designs, such as the rough-riding "boneshaker" and later-model "safety" bikes, which featured two wheels of roughly equal size. Despite its silly look, the ordinary bike's big wheel was a breakthrough at the time. Before the invention of bicycle chains and gears, which boost a bicyclist's pedaling power, bike pedals were often connected directly to the front tire. The larger the front tire, the more power it gave the rider, and ordinary bicycle riders had the biggest front tire of all.

How did people even ride these bikes without wrecking them?

After a lot of practice. Ordinary bike riders were an elite group of daredevils, called wheelmen, and they thrilled at how fast they could travel on their big-wheeled machines. But clambering up into that high-riding seat required feats of balance and acrobatics. And small bumps in the road or sudden stops could send riders hurtling over the handlebars. Despite the dangers (or perhaps because of them), ordinary bikes are still popular with thrill-seeking wheelmen today, who stage annual races.

Why don't we have pedal-powered flying machines?

You're far from the first person to dream up the idea of using muscle power alone to propel yourself into the clouds. In the late 1400s, Italian artist Leonardo da Vinci studied birds to sketch an "ornithopter" flying machine with flapping wings powered by levers. Many such human-powered aircraft have been developed since, but none of these ingenious flying machines has soared with the greatest of ease. It takes an athletic pilot with Olympic-level endurance to pedal such a craft into the air and keep it there. The farthest-flying pedal-powered aircraft is the Daedalus, an ultralight plane—less than 60 pounds (27 kg)—with wings spanning more than 100 feet (30 m) and pedals that the pilot pumps to spin the propeller. It set a distance record in 1988 when its pilot, a Greek cycling champion, pedaled it 74 miles (119 km) across the Mediterranean Sea.

PEDAL PUSHERS

A BICYCLE TIMELINE

1817 THE DRAISINE, OR "HOBBYHORSE"

This early two-wheeled contraption looked like a wooden bike without any pedals. Riders made it go by kicking their feet along the ground, as if they were bounding along on a hobbyhorse (which explains the machine's nickname).

1858 THE VELOCIPEDE, OR "BONESHAKER"

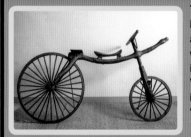

Tinkerers added pedals to the Draisine's design to give riders a means of moving the front wheels. Because every bump in the road carried through the Velocipede's rigid frame and iron wheels, riders called it the "boneshaker."

1872 THE ORDINARY, OR "PENNY-FARTHING"

The first big-wheeled bikes begin selling in England and were soon imported to the United States. Their popularity kicked off the new sport of bicycling and triggered a demand for better roads.

1885 THE SAFETY BICYCLE

Developed as a safer alternative to the rider-bucking big-wheeled bikes, the "safety bicycles" featured wheels about the same size. An innovative gear-and-chain system transferred the pedal's pumping power to the rear wheel instead of the front, making the bike safer to ride (front-pedaling bikes like the ordinary were much harder to steer); inflatable-tube tires smoothed out the ride. Safety bikes aren't much different from what you ride today.

SILLY QUESTION, SERIOUS ANSWER

Why can't I fly by flapping my arms?

Scientists estimate that a human would need a wingspan of more than 22 feet (7 m)—possibly up to 80 feet (24 m)—to create enough lifting force to propel us into the air. Unlike with birds, our bones are strong but dense, and our heavy muscles weigh us down. But students from the University of Toronto Institute for Aeronautical Studies were keen to create a human-powered machine propelled by flapping wings. Their creation, called the *Snowbird*, is a mishmash of bird and plane. It uses pedals and cables to flap its massive wings—half the wingspan of a jumbo jet's—downward and forward, providing the thrust necessary to stay airborne. But even though the *Snowbird* is made of super-lightweight materials and its pilot stuck to a strict diet to trim his bodyweight for flight, the plane flapped through the air for less than a minute before losing speed and touching down, one small step for human-powered wings.

WHY don't we TRAVEL in these things anymore?

In the early days of air travel, enormous airships were the only way to fly. Decked out with restaurants, libraries, showers, bunks, and even piano lounges inside their cavernous tube-shape hulls, they were like inflated cruise ships that soared at 650 feet (198 m). Airships ruled the skies in the early 1900s, but the technology that kept these vessels afloat is based on dangerous principles. Airships relied on lighter-than-air gas—particularly hydrogen—stored in cells within the ship to stay afloat, while propellers pushed them through the air at around 85 miles an hour (137 km/h). Hydrogen is highly flammable; just one small leak combined with a spark could turn these flying cruise ships into flaming hulks.

Dozens of airships burned and crashed in the early 20th century. The most famous accident happened on May 6, 1937, when the German airship *Hindenburg* caught fire 200 feet (61 m) above its destination airfield in Lakehurst, New Jersey, U.S.A., after a trip across the Atlantic. In less than a minute, the largest vessel ever airborne was consumed in a ball of flame. More than half of the airship's 97 passengers and crewmembers managed to leap to safety, but media coverage of the *Hindenburg*'s fiery demise helped convince the public to travel by newfangled airplanes, which could cross an ocean in less than 12 hours. (A typical transatlantic airship trip took nearly five days.)

Why don't
we travel by jetpack?

Great news! The jetpack is a real thing that's been zipping around since the 1960s. But unfortunately you won't be strapping one on for your commute to school anytime soon. The original model—dubbed the "Rocket Belt" by developer Bell Aerosystems—relies on chemical reactions to squirt a stream of steam through exhaust nozzles. Using joysticks to control these nozzles, the pilot can take off, spin in midair, zip in any direction, and land—preferably before the fuel runs out, which doesn't take very long. The Rocket Belt carries enough fuel (pressurized hydrogen peroxide) for only about 20 seconds of flight time, or about the length of a city block. It's also tricky to fly and requires years of training. Unlike planes and helicopters that have emergency procedures for gliding to the ground, Rocket Belts drop like rocks when they run into problems. One pilot broke his jaw and needed 27 stitches after a hard landing in 2016.

So are jetpacks a lost cause?

Maybe not. At least one company is betting that jetpack technology will finally get off the ground. After 40 years of tinkering, California-based JetPack Aviation has developed what it calls the "world's first true jetpack": an 85-pound (39-kg) backpack built from a lightweight frame equipped with two miniature jet engines that roar louder than a Harley-Davidson motorcycle at full rev. These tiny turbojets pack a lot of power, propelling the prototype jetpack up to 100 miles an hour (161 km/h). More importantly, the pack carries enough fuel to fly for about 10 minutes—still not practical for day-to-day travel but certainly a step up from the Rocket Belt's 20 seconds in the air. The company hopes to equip future models with an emergency parachute and an electric power source, which would boost flight time considerably. The thrill of personal flight won't come cheap, though: Each jetpack will cost about $250,000.

SKYWALKERS
JETPACK Alternatives

JETLEV-FLYER

Jetpacks are impractical because they require so much fuel and are tricky to pilot. The Jetlev-Flyer solves one problem and minimizes the other. It rides on dual streams of pressurized water (sort of like two firehoses at full blast), which it pulls from a hose connected to a pump towed behind it. And because Jetlev-Flyer pilots can travel only above lakes and the ocean, they're at least guaranteed a softer landing when they crash. Jetlevs cost around $100,000 each, although they're becoming the hot thing at beach resorts.

FLYBOARD AIR

Less a jetpack and more like a supercharged version of the "hoverboard" seen in the Back to the Future films, the Flyboard Air rides on four screaming jet engines that propel the machine up to speeds of 93 miles an hour (150 km/h) and thousands of feet in the air. The pilot straps into the board with special boots and controls it through a combination of balance and a handheld throttle. Meanwhile, a computerized control system stabilizes flight and keeps the Flyboard from spinning out of control. The Flyboard Air has already set a Guinness world record for the farthest hoverboard flight, soaring more than a mile off the coast of France in 2016.

JETMAN

Invented by Swiss pilot Yves Rossy, this personal flying machine is less a jetpack and more like a jet-powered wing he straps to his body. Rossy "takes off" by leaping from a helicopter and steers with subtle movements of his body. The craft carries enough fuel to fly for 10 minutes before Rossy must deploy a parachute and float gently back to Earth.

WHY can't planes hover like HELICOPTERS?

Helicopters are the hummingbirds of aircraft, able to take off in a single vertical bound, hover, dart in all directions, and then land on any convenient patch of turf. Most conventional airplanes require runways to take off and land, and they fall from the sky if they go too slow. Why do planes sink while helicopters soar?

The difference is in their wings. Airplanes have large, flat wings attached to their long, skinny bodies. An airplane's engine generates thrust that pushes the plane forward. Air begins moving over the plane's wings, which are shaped in such a way that pressure builds below them. As the plane's forward speed increases, the pressure beneath the wings builds and lifts the wings—and the rest of the plane—into the air. As long as a plane has enough thrust and forward motion to keep air moving over the wings, it will stay in flight. Helicopters rely on the same forces—thrust and lift—to fly, and they have wings just like planes, except their wings are on the propellers—or "rotors"—that whirl above the whirlybird. The helicopter's engine spins the rotors, which thrusts them through the air and creates lift, pulling the helicopter vertically into the air. The pilot can control the shape of the rotors to control the amount of lift, as well as angle them forward or backward to determine the direction of flight.

Why can't planes fly all the way into space?

The Earth's atmosphere becomes thinner as you travel farther from the planet's surface. So the higher a plane flies, the less air it actually flies through. Eventually, the air traveling over the wings becomes so wispy that they can't generate any lift. Engines fail to produce sufficient thrust in the thin air, as well. At this point the plane has reached its maximum altitude, or "ceiling." Commercial airlines can't travel much higher than seven miles (11 km), although planes with especially large wings and more powerful engines can squeeze every bit of lift out of the thin air at extreme altitudes. A NASA plane called Helios reached a record-breaking altitude of just above 18 miles (29 km), but that's still 44 miles (71 km) short of the official boundary of outer space.

Why don't all planes leave trails of smoke when they're flying up high?

Those white lines you see lingering in the air behind airliners aren't smoke. They're "contrails," or trails of condensation that form when the hot exhaust of jet engines warms the freezing air around them at high altitudes. The engine heat sucks the moisture out of the air—a process called condensation—and this moisture then freezes into a trail of tiny ice crystals. These are the same types of crystals in high-altitude cirrus clouds. In other words, airliners create their own clouds as they fly! Contrails only form in moist air, and not all plane engines are hot enough to create them.

But why can rockets fly into space if planes can't?

Unlike planes and helicopters, rockets don't rely on wings to fly or even air to fly through. They carry everything they need to blast through the atmosphere and into space. Rocket propulsion is based on one of science's most famous principles, put forth as the third law of motion by 17th-century English physicist Sir Isaac Newton: For every action, there is an equal and opposite reaction. A rocket's engine mixes fuel and oxygen to create a powerful downward exhaust, which in turn propels the rocket upward in the opposite direction.

high FLIERS

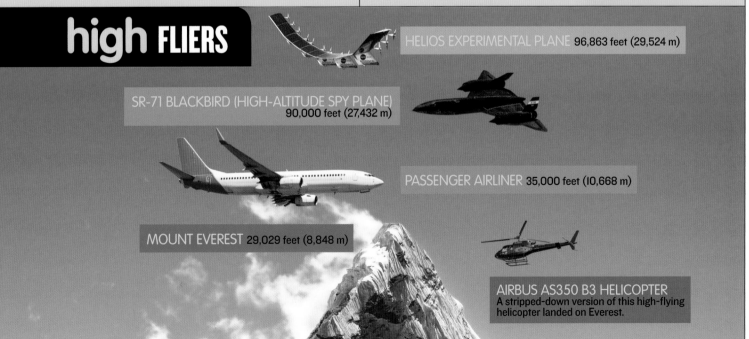

HELIOS EXPERIMENTAL PLANE 96,863 feet (29,524 m)

SR-71 BLACKBIRD (HIGH-ALTITUDE SPY PLANE) 90,000 feet (27,432 m)

PASSENGER AIRLINER 35,000 feet (10,668 m)

MOUNT EVEREST 29,029 feet (8,848 m)

AIRBUS AS350 B3 HELICOPTER
A stripped-down version of this high-flying helicopter landed on Everest.

WHY can't I open the WINDOW in an airliner?

For the same reason you can't climb Mount Everest in a T-shirt and shorts: Because you would freeze and pass out—and maybe even die! Despite its soothing blue hue and fluffy cloudscapes, the sky is unfriendly to human life above 15,000 feet (4,572 m). A quick lesson in air pressure will help you understand why. On the surface of the Earth, the air around you is heavy. But way up high, it's really light.

Wait, air has weight?

The force of gravity is constantly pulling Earth's atmosphere downward and toward the planet's center, and the weight of all that air above you creates pressure that builds as you get closer to the ground. Air is thickest and heaviest at sea level, where humans evolved to live. As you gain altitude—either by climbing a mountain or soaring up and away—the air becomes thinner and holds less oxygen and heat. At just 8,000 feet (2,438 m), the air is still breathable, but freezing. At 26,000 feet (7,925 m), the air holds only a third of the oxygen we inhale at sea level. Anyone without an air tank begins suffering from "hypoxia," or lack of oxygen, and will pass out within half an hour. By the time you climb to the altitudes flown by airliners, at 35,000 feet (10,668 m), the air temperature has dropped to nearly minus 100°F (-73°C). Any exposed skin freezes fast and suffers from a painful condition called frostbite.

So what would happen if I could open an airplane window?

Airplane cabins are pressurized to simulate altitudes closer to sea level; opening a window would trigger "explosive decompression," which is as scary as it sounds! All that pressurized air inside the cabin would immediately whoosh outside, like air released through the opened valve of a scuba tank. You wouldn't get sucked out the window (you're too big, for one thing, and your seat belt would hold you in your seat), but the pressure and environmental conditions inside and outside the plane would quickly equalize, or become the same. Emergency breathing masks would drop from the ceiling to provide oxygen (otherwise you would pass out in less than a minute), but you would be left shivering in cabin temperatures colder than the Arctic.

MYTH MASHED

Why CAN I OPEN A PLANE'S EMERGENCY DOORS IF YOU CAN'T OPEN THE WINDOWS?

You can't, actually—not at 35,000 feet (10,668 m), anyway. All the terrible things that would happen if you could open a window on a passenger plane at high altitude—explosive decompression, the blast of freezing air, lack of oxygen, and so on—would ensue the second you cracked the seal on a plane's emergency door, except on an even worse scale: The door is actually large enough for you to get sucked through! Fortunately for flight passengers, emergency doors are impossible to open once the cabin is pressurized. Plane doors open inward, and all that air pressure inside the cabin presses the door shut, kind of like how the water pressure in a bathtub makes the rubber plug in the drain harder to pull out. Unless the Incredible Hulk's sitting in first class, no passenger on the plan has the strength to open an emergency door before the flight crew depressurizes the cabin (which they do upon landing).

GREAT PANES

A GALLERY OF windows

HOLES IN THE WALL

The first windows were just gaps left in the walls of primitive houses, sometimes covered with animal hides or wooden shutters to keep out rain and bugs.

DEFENSIVE MEASURES

Windows evolved to fulfill specific functions in castles of the 12th century. Narrow vertical slits called "arrow loops" allowed castle defenders to launch arrows without exposing themselves to enemy fire.

WINDOW DRESSING

Glass technology has come a long way since the first panes—made of cloudy colored glass that let in light but didn't offer a view—were used in the windows of ancient Rome around the first century A.D. Modern house windows usually have two panes of glass just one-sixteenth of an inch (1.6 mm) thick, with a small gap of air in between to help block outside sounds and keep the house a cozy temperature.

MASTER GLASS

The most advanced windows made on Earth are in orbit aboard the International Space Station. Made of four panes of high-tech glass averaging about an inch (2.5 cm) thick and capped by aluminum shutters, these windows have withstood hits from micrometeorites that strike with the force of a bullet.

Wait, why is there a little hole in airplane windows?

Snag the window seat on a plane trip and you can really see it all: clouds, mountains, rivers, the tiny hole at the bottom of your window, beaches, forests—wait … what? Why does the window have a hole in it?! Relax. It's supposed to be there! Airplane windows are made of three panes. The inner pane is just a simple sheet of plastic designed to keep you from smudging up the middle pane, which is home to that little hole. Aircraft designers call it a "breather hole," and it's there to maintain the cabin's pressure against the outer windowpane, which is more than strong enough to hold in all that pressurized air. That little hole also keeps the window fog free, so you get a clear vista of all those clouds, rivers, mountains, and beaches.

WHY don't we have FLYING CARS yet?

If you've always dreamed of leaping over traffic jams in a jet-powered sedan, you might want to bring those expectations back down to Earth. Flying cars will probably never get off the ground, at least not on a large scale. Despite dozens of promising prototypes built over the decades—including the

sleek AeroMobil, which looks like a sports car with folding wings—flying cars are still too tricky for the average driver to operate without a pilot's license. And then there's the safety factor: When cars break down, drivers can simply pull over to the side of the road. Pilots in malfunctioning flying cars have nowhere to go but down.

So we're stuck in rush-hour traffic forever?

Not necessarily, but you'll need to rethink your definition of a flying car. Companies such as Uber, Google, and Tesla are taking the flying-car concept in a different direction, combining autopilot technologies with new aircraft designs to create flying drone taxis that will carry passengers or make deliveries. These won't be flying cars; they won't have tires or drive on roads before switching to flight modes. They'll look like giant versions of the toy drone you probably wrecked in your backyard tree. But because these drones will be controlled by autopilot systems that have been tested in the airline industry for decades, they'll be less likely to crash or collide. Drones will also run on quiet battery power and won't burn gasoline like regular planes, helicopters, or cars. Uber hopes to get its first flying taxis into the air by 2030.

READY FOR TAKEOFF

TWO DIFFERENT TAKES ON THE **flying car**

AEROMOBIL

MAX AIRSPEED
124 miles an hour (200 km/h)

MAX RANGE
435 miles (700 km)

PILOT'S LICENSE NEEDED?
Yes

Like many flying car prototypes, the AeroMobil has wings that fold back for travel on the road and extend for takeoff from any short runway.

EHANG184 AAV

CRUISING AIRSPEED
37 miles an hour (60 km/h)

MAX RANGE
25 minutes of flying time

PILOT'S LICENSE NEEDED?
No (because it doesn't have a pilot)

This electric robo-piloted prototype has room for a single passenger and is designed as a flying taxi for cities. It can land vertically when summoned by smartphone.

Why don't cars travel on water?

Conventional cars—the kinds with old-fashioned "combustion" engines—need more than gas to make them go. They also need air to mix with the gas in the car's engine, where a small spark ignites the mixture to push a series of pistons and make the car move. A car driving on a lake or ocean runs the risk of water flooding its air intakes and ruining the engine (which is why drivers should never drive down flooded streets). Still, carmakers have designed special "amphibious" cars with air intakes high above the water's surface. U.S. president Lyndon B. Johnson even had one of these novelty cars on his Texas ranch, where he loved to startle unsuspecting guests by pretending to crash his "Amphicar" into a lake. Intended as an all-terrain replacement for the family car, the Amphicar never became more than a novelty—probably because it tended to spring leaks and traveled about as fast as a rowboat.

WHY aren't all cars ELECTRIC cars?

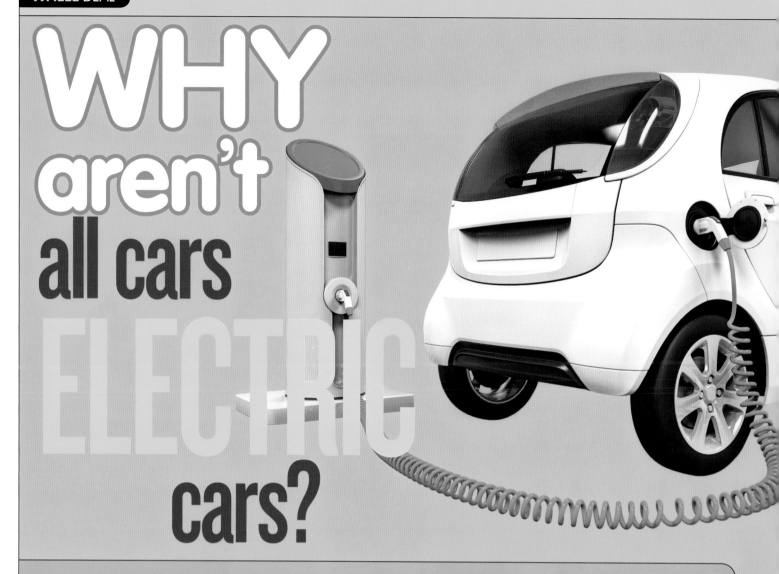

You might think electric cars are the hot new thing, which is why they're still fairly rare on the road. But they were actually invented more than a hundred years ago, around the same time as conventional gas-powered automobiles. In fact, Americans who were ready to upgrade from the horse and buggy in the early 1900s had three power options to consider for the newfangled automobile: gas, electricity, and steam! Each had its downsides. Steam-powered cars could take nearly an hour to warm up and get moving. Gasoline-powered cars were noisy and hard to start (early models had to be hand-cranked into action). Electric cars had a limited range and relied on bulky batteries. In the end, the entrepreneurial genius of Henry Ford, a pioneer in the mass production of automobiles, steered the world toward gas-powered cars. When his Model T rolled off the assembly lines in 1908, it sold for just $650—a third of the price of electric cars. Soon, gas-powered cars became an essential part of daily life, and gas stations began popping up everywhere to fuel them.

Will electric cars ever replace gas-powered cars?

Probably, but it won't happen anytime soon. Electric cars—and particularly "hybrid" cars that charge their own batteries with gasoline-powered motors—are gaining momentum. One key reason is they're considered "green," or friendly to the environment. Gasoline engines emit carbon monoxide and dioxide gases that contribute to a dangerous rise in global temperatures, whereas electric cars don't even have an exhaust pipe. But the old challenges facing electric cars remain: They cost more than gas-powered cars and have a limited range. These cars are easy to charge in suburbs where owners can plug them into special outlets in the garage, but many city dwellers must park on the street. As of 2017, electric and hybrid cars represent only about 1.5 percent of all the cars driven in America.

But car manufacturers from BMW to Volkswagen are getting behind the electric-car trend, putting more models on the market. Electric-car prices are falling while their driving range increases from more efficient battery technologies. Meanwhile, more charging centers are popping up in parking lots across the country. All the pieces are falling into place for a green revolution in car propulsion. If you're waiting for steam-powered cars to make a comeback, though, you're probably out of luck.

Why don't our cars drive themselves yet?

Self-driving cars have been in development for decades, and several models are on the road now. Some offer basic features that assist drivers with simple tasks such as parallel parking and emergency braking. More expensive cars handle all the driving duties while allowing human drivers to take over at any time. These so-called autonomous cars still have steering wheels and other controls similar to standard cars, and people can still drive the old-fashioned way if they want to. True "self-driving" cars, set for the near future, won't have steering wheels or pedals at all. Travelers will use their smartphones to summon one of these driverless taxis from a fleet of robotic cars. Because these smart cars lack bulky controls, all passengers will have more room to stretch out and enjoy the ride.

Will self-driving cars be safe?

Safer than any human driver you know. People pick up bad habits behind the wheel, such as driving too fast or getting distracted by their smartphones. And human drivers must rely on their limited senses—sight, sound, and the feel of the road through the steering wheel. But robo-chauffeurs use cameras, radar, and lasers to see in all directions and scan far ahead for oncoming dangers. They can track all the cars in surrounding traffic—even those that would fall into a human driver's "blind spots." Each car's computer can access traffic data online and combine that information with a GPS system to plot the shortest routes to destinations. These amazing autos can even communicate with each other using rapid bursts of data to warn of lane changes or sudden stops. And, unlike human drivers, robot chauffeurs give their undivided attention to the task at hand: getting you to your destination safely.

WHY aren't all trains BULLET TRAINS?

Blazing through the countryside at up to 400 miles an hour (644 km/h), high-speed trains are a common sight in Japan, China, Europe, and elsewhere. But in the United States and other parts of the world, they're almost unheard of. One roadblock is the vast distances these trains must cover in a large country such as the United States. In smaller nations, such as Japan or France, high-speed trains typically only travel a few hundred miles, making the trip comparable in speed to air travel. In America, travel across the country—even by a high-speed train—could take more than a day, much longer than air travel. Building the special tracks for these trains (some require special electrical magnets) is expensive, and governments would rather put that money toward fixing aging roads and bridges. But speedy train travel might still become a reality in some parts of the United States. Plans are under way for  high-speed lines connecting San Francisco and Los Angeles on the West Coast (with a travel time of less than three hours, comparable to air travel when you throw in security lines and luggage check-in at airports), and New York City and Boston on the East Coast. The middle of the country, meanwhile, will most likely still rely on regular old train, plane, and automobile travel—at least until someone perfects teleportation.

Why don't all passenger planes fly faster than the speed of sound?

More than 40 years ago, a futuristic-looking British-French passenger jet called the Concorde roared across the Atlantic Ocean at more than twice the speed of sound, carrying passengers from New York to London in three and a half hours (a similar flight takes at least seven hours today). It stopped flying in 2003, and today's airliners typically cruise no faster than 600 miles an hour (966 km/h), close to but not quite breaking the sound barrier. Why has air travel slowed down while other technologies have sped up? The answer won't set your imagination soaring. It's just a matter of economics! Supersonic (or faster than the speed of sound) flight requires a lot of fuel—about a ton (0.9 t) per passenger—and jet fuel costs a lot of money. Those costs are passed on to the passengers in the form of expensive tickets. Most passengers would rather save their money and spend a few extra hours in a conventional airliner, which at least offers diversions such as Wi-Fi and in-flight movies to pass the time.

SPEED DEMONS
THE **fastest** BULLET TRAINS

AMTRAK ACELA EXPRESS **FAST**

TOP SPEED 150 miles an hour (241 km/h)

The closest thing the United States has to a high-speed rail system is this passenger train that runs from Boston to Washington, D.C., in about seven hours, using a standard electrically powered propulsion system. Ticket sales exploded when this route began running in 2000 while sales for plane tickets for the same route plummeted, proving that bullet trains are a sought-after alternative to air travel.

SHANGHAI MAGLEV **FASTER**

TOP SPEED 267 miles an hour (430 km/h)

The world's fastest train operating today is more of a taxi service, ferrying passengers just 19 miles (31 km) from a train station near Shanghai, China, to the nearby Pudong International Airport. The train completes the journey in just seven minutes and costs only $8 per person. As a "magnetic levitation" train, the Maglev rides on a cushion of magnetic force, which reduces friction and allows for an incredibly smooth ride.

JAPAN'S MAGLEV **EVEN FASTER**

TOP SPEED 374 miles an hour (602 km/h)

Japanese engineers invented high-speed rail travel more than 50 years ago, so it's no surprise this made-in-Japan bullet train would be the world's speediest—traveling up to a mile (1.6 km) every 10 seconds! The train is currently just a prototype and won't enter service until 2027.

HYPERLOOP **FASTEST**

TOP SPEED 4,000 miles an hour (6,437 km/h)

Strap in for the next giant leap in high-speed transit. Instead of riding on rails, Hyperloop cars travel inside giant tubes that are pumped clear of air. Without air friction to slow them down, and propelled by magnetic levitation, Hyperloop cars can travel even faster than passenger airlines, crossing entire continents in less time than a typical commute to work. The technology is just in the experimental stages now and will require expensive networks of tubes, but the first cars may be ready by 2020 to ferry passengers within California, U.S.A., at more modest (but still impressive!) top speeds of around 700 miles an hour (1,127 km/h).

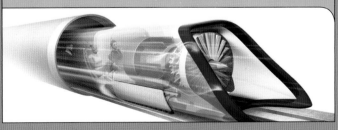

WHY doesn't my SMARTPHONE stay connected?

Today's smartphones do a lot more than let you gab on the go. Loaded with social media apps and Internet browsing services, they serve as your link to the world wherever you wander. Well, almost. Travel too far into the wilderness or head underground into a parking garage and your phone's signal meter begins to shrivel: five bars, three bars, one bar ... Uh-oh! Where'd the service go? Although it's a complex little machine—a miniature computer, really—your smartphone is just a radio. And like any radio, it has its limitations.

How do cell phones communicate?

Your phone is called a "cell phone" because it relies on a giant network of tiny service areas—called cells—that work together to provide uninterrupted phone and Internet service. Each cell area is weak by radio signal standards; most cell towers barely pack enough power to cover a square mile (2.6 sq km). That's also the range of your phone's radio receiving and broadcasting abilities. Why itty-bitty cells rather than one powerful tower that could cover an entire city? Radio signals travel on a limited number of "frequencies," and cell phone companies have access to only about 800 of them. These must be split into frequencies for transmitting (talking or sending data) and receiving (listening or receiving data), which means only about 400 people could carry on a conversation within range of a radio tower at the same time. By dividing the entire network into smaller cells that aren't strong enough to "shine" into neighboring ones, radio frequencies can be reused again and again across the entire network.

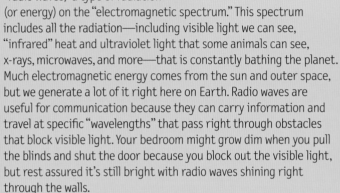

So **how does** a radio work?

Radios such as your phone, walkie-talkies, and CB radios communicate by sending and receiving "radio waves," a type of radiation (or energy) on the "electromagnetic spectrum." This spectrum includes all the radiation—including visible light we can see, "infrared" heat and ultraviolet light that some animals can see, x-rays, microwaves, and more—that is constantly bathing the planet. Much electromagnetic energy comes from the sun and outer space, but we generate a lot of it right here on Earth. Radio waves are useful for communication because they can carry information and travel at specific "wavelengths" that pass right through obstacles that block visible light. Your bedroom might grow dim when you pull the blinds and shut the door because you block out the visible light, but rest assured it's still bright with radio waves shining right through the walls.

Radio waves still have their limits, though. They can't penetrate the layers of concrete and soil to reach deep underground, which is why your phone loses its signal in parking garages or even in elevators (some metals block radio signals). Drive far enough away from the source of the radio waves and they lose their intensity, just like a flashlight looks dimmer the farther you stand from its bulb. The radio signals used in cell phone communication are already relatively wimpy to begin with—and that's by design. Strong radio signals would flood the entire cell phone communication system with deafening static!

Why can't I use my phone on a plane?

Remember: Your phone is actually a tiny radio station, and those radio signals have a slight chance of interfering with a plane's own radios and instruments. Pilots don't want to take that chance—particularly during takeoff and landing—which is why flight attendants ask you to put your phone into "airplane mode," which limits its broadcasting abilities.

SMALL TALK

CELL PHONE COMMUNICATION IN **four steps**

Step 1. When you turn on your phone, it sends a signal to the nearest cell tower letting the system know your phone's unique ID code and location in the network. This way it can find you when someone calls or pass you off to the next cell tower—called a "handoff"—as you travel from one cell to the next.

Step 2. When you make a call by punching in someone's phone number, your phone's transmitter broadcasts that request at the speed of light by radio signal to the nearest cell tower. That tower routes the request down into its base station, which then sends it (usually by a wire buried underground) into the core of the cell company's network.

Step 3. The company's computers locate the person you're calling by finding that person's nearest cell tower (based on their own unique ID code). It then broadcasts a signal from that tower to ring the person's phone while also identifying you as the caller. Your friend pulls out the phone, sees your name on the screen, and decides to answer (you hope). "Hey!" she might say. Communications companies share towers and coordinate to find callers on different networks; they also connect with old-fashioned landline networks to connect you with callers who don't have a cell phone.

Step 4. Your friend's cell phone transmits their "hey!" via radio signal back to the nearest tower, which then routes the message through the network to your nearest cell tower, where it's transmitted to your phone's radio receiver. You and your friend are now linked and communicating, you from your cell area and your friend in hers, perhaps on opposite ends of the city, country, or even the world! The process seems simple—you call, chat, and hang up when you're done. But now you know that a lot happens behind the smartphone screen!

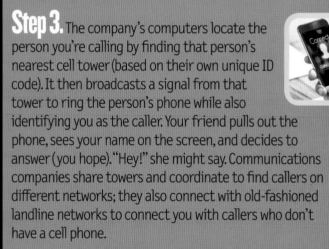

SILLY QUESTION, SERIOUS ANSWER

If cell towers are everywhere, why can't I see them?

Sometimes you can. They look like towers with triangular structures clustered near the top. These are the transmitters and receivers of the different cellular carriers. In some places, cell towers are hiding in plain sight: disguised as trees so they're less of an eyesore.

WHY does my voice SOUND DIFFERENT when I hear it in a video or recording?

When you hear your speech as you talk, you're actually hearing it from both outside and inside your body. The sound waves of your voice enter your ears from the outside like any other sound, striking membranes called eardrums that transmit vibrations to tiny bones and hairs inside your ears, which in turn transmit sound information to your brain for processing. But when you talk, the vocal cords in your throat—the source of your voice—unleash tiny shock waves through your skull, which acts as a sort of subwoofer that lowers the pitch of your voice before it reaches those tiny hearing bones and hairs inside your ear. When the sounds of your outside and inside voice combine, the audio mix comes across as slightly deeper in your own head. When you play your voice back on a recording, you're only hearing your voice from the outside. It sounds shockingly higher and different, a true representation of your speaking voice. Like it or not, that's what everyone else hears when you talk.

Why don't I look quite like myself in selfies (and other photographs)?

Think about where you usually look at yourself as you go about your day, whether you're brushing your teeth or styling your hair or maybe checking your teeth for bits of breakfast. It's in the mirror, and mirrored images are reversed from real life. Part your hair to the right in the mirror and everyone else sees it parted on the left. Everyone's face is asymmetrical, meaning the left and right sides are slightly different. When you examine your face in a photograph, you're seeing your asymmetrical face the way

everyone else sees it, but to you it looks reversed from what you normally see in the mirror. Even subtle differences are enough to throw off how your brain perceives and processes your appearance. As you've read elsewhere in this book, humans tend to like things that are familiar. Your reversed image in the mirror is familiar; your nonreversed image captured in selfies is less familiar. And studies show that people rate the mirror images of their faces as more attractive than what's captured in photographs. This perception works in the other direction: Studies show that people rate the mirrored images of famous faces as less attractive than their true, nonreversed appearance. You can try this yourself by standing next to someone you know well—perhaps your best friend or a sibling—in a large mirror. Do they look at little off? You're seeing them as they see themselves in the mirror. If they don't look fine, just remember it's a trick of the mind.

How DO I TAKE THE PERFECT SELFIE?

- **FIND THE RIGHT ANGLE:** Hold your camera in front of you and slightly above. Avoid snapping from too high of an angle, though, which makes for too much space around your face and can distort your features.
- **STRIKE THE RIGHT POSE:** Head-on photos can make your face look flat. Turn your head slightly to the right or left (show more of your "good side" if you think you have one) to accentuate your features.
- **SEEK THE RIGHT LIGHT:** Natural sunlight will give your skin an even glow and bring out the shine in your hair. If you're inside, take your selfie looking out a window or door.
- **EXPERIMENT AND HAVE FUN!** Researchers think one reason selfie-taking is so popular is because it lets us snap photos over and over until we find the images we like, unlike the old days when cameras required expensive film and weren't built into everyday devices. So by all means experiment with different expressions and angles until you find the photo that makes you happy.

THREE special SELFIES

THE WORLD'S FIRST SELFIE

A selfie is defined as any picture that photographers take of themselves. By that definition, the first known selfie was snapped in 1839 by a Pennsylvania, U.S.A., photography enthusiast named Robert Cornelius. Snapping photos on primitive cameras back then involved a lot more than pointing and shooting. Cornelius had to remove the lens from his camera, stand in front of it for about a minute, then replace the lens.

THE SELFIE MASTERPIECE

When Helen Meldahl takes a selfie, she makes a scene—literally. This Norwegian Instagram artist uses chalk and paint to create fanciful scenery on a mirror. She then poses in the mirror and snaps a selfie of her reflection interacting with her art, creating amazing selfies that blend the real with the surreal.

THE MONKEY MASTERPIECE

British nature photographer David Slater came home with this great shot when he traveled to Indonesia to take pictures of monkeys—and he didn't even need to snap the picture himself. Slater set up his camera on a tripod and left the remote trigger within reach of a female Celebes crested macaque. The curious monkey reached for the trigger and snapped a series of photos, one of them this perfect monkey selfie.

WHY aren't all computers "SUPERCOMPUTERS"?

The world's first general-purpose electronic computer—called the **ENIAC** (or Electronic Numerical Integrator and Computer)—was literally the size of a **house** when it was built in 1943. It could perform thousands of calculations in a second, weighed more than 30 tons (27 t), and required so much electricity to operate that it made the lights flicker in nearby Philadelphia, Pennsylvania, U.S.A. Today, your smartphone can perform hundreds of millions of calculations per second, fits in the pocket of your jeans, and runs for hours off a small rechargeable battery. So why isn't your phone—or your laptop or game system, for that matter—considered a "supercomputer"? It turns out a supercomputer is a specific type of computer, one that's not made to surf social media or play *Super Mario Kart*.

What are supercomputers used for?

PREDICTING THE WEATHER
Supercomputers can crunch climate data from around the world to forecast the weather and model the effects of a warming planet.

MEDICAL SCIENCE
Only supercomputers are powerful enough to catalog and analyze organic systems as complex as the human brain or our genetic structure.

Okay, so **what** is a supercomputer?

Put in the very simplest terms, a supercomputer is like millions of computers in one. Your typical laptop computer or smartphone contains a chip called a central processing unit (CPU). When you play a game or surf the Web on your smartphone, you're actually running a program that relies on numerical calculations and other instructions, all performed by the CPU. Think of it as the brain of your device. Many modern CPUs might have two or four or even up to twelve "cores" that work like additional CPUs to boost the device's computing power.

A supercomputer has millions and millions of cores, controlled by special hardware and software that allows all these mini-brains to work together smoothly. Remember how we said your smartphone can perform hundreds of millions of calculations per second? China's Sunway TaihuLight, one of the world's most powerful supercomputers, can perform 93 quadrillion calculations per second. (A quadrillion is a thousand trillion or a million billion.) But all that power comes at a price: The Sunway TaihuLight cost nearly $300 million! Supercomputers are also huge, dwarfing even the house-size ENIAC from 1943. They require enormous amounts of electricity to power all those cores. The electric bill for IBM's Sequoia supercomputer is more than $6 million a year!

What ABOUT SUPERCOMPUTER GAMES?

Hey, if Mario looks great on your Nintendo Switch, imagine playing it on a machine that's quadrillions of times more powerful! But although supercomputers could certainly be programmed to play *The Legend of Zelda,* their electricity needs and computational power make them much too expensive and powerful to waste on fun and games. Scientists vie for supercomputer time and must apply for it years in advance. There just aren't enough of these expensive, complex machines to go around. Even Watson, the IBM computer that beat those *Jeopardy!* contestants, has been put to work analyzing diseases and helping find cures.

DIY SUPERCOMPUTER

You might think you could build your own supercomputer by linking all your friends' PCs together and putting them to work on a specific task, but that type of networking already has a name: "distributed computing." It offers a fraction of the power of supercomputers but none of the speed. Distributed computers must communicate over the Internet, which is much slower than the direct connections of a supercomputer's millions of cores.

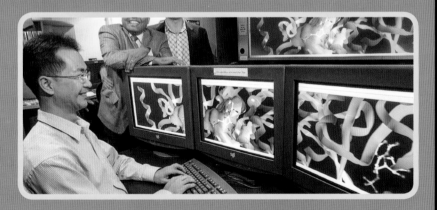

SIMULATING ... EVERYTHING

Scientists use supercomputers to simulate the places they can't visit or even see with their own eyes, such as the structures of itty-bitty atoms or the inner workings of the sun.

ENTERTAINING US

IBM has created supercomputers powerful enough to beat chess champions and even genius contestants of the game show *Jeopardy!*

WHY aren't computers making GREAT LEAPS in power like they used to?

Computers began shrinking in size and growing in power in the 1950s not long after the invention of the transistor, a tiny device that controls electrical signals and a crucial component in all modern electronics. A single transistor can't do much—it's just an ultrasmall version of your wall light switch, either on or off. But by working together on a silicon microchip, transistors can perform complex calculations that in turn process vast amounts of information. Their power comes in their numbers: The more transistors that can fit on a chip, the more calculations that chip can perform.

Like most gizmos, transistors shrunk as the technology improved. The first transistors were the size of a roll of pennies; today's transistors are 500 times smaller than a cell in your body. In 1971, computer makers could fit only about 4,000 transistors on a chip. By 2011, they could cram in more than 2.5 billion. But today's engineers fear they've reached the dinkiest shrinking point for transistors, which would lose their ability to control electricity if they shrunk any smaller. Consequently, computers have stopped shriveling in size, and they're no longer making great leaps in power, and that has engineers looking for the transistor's replacement.

So **what** will the next computers look like?

With transistors reaching their physical limits, computer engineers are thinking small to create the next big thing: the "quantum computer." This mysterious machine marks a departure in how computers process data. Remember: A normal transistor is just a tiny switch that represents information in one of two states (either on or off). Instead of relying on transistors, however, a quantum computer harnesses the mysterious properties of subatomic particles—the smallest known particles—which are capable of representing information in a much greater variety of states (not just on or off). That translates into more computing power squeezed into much less space, making quantum computers many millions of times faster than current machines for certain tasks. These machines represent a new (and in many ways mysterious) frontier in computing. So far, quantum computers have only existed in small prototypes, although an international team of researchers is working on building one. As with the early conventional computers such as ENIAC, the first quantum computers will be huge—the size of an office building—but someday all that power could fit into a device the size of a toaster.

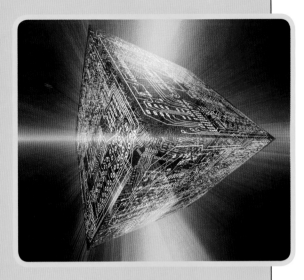

Why can't we control computers with our minds yet?

Actually, at least one computer controller grants players mind control in the virtual world of video games. The Emotiv Epoc headset bristles with sensors that translate thoughts into actions on the computer screen, such as rotating blocks or moving rocks. Think to yourself, "Push that boulder!" and the on-screen boulder will respond to your mental magic. But although brainpower might seem like the ultimate video game interface, it can't really replace the mouse or joystick for moving your character around and performing actions (like jumping or shooting) that require good ol' hand-eye coordination. Players must first train the brain-reader to associate mental commands with on-screen actions, and these commands can be hard to recall in the heat of the game. When games get hectic, after all, it's hard to think straight!

QUANTUM COMPUTERS NOT EXOTIC ENOUGH FOR YOU? How about a cyborg hard drive made from your DNA? Researchers are also looking into how to turn the genetic material of all living things into a data-storage device. If you'll remember from chapter 5, every cell in your body contains tiny strips of chemicals called genes that instruct your cells how to work together, build the body, and make it run smoothly. Genes are components of spiral-shaped molecules of DNA, and each molecule encodes all the instructions necessary to build your entire body. That's an astounding amount of information packed into a teeny-tiny space. In fact, one teaspoon of genetic material could store every book, movie, TV show, photo, and cute doggie video ever created in the history of the world! Scientists have already figured out how to create DNA strands and encode them with information, then fossilize the strands to preserve the data for millions of years.

WHY don't we have ROBOTIC BUDDIES yet?

Who wouldn't want their own R2-D2, a helpful little robot pal who's always there to lend a tool for every task? Actually, the robot invasion began decades ago, and today robots are everywhere: from the motorized vacuum that slurps dust bunnies from beneath your bed to the millions of machines building everything from cars to candy bars in factories across the world. But aside from a few gimmicky dancing toys or cute robo-pets, the household robot promised in science fiction has yet to come lumbering into your bedroom with a tray of robot-baked cookies. The big holdup is a lack of smarts. Computer intelligence hasn't reached the point where machines are autonomous, or able to think for themselves. Instead of an all-purpose pal like R2-D2 that can read your moods and respond to any request, modern household robots are built for specific jobs—such as vacuuming the floor or cleaning the bottom of your pool.

A ROBOT IS ANY MACHINE created to perform a series of actions, from delivering packages by air to exploring the surface of Mars. And, by that broad definition, robots have been around for a lot longer than you think. In fact, historians believe the first robot was created more than 2,000 years ago by a Greek mathematician named Archytas, who built a birdlike machine that could fly the length of two football fields on its own! Historians know little about this primitive drone's design or what propelled it, although some believe it might have been steam powered!

WALKING TALL
THREE humanoid ROBOTS

Robots come in all shapes and sizes, from buzzing robo-bugs to tool-tipped metal arms used on assembly lines. But humanoid robots—or robots shaped like people (think C-3PO instead of R2-D2)—are becoming more common as engineers experiment with machines that serve as playmates or perform jobs too dangerous for people. Here are three of these amazing walking (and in some cases, talking) machines ...

ASIMO

Billed as the world's most advanced humanoid robot, Honda's ASIMO (short for Advanced Step in Innovative Mobility) was designed as an ambassador for robotkind. It can talk in several languages, walk up stairs, jog, recognize faces, shake hands, and help with some basic tasks like turning on light switches and pouring drinks.

ASIMO

NAO

Hyperintelligent humanoid robots of the future might look back and consider NAO (pronounced "now") their great-great-granddroid. This robot is small (about as tall as your thigh) but big on abilities: It can walk, dance, hear, see, talk, and even touch with its three-fingered hands. But NAO is intended more as a tool than a toy; students and hobbyists at schools across the world are using it to learn about robotics and contribute to its skills, a type of collaborative development known as crowdsourcing.

ATLAS

This tough, rough-looking human-size robot isn't pretty—or particularly smart—but it can sure get around. Atlas relies on an advanced balancing system to lumber over rough outdoor terrain, including slippery snow, that would trip up other robots. Atlas can handle tough falls and scramble back to its feet using its strong arms and legs. The robot is designed to perform rescue missions or emergency tasks—such as shutting off valves or lifting debris—in hazardous environments.

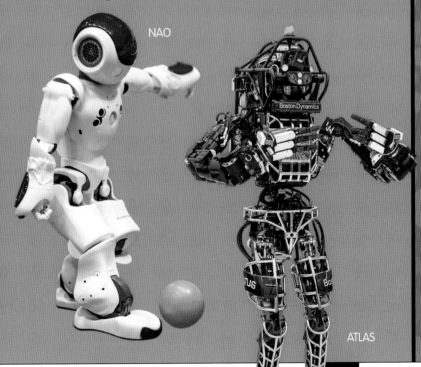

NAO

ATLAS

PLAYING FOR KEEPS

Each year, teams of humanoid robots from around the world compete in a soccer competition known as RoboCup, which has the goal of one day pitting the RoboCup champions against the winners of the most recent World Cup—and beating them. (RoboCup organizers hope to achieve this goal by 2050.) Such events aren't just for kicks; they help roboticists pioneer new ways for robots to work, play, and think.

PERSON OF INTEREST

WHO?
Grace Murray Hopper

WHAT is she famous for?
Making computers easier to program

WHEN?
1940s

WHERE?
United States

WHY is she important?

As a kid growing up in New York City, Grace Murray Hopper liked taking alarm clocks apart just to see what made them tick. She carried this curiosity—and a doctorate in mathematics—along with her when she joined the U.S. Navy in World War II. She was assigned to program one of the first computers, called the Mark I, which took its instructions from complex mathematical code printed on paper rolls. Hopper believed computers could do more than just military tasks if they were easier to program, so she later helped devise a more user-friendly programming language that used English words. Her work helped popularize computers and is one of the reasons we carry them with us everywhere today.

WHY aren't
computers as SMART as humans?

You see it every time your robot vacuum dodges your dog or you start up a conversation with your smartphone's voice-recognition system: "artificial intelligence," or AI. Ever since the term was coined in 1956 to describe the new field of building intelligent machines, computer scientists have devised robots and computers that mimic our abilities, from beating chess champions to translating foreign languages as they're spoken. But as brainy as computers might seem, they just can't process the deep thoughts of a human brain.

One crucial concept that remains beyond the reach of thinking machines is "self-awareness." It's more than the ability to think—it's the ability to think *about* thinking—and it's not the sort of command or concept that can be programmed into a computer from the "top down," as computer scientists call coding specific functions into a machine. A true self-aware machine must be designed from the "bottom up" to simulate a human brain. Instead of being programmed, such a machine would learn on its own. That would take some seriously powerful hardware that doesn't exist yet.

Brainy INSPIRATION

The human brain is a network of 100 billion "neuron" nerve cells (also known as a neural network) that processes and stores information; our most powerful supercomputers in many ways mimic that neural network between your ears. IBM's supercomputer Watson, for example, was built in 2005 using thousands of processing cores and dozens of servers. Programmers used a bottom-up approach to teach the machine to understand spoken questions and retrieve the answers from its vast memory banks. But Watson is still just a machine performing an impressive trick, falling far short of demonstrating self-awareness and true human intelligence.

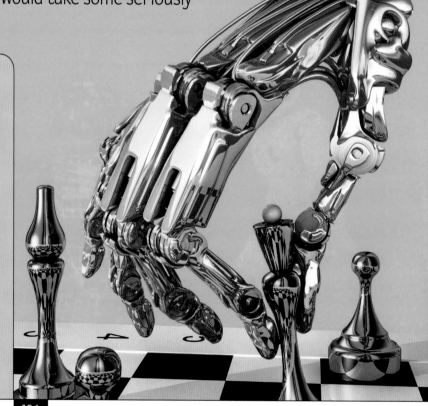

So **when** might computers become as smart as people?

Not anytime soon. Some computer scientists point to the development of powerful quantum computers and predict we'll have self-aware, human-smart machines by 2050—or sooner. But not everyone is as optimistic. "Software does not improve as smoothly as hardware," says roboticist Hod Lipson, director of the Creative Machines Lab at Columbia University in New York, U.S.A. To get a better idea of the timeline for self-aware AI, he thinks we should look at how intelligence evolved in nature over millions of years rather than how computers grew in power over the past few decades. Drawing on that analogy, Lipson doesn't think computers will achieve human-level, self-aware intelligence for another 500 years.

Would supersmart computers threaten humanity?

Breathe easy. A machine capable of human-level thought is more likely to save humanity than harm it. Such an artificial intelligence would combine a human's ability to learn with a computer's superhuman processing speed and perfect memory recall—without ever needing to snooze or even take a bathroom break. Installed in a medical laboratory, for instance, an artificial intelligence could analyze the entire case history of all cancers or some other disease to find a cure. Intelligent machines could study and offer solutions to humanity's greatest problems, from climate change to species extinctions. Installed on a space ship, an AI would serve as our eyes and ears—and brains—as it unravels the mysteries of the solar system.

How does my computer or phone understand what I'm saying?

When you speak a command to a smartphone, computer, or other device and it does what you ask (such as search the Internet or send a text), it's actually demonstrating a major breakthrough in artificial intelligence: the ability to understand speech. Here's how "speech recognition" works, in four phases ...

LISTEN UP: Your devices listen to what you have to say and break each word into pieces of digital information, or numbers, the language of computers.

WORD SEARCH: Your device compares this digital information against its own memory to determine which words you said, selecting the most likely matches.

LANGUAGE ARTS: Once it figures out your words, the computer analyzes the order in which you spoke them to determine what you want. This is the trickiest part of the process, involving an understanding of sentence structure and the rules of grammar and spelling (distinguishing "there" from "their" or "two" from "too," for instance).

TALKING BACK: Now the device will respond to you with the requested information. It searches its memory for the correct response, which it assembles and speaks back to you in a language you understand. Speech-recognition technology has improved so rapidly (tech company Apple claimed in 2015 that its speech-recognition system makes mistakes only 5 percent of the time) that it can listen to other languages and translate them back in your own. Soon, all you'll need to say "hello" or "where's the bathroom?" in any country is a universal translator app for your phone.

WHY don't we have three-dimensional HOLOGRAMS like in sci-fi movies?

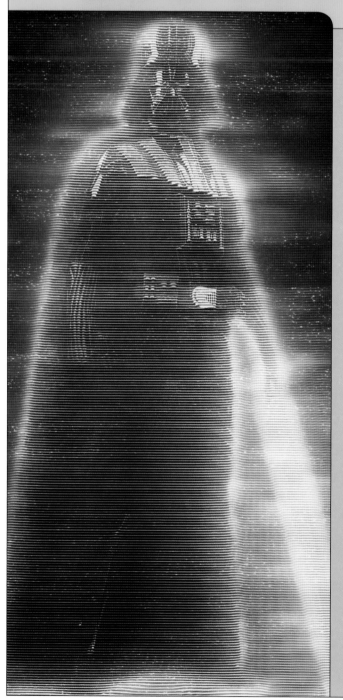

You've seen them on-screen in everything from Star Wars to Iron Man: three-dimensional images of people, spaceships, and control panels that shimmer to life in midair. They're holograms, or projections that can be viewed from any angle. Such technology would revolutionize the way we communicate and watch movies. Faraway family members could project their holographic form in your living rooms for face-to-face meetings.

Hologram technology has actually been around since the 1970s and comes in many varieties. That 3-D security sticker on Dad's credit card? Hologram. The shimmering logo on the back of your favorite baseball team's official cap? Hologram. But these shiny novelties are dull compared to the full-color 3-D midair displays in sci-fi movies. Unfortunately, those types of floating projections aren't really possible, at least not with today's technology. Light can't just hover in midair; it needs to reflect off something to bounce back to your eye. But don't lose hope for that 3-D holo-theater just yet! Here's how hologram (or hologram-like) technologies might replicate the experience in the very near future ...

SEEING THINGS

THREE 3-D displays

CLASSIC HOLOGRAMS

True holograms have been around for decades and rely on a complicated combination of lasers and mirrors to project 3-D images onto a surface, such as film or glass. The technology is limited by the size of the surface it's projected on. A Star Wars–style hologram would require a screen as large as a room, and even then you could view it only from certain angles.

LASER HOLOGRAMS

A laser is more than just an alien-blasting weapon from sci-fi movies. Real-life lasers use mirrors to focus light into a concentrated beam. Engineers have figured out how to pulse these beams to "ionize" air molecules, creating tiny bursts of light. A group of pulse lasers focused just right can create hologram-like images in midair without needing to bounce them off a surface. The images are simple for now—more like floating connect-the-dot shapes—but as laser technology improves, so will the visuals.

VISOR-BASED HOLOGRAMS

The closest you can get to seeing Star Wars–style holograms right now is a technology that doesn't involve holograms at all. Tech companies like Microsoft and Florida-based Magic Leap are creating visors that superimpose detailed holograms over the real-world environment (in the case of Magic Leap, the images are beamed directly into your eyes). Think of it as a mash-up of virtual reality and real reality (the actual term for it is "augmented reality"). The downside, of course, is you can't see the holograms unless you have a visor—which also means you look silly to anyone watching you gawking and pawing at empty space.

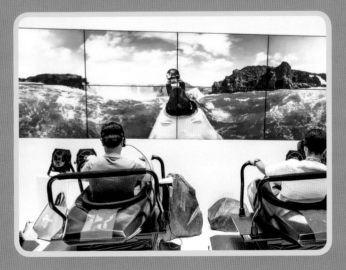

Why can't I experience virtual reality without losing my lunch?

Virtual reality (VR) goggles can boggle the mind, offering an escape into wickedly nifty computer-generated worlds where you might soar like Superman or save the world from tentacled aliens. In real life, meanwhile, you might not feel so heroic. Your skin becomes clammy. Your stomach grows queasy. Your throat goes dry. And then, *BLAARRRGH!* You feel like the game just beat you. You just experienced what scientists call "simulator sickness," a close relative of the motion sickness you might feel on a rocking boat or as a passenger in a car on windy roads. VR goggles are so effective at transporting you to fantasy worlds because their high-definition screens—one for each eyeball—fool your eyes into believing you're in another place. But your brain will always know better. Your ears contain special organs that detect your motion, tell up from down, and keep you from tumbling when you trip. While your eyes might be telling you you're leaping mountains and dodging lasers in virtual reality, your body knows that you're standing, sitting, or moving differently in the real world. That difference between your perceived motion and real motion is what makes you feel motion sick.

How do I avoid VR motion sickness?

If you're prone to motion sickness, there's no easy fix. Repetitive exposure to motion sickness—inducing situations such as virtual reality will eventually make your body accustomed to them. That's why fighter pilots can pull loop-the-loops without losing their cookies and ship captains can sail rough seas without spending half the trip hurling over the rail. VR experiences with smoother graphics will also help diminish the disconnect between what you're seeing and what you're feeling, which will help limit those un-fun feelings.

WHY don't VIDEO GAME GRAPHICS look just like real life?

Your gaming device creates virtual worlds through a process called "rendering," which assembles everything you see on the screen—heroes, villains, their gear, and the worlds they inhabit—from three-dimensional shapes called polygons. These polygons are then digitally painted with "textures" that give them details: skin, scales, buttons, rocks, rivets, rust, and so on. The process happens dozens or even hundreds of times each second, depending on the power of the graphics hardware, creating an environment that looks real although still not 100 percent realistic. Many times the artists who create virtual worlds aren't even trying to design "photorealistic" graphics that mimic real life; cartoony environments and characters might better fit a game's theme. (After all, would you really want to control a realistic Mario who sports a five o'clock shadow and wears overalls covered in work stains?) But when artists try to create photorealistic environments and characters, they're still hampered by the technical limitations explained on the right.

When will computer graphics become indistinguishable from real life?

Computer experts predict that graphics hardware will become powerful enough to render 100 percent realistic scenery by 2023, although game physics and human characters—with their expressive faces and body language—might take much longer to get just right.

Why aren't the computer-controlled opponents in games more intelligent?

Be careful what you wish for. When game designers create the behaviors of enemies and other characters in their games, they're not trying to create an artificial intelligence that rivals your own. Game makers are trying to create the illusion of intelligence for very specific situations, such as racing a player in a go-kart or sneaking up close for an attack. Video games are supposed to be fun, after all; if foes are too brainy, players will gripe and even chuck their controllers in frustration. So programmers and designers come up with AI techniques that give players a chance. One such trick—known as "rubber-band AI"—limits how far opponents in racing games will pull ahead if they're winning the race. For instance, they might accidentally crash or slow down to give you a chance to catch up. The end result is a close race and possibly one less controller chucked across the room.

EYESORES

WHY GAME GRAPHICS DON'T MATCH real life

RESOLUTION SOLUTIONS

The term "resolution" refers to the number of picture elements—or pixels—that a computer, game console, or virtual reality system can display. The most powerful hardware can produce images around eight megapixels (or eight million pixels), and imaging experts believe the human eye can take in about 70 times as much information. Still, scientists argue that our eyes can focus on only about seven megapixels at a time, which means display technology may have caught up with the capabilities of our eyes.

PHYSICS LESSONS

When objects in a virtual world don't fall or roll or otherwise react according to real-world physical laws such as gravity, it can shatter a game's illusion of reality. Programmers are working on game worlds in which every object exists in a framework of physics—virtual leaves will sway in the virtual breeze, for instance—and engineers are creating special "physics processors" to run these programs, but the technology isn't quite there yet.

LIGHTS ON

You see what you see in the real world because light bounces off objects in the environment into your eyes. Artists often fake this in virtual worlds by painting light and shadows in the environment—a technique that doesn't quite fool the eye. As hardware becomes more powerful, however, they'll be able to render game scenes with virtual light sources that create realistic shadows and reflections.

FUNNY FACES

Digital artists can create convincing animals, monsters, cities, and objects, but one species still presents a challenge: humans. Because we see flesh-and-blood people on a daily basis—particularly their eyes, our primary point of eye contact—we're especially good at noticing the slightest imperfections in computer-generated people. The result: Realistic human characters in games look slightly off, stuck in zone that computer artists call the "uncanny valley."

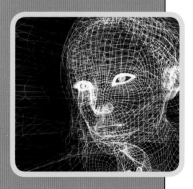

POP **CULTURE**

NOT ALL OF THE UNIVERSE'S GREAT-EST MYSTERIES ACTUALLY INVOLVE THE UNIVERSE, or the origins of life on Earth, or all the goings-on beneath the skin of your own body. Sometimes, you just want to know the basics behind the stuff of everyday life (why are fire trucks red and school buses yellow?) or the answers to the questions that keep you up at night (why don't airplanes come with parachutes?). In this chapter, you're peeling back the onion of popular culture—uncovering the big answers to the little questions about sports, myths, movies, toys, and even fashions to (literally) die for.

KNOW-IT-ALL 7

WHY can't I surf on a TSUNAMI?

Because this type of surf would slam you into the turf! Tsunamis aren't formed like normal waves, which begin as ripples blown across the sea's surface hundreds or even thousands of miles away. Tsunamis are spawned by coastal or undersea earthquakes, submerged landslides, volcanic eruptions, or even asteroid impacts. Such earth-shaking events displace ocean water around or above them, triggering knee-high swells that zoom across the ocean at the speed of a jet airplane—fast enough to cross the entire Pacific Ocean (where tsunamis are most common) in less than a day. When these energy-packed waves reach shallow waters, they undergo a terrifying transformation. The low point of a tsunami wave—called its trough—reaches shore first, causing waters on beaches and harbors to retreat and expose the seafloor. Coastal residents who recognize this warning sign know it's time to race inland rather than wax their boards. Any surfers trying to ride this gnarly wave would first get sucked out to sea, then shoved back to shore by a wall of water as high as 100 feet (30 m).

Why can't
I skydive without a parachute?

Gravity and falls from great heights typically make for a bad combination. Although air resistance cushions our bodies in a fall, skydivers still reach a terminal velocity of around 120 miles an hour (193 km/h) just 12 seconds after stepping out of the plane. Hitting the ground at that speed would be like stepping in front of a bullet train, and tumbling into a lake or ocean is no better: Water doesn't squish into itself like air or swampy muck or that foam in your bubble bath, so plummeting into the sea would be as bad as landing in a parking lot. Survivors of skydiving accidents owe their lives to the luckiest of landings. When British bomber gunner Nicholas Alkemade survived a plummet of 18,000 feet (5,486 m) from his blasted bomber in World War II, it was because his fall was broken by tree branches, brush, and drifts of snow. In 1993, a New Zealand skydiver named Klint Freemantle fell 3,600 feet (1,097 m) when both his parachute and emergency parachute failed. He walked away with just a cut over his left eye after splashing down into a mucky duck pond—a softer landing spot than a body of water.

Why do wingsuit skydivers still even need a parachute?

You've probably seen the stomach-churning videos: Wingsuit skydivers, wearing special jumpsuits equipped with inflatable "wings" stretched between their arms and legs, seem to soar like Superman. But they can't land like Superman, which is why they still need to wear parachutes. These elite jumpers can control their direction better and stay aloft longer than conventional skydivers, but they still fall as they fly—which is why they typically skim down the slopes of mountainsides. They also travel about 100 miles an hour (161 km/h), leaving no room for error as they dodge terrain and deploy their parachutes for a soft landing.

Why don't airliners come with parachutes for the passengers?

Frequent fliers have heard this safety spiel dozens of times: "In the event of a water landing, your seat cushion can be used as a flotation device." Good to know! But wouldn't it also be reassuring if your seatback doubled as a parachute in the event of engine failure? Actually, no. Unlike a simple flotation device, parachutes are bulky and need extensive training to use safely. They would also require the calm cooperation of more than a hundred panicked passengers during the chaos of an in-flight emergency. Passengers would have to strap on their parachutes (a process that takes minutes), wait for the captain to depressurize the cabin, then calmly walk to an emergency exit and leap into a blast of wind whipping by up to 600 miles an hour (966 km/h). Everyone in free fall would need to keep their parachutes from tangling in a sky full of fellow passengers suddenly turned into untrained skydivers. Such a feat would be tricky even if the captain could keep the plane flying level and slow enough for a safe exit—unlikely in a crashing aircraft.

Happy LANDING

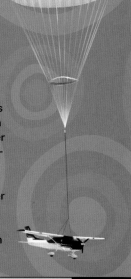

Although individual emergency parachutes for airline passengers are impractical in an air emergency, giant parachutes for smaller planes—those that carry five or fewer passengers—have actually saved these craft from crashing. At least one company is developing parachutes for larger commuter planes capable of carrying 20 people. Eventually parachutes might help full-size passenger planes drift safely back to Earth in an emergency.

RIDING A MONSTER WAVE ON A SURFBOARD is scary enough. But Australian motocross star Robbie Maddison (aka Maddo) managed to rev it up even further: He surfed a big wave in Tahiti on a special ski-equipped dirt bike modified to race across the water.

SAY WHAT?!

WHY don't we wear blue for ST. PATRICK'S DAY?

Actually, blue was the original color of choice to celebrate Ireland's patron saint (the hue is actually called St. Patrick's blue, after it was chosen by kingdom officials in the 18th century), but green eventually won out for several reasons: Ireland's nickname is the Emerald Isle, the clover is associated with St. Patrick (who, according to legend, drove all the snakes from Ireland), and green dominates Ireland's flag. Oh, and according to another legend, leprechauns can't see you if you wear green.

Why isn't the Incredible Hulk gray?

Gray?! Ha! Everyone knows the Hulk is a mean green smashing machine, right? Well, not always. When comic book writer Stan Lee created the character in 1962, he wanted the Hulk—the angry alter ego of mild-mannered scientist Dr. Bruce Banner—to sport a skin color that wouldn't be confused with the Fantastic Four's Thing, a mountainous orange rock monster. Lee and the comic's colorist considered making the Hulk red and even green, but Lee decided to go with gray. Unfortunately, gray was a tricky color to print consistently in comic books at the time; in his debut comic, the Hulk appeared in various shades of gray throughout the issue and even green in one panel. Green was an easier color to print consistently, so from the second issue onward—and in his various TV and movie appearances—the Hulk is green. Well, usually. Every once in a while the Hulk reverts to his original gray color for various plot twists.

Why is the White House white?

It's a common myth that the White House—home of United States' presidents since 1800—was painted white to cover up fire damage from a British raid in 1814. But the mansion at 1600 Pennsylvania Avenue was actually always white, coated with whitewash since before it was finished in 1798 to protect its stone walls from Washington, D.C.'s freezing winters. It was painted with white paint in 1818 and unofficially known as the White House until President Theodore Roosevelt made the name official in 1901.

Why aren't school buses red like fire trucks?

Wait, why are fire trucks red in the first place? Unfortunately, no one is quite sure. The most plausible theory is that the first fire engines were painted red so they would stand out from early automobiles, which were mostly black in the early 1900s. Later research showed that bright colors such as yellow and lime green actually pop more in your peripheral (or side) vision, particularly in the early morning hours, so school buses were painted yellow (actually, more of a yellow-orange) to make them easier for other drivers sharing the road to see. Some fire departments across the country are following suit, which is why you might see a yellow fire truck racing by. It's certainly hard to miss!

SAY WHAT?!

WHEN A PLANT GROWS FRUIT, everybody wins. Animals gobble up the sweet energy-rich treat and then wander off to spread the seeds far and wide through their ... ahem ... waste. Now imagine a tree that grows an entire produce section of different fruits. An American artist and professor named Sam Van Aken has created more than a dozen of these magical multicolored trees. First he cuts the branches from various donor trees, then painstakingly attaches them to a single tree using tape and special cutting techniques. The "grafted" branches take hold and heal, forming a living work of art that blossoms in a rainbow of colors and bears 40 different kinds of fruit!

WHY don't we
DRESS LIKE THIS
anymore?

The goofy getups in this picture might make you giggle, but once upon a time these styles were all the rage. When it comes to fashion—that flavor-of-the-moment combination of clothes, hairstyles, makeup, and jewelry—the only thing that stays the same is constant change. Shifts in cultural and political beliefs drive fashion. Coats and scarves made of exotic animal furs and skins were once considered luxurious symbols of high status, for example; now considered cruel, they have been replaced with faux, or imitation, fur and human-made materials.

But fashion is mostly dictated by the so-called influencers: movie stars, pop singers, politicians, athletes, and other celebrities. In the 1990s, millions paid hundreds for a pair of Air Jordans so they could "be like Mike" (aka basketball legend Michael Jordan). Singer Madonna influenced a generation to don lace and rubber bracelets—a pop-punk look that defined fashions in the 1980s. And in today's world shrunk by social media and linked with instant access to the latest trends, fashion fluctuates faster than ever. Maybe you're a slave to fashion, or maybe you don't care. Even refusing to follow the latest fashions is itself a fashion statement.

EXTREME STYLES

History's MOST
OUTRAGEOUS FASHION STATEMENTS

SKY-HIGH SHOES

WHERE: Venice and Spain

WHEN: 15th to 17th centuries

Platform pumps known as chopines originated as sensible shoes, giving well-to-do ladies in Venice a slight boost above streets streaked with mud. But soon the chopines' function took a backseat to outrageous form, with ladies competing for a height advantage. Some shoes towered 20 inches (51 cm) above the ground, requiring a team of servant spotters to flank fashion mavens and steady them from tumbling.

SOOTY SMILES

WHERE: England

WHEN: Late 1600s

Sugar was an expensive new luxury in England in the late 1600s, and Queen Elizabeth I discovered she had a sweet tooth. Dental hygiene, on the other hand, was much less fashionable; Elizabeth's teeth soon grew dark from decay. Black teeth became a symbol of wealth—a hallmark of the hoity-toity who could afford expensive sugar—so ladies across England began blackening their pearly whites to imitate the rotten-toothed aristocracy.

BIG WIGS

WHERE: Europe

WHEN: Mid-1700s

Ancestors of modern hipsters, macaronis (named for their love of the Italian noodle) were young 18th-century Englishmen famous for their silly sense of humor and a fashion sense that was literally over the top. They wore towering wigs covered in sweet-smelling white powder and crowned with teeny-tiny hats that could only be removed with a long stick or the tip of a sword.

EXPLOSIVE SKIRTS

WHERE: United States

WHEN: 1800s

An extreme example of form over function, crinolines were massive skirts draped over bell-shaped cages of metal rings to keep their rigid shape. They were popular among women of all ages and classes but hardly practical. The rigid cage made it nearly impossible to sit or even squeeze through some doorways. Stiff updrafts could tip women head over heels. Navigating in the ungainly, flammable dresses was especially perilous in the days when homes were lit and heated with candles, oil lamps, and fireplaces. According to an 1858 *New York Times* story, an average of three women a week perished in crinoline fires.

MAD HATS

WHERE: United States

WHEN: 1800s

Crinolines weren't history's only dangerous duds. Trendsetters of the past used deadly poisons such as arsenic to dye clothes and toxic lead to create cosmetics. Hatmakers had it particularly bad. To glue animal furs into felt, they brushed the furs with mercury, a substance toxic to the touch or if its fumes are inhaled. A hat's lining protected the wearer from toxic exposure, but hatmakers suffered from mercury poisoning, which made them paranoid and angry (the origin of the phrase "mad as a hatter"). Prolonged contact led to an early death. Despite the dangers, mercury was still used in hatmaking well into the 18th century. Hatmakers considered exposure just part of the job.

WHY isn't DONKEY KONG a donkey?

Most gamers know Donkey Kong as the top gorilla in a sprawling family tree of vine-swinging, go-kart-racing, party-game-playing apes, from fun-loving nephew Diddy Kong to sneaky distant cousin Ninja Kong. But long before these other Kongs came along, Donkey Kong was just the girlfriend-swiping rival of mustachioed plumber Mario, hero of 1981's *Donkey Kong* arcade game. It was the first big hit for Nintendo game designer Shigeru Miyamoto (who went on to design the legendary *Legend of Zelda* series). Miyamoto always intended for the game to feature an ape villain—a riff on the classic Hollywood monster fable *King Kong*. When it came time to name his game's stubborn gorilla, Miyamoto (who's Japanese and spoke little English at the time) flipped through a Japanese-English translation book. He found the word "donkey" implied stubbornness and the word "kong" called to mind an ape. He put the words together and a gaming superstar got its unusual name.

Why don't Nintendo, Sony, and Microsoft just make one super game console?

Imagine needing to buy only one game system to play games featuring all your favorite characters, from Mario to Master Chief, Pikachu to Sonic the Hedgehog. Actually, console manufacturers have considered collaborations in the past (Nintendo once designed a prototype CD-based system with Sony, and Microsoft talked with both Nintendo and Sony about building a console before the debut of the first Xbox), but such plans never left the drawing board or the boardroom. The gaming business isn't all fun and games: It's a multibillion-dollar industry. The console makers make money—in the form of a fee charged to the game publishers—on each game that sells for their respective system. Joining forces behind one system would mean sharing these fees, which the hardware makers just aren't willing to do. So for now you'll need to choose your game console based on which one offers the exclusive games and characters you connect with.

Why isn't Nintendo's famous plumber Mario clean-shaven instead of mustachioed?

Before he was even named "Mario" (for his debut in 1981's *Donkey Kong*, Mario was simply a carpenter called Jumpman), Nintendo's mascot sported a bushy mustache to go along with his blue overalls, black hair, and red cap. Using the primitive blocky graphics of 1980s computer technology, digital artists had only so many tiny blocks—called pixels, or picture elements—to draw with when designing game characters and their facial features. For Mario, Nintendo's artists made the most of their limitations by using just a few blocks to draw a large mustache and red cap, bold features that gave their tiny character a big personality compared to rival game heroes of the day. The mustache became Mario's defining feature, Jumpman was soon renamed Mario, and he was given an Italian accent in later games.

PERSON OF INTEREST

WHO?
Jerry Lawson

WHAT is he famous for?
Pioneering vital video game features

WHEN?
1970s

WHERE?
United States

WHY is he important?
This engineer from New York City didn't invent the first video game console, but he came up with all the features you can't live without today. Before Lawson helped develop the Fairchild Channel F system in 1976, consoles could play only a few built-in games for two players only. Lawson helped pioneer games that fit on cartridges, which players could swap in and out of their system, expanding their game libraries immensely. He also designed his system with enough memory to allow for artificial intelligence, so players could challenge the computer instead of just friends. Oh, and Lawson's other innovation might be the most important of all for any gamer who has ever needed a bathroom break: the pause button.

SAY WHAT?!

PIKACHU, THE MOST FAMOUS—AND POSSIBLY THE MOST ADORABLE—OF THE POKÉMON CREATURES, was named after the Japanese sounds of an electric spark (*pika*) and the soft *choo*-ing sound of a mouse. (Wait, mice make a *choo*-ing sound? In Japan they do, and we'll explain why later in the chapter.)

WHY aren't GOLF BALLS smooth?

Golf might seem like the simplest of sports: Players swing a long club at a small ball in an attempt to knock it into a distant hole. But serious science went into making that ball soar higher and farther. Each golf ball is dented with between 300 to 500 tiny dimples, which churn the air around them in mid-flight to create a wraparound cushion of rough air. This turbulent layer creates a kind of force field that reduces drag on the ball while pushing it higher, a little like how an airplane's wing shape generates lift. The result: Dimpled golf balls fly twice as far as smooth ones.

Why aren't basketballs brown?

Well, they used to be, until the late 1950s. That's when a university basketball coach named Tony Hinkle discovered that an orange ball is easier for players, fans, and referees to see. The National Collegiate Athletic Association liked the orange ball so much it made it the standard ball.

Why aren't footballs round?

In the earliest days of the sport, when players used their feet as well as their hands to move the ball around, footballs were just ordinary round balls. It wasn't until the first college match between Princeton and Rutgers in 1869 that the ball took on the familiar oblong shape—and that happened only by accident (the ball had leaked and sagged into more of a lopsided lump). As the sport evolved into more of a passing game (forward passes weren't even allowed until 1906), its ball evolved with it, becoming the classic "pigskin" we know today.

Why aren't
all baseball stadiums the same?

Seen from above, most Major League Baseball (MLB) ballparks look like diamonds in the rough: built with oddly bent angles, mismatched halves, and outfield walls of varying heights. Soccer and football fields are laid out according to precise dimensions, so why is ballpark design so willy-nilly? These stadiums are the products of regional geography and history. Many major league ballparks are located in cities where space is limited and stadiums butt up against streets and buildings. Setting a standardized "footprint" for all 30 ballparks would be impossible, so MLB rules allow wiggle room when it comes to the layouts of outfields and foul-ball zones. The distances between bases and location of the pitcher's mound on the actual diamond, however, must all be the same. Each field's unique shape and quirks are just part of baseball's charm—and strategy. In no other sport does the home team have a greater advantage.

OBSTACLES IN THE OUTFIELD

Ballpark LANDMARKS

TAL'S HILL

HOME TEAM: Houston Astros

Outfielders in Minute Maid Park in Houston, Texas, U.S.A., not only have to deal with a 90-foot (27-m)-wide hill in center field when they scramble for pop flies, they also have to dodge a flagpole that can deflect the ball in unpredictable ways.

OUTFIELD IVY

HOME TEAM: Chicago Cubs

The ivy-covered brick walls in Chicago's Wrigley Field, added in 1937 to support outfield bleachers, are one of the ballpark's signature features—and a huge hassle for outfielders who must sometimes dig out the ball from the thick wall of greenery.

GREEN MONSTER

HOME TEAM: Boston Red Sox

The most famous ballpark landmark, this 37-foot (11-m)-high wall stretching along left field of Boston's Fenway Park is famous for its manually operated scoreboard, mysterious interior (visiting outfielders cannot resist peeking their head inside the scoreboard), and imposing height. Left-handed batters here have an advantage knocking the ball out of the park over the lower right-field wall.

WHY is TUG-OF-WAR no longer an Olympic event?

Wait, tug-of-war was once an Olympic event? Yep—with medals and everything—and we're not talking about the original games first played in ancient Greece 2,700 years ago. Teams from around the world competed in tug-of-war as recently as the 1920 Summer Games. The United States' team actually swept the gold, silver, and bronze medals in 1904. But as interest in the sport waned and the Olympics governing body began to whittle down the number of events, tug-of-war got the heave-ho. But just because it's no longer a medal-worthy event doesn't mean people don't take tug-of-war seriously. The Tug of War International Federation has more than 60 teams worldwide and an annual world championship.

SAY WHAT?!

TUG-OF-WAR IS HARDLY THE ONLY ODDBALL OLYMPIC EVENT that's fallen by the wayside. In the swimming obstacle course, featured in the 1900 Summer Olympics in Paris, swimmers raced 200 meters in the Seine River while dodging boats and climbing a pole at the end. Competitors in rope climbing, discontinued in 1932, raced up a rope similar to the one you might scramble up in gym class. In racewalking, racers mosey around the course as fast as possible while keeping one foot in contact with the ground at all times and their front leg rigidly straight until they can move their back leg in front of it. If that sounds easy, it's not—but racewalking is still an Olympic event if you want to put your best foot forward and give it a shot (just remember to keep that leg straight)!

Why aren't sumo wrestlers skinny?

Size equates to power in this sacred Japanese sport, in which two behemoth men (women aren't allowed in professional sumo wrestling, despite a growing number of amateur female competitors) attempt to manhandle each other across the boundary of a small circular ring. But despite their blubbery bodies and ground-shaking weight—some more than 400 pounds (181 kg)—sumo wrestlers don't spend the day scarfing down junk food. They're athletes, and like any athlete they need to eat right to stay in shape. The breakfast, lunch, and dinner of sumo champions is *chankonabe*, a protein-rich stew overflowing with beef, vegetables, and fish. Sumos in training consume chankonabe in great quantities to build muscle. They eat heaping side dishes of white rice, then follow each meal with a nap. Snoozing so soon after eating lowers the body's metabolism. All that rice is stored as fat, turning each sumo wrestler into a mountain of a man!

Why aren't competitive eaters hefty?

Because as strange as it might sound, staying skinny helps these "gastro-athletes" eat more. Competitive eaters carefully train their stomachs to stretch beyond doctor-approved limits, and their bellies can stretch even more if they're not held back by a layer of flab taking up space in the abdomen. Most contest foods are of the unhealthy variety, such as hot dogs, chicken wings, hard-boiled eggs, and even mayonnaise from various sponsors organizing the events. Eating these calorie bombs too often would put competitive athletes at risk of high blood pressure, heart diseases, diabetes, and obesity. So most gastro-athletes stuff themselves with healthier foods—fruits and vegetables—to stretch their stomachs between contests. That's why top champs such as American Joey Chestnut (who holds the world record for eating 70 hot dogs) and South Korea's Sonya Thomas (who holds the women's record at 45 hot dogs) are fit and trim, always in fighting shape for the next big stomach-stuffing event.

Weird World
OF SPORTS

COW CHIP TOSSING

The globe's best chip chuckers gather every April in Beaver, Oklahoma, U.S.A., for the World Championship Cow Chip Throw. Here they select projectiles of sun-dried cow plops at least six inches (15 cm) in diameter from an official chip wagon that's guarded around the clock to prevent poop tampering. Competitors get two chips each to toss however they like—as long as they don't cross the foul line while hurling these disgusting disks up and away.

WORM CHARMING

Working in two- or three-person teams, competitors at the World Worm Charming Championships in the soggy English countryside (and elsewhere) have 30 minutes to coax as many squiggling earthworms as they can from the muddy ground using nothing but sound. Implements include pitchforks, knitting needles, musical instruments, subwoofers—any tools that woo worms using vibration. By the end of a typical competition, the ground is absolutely oozing with slippery dirt-covered night crawlers!

COCKROACH RACING

Buckets of squirming roaches, each individually numbered and given names like "Lord of the Drains," are sent scurrying as a spectator sport at Brisbane, Australia's Story Bridge Hotel. Roaches compete in various themed races, including hurdling events in which the bugs have to clamber over garden hoses. Roach wranglers scoop up the first bug to leave the ring and declare it the winner. Performance-enhancing substances such as sugar and coffee are strictly forbidden for the six-legged contestants.

WHY can't I go over NIAGARA FALLS in a barrel?

Straddling the Canadian border with the United States, Niagara Falls attracts millions of vacationers and honeymooners each year with its inspiring natural beauty and power. Enough water pours over the falls every second to fill 13,000 bathtubs! For more than a century, the falls have attracted another type of visitor: daredevils. At least 15 people have intentionally plunged over the falls in barrels and other homemade contraptions since 1901. It's a suicidal stunt. The falls plunge 180 feet (55 m) into a treacherous pool of submerged rocks and swirling currents. About one out of four daredevils don't survive the fall. If that's not enough to scare you away, Niagara fallers face $10,000 in fines and must pay for their own rescue.

Why aren't
these people terrified?

Don't worry! These smiling swimmers might look like they're seconds away from a deadly drop, but they're actually just posing for a photo op. They've bellied up to the edge of Devil's Pool, a naturally formed tub at the edge of Victoria Falls in Zambia, Africa. A slippery rock ledge prevents people from being swept over the falls during the region's dry months (from May to October), allowing a front-row seat to a 300-foot (91-m) drop and the rainbow-colored plume created by the world's largest waterfall.

SILLY QUESTION, SERIOUS ANSWER

Why can't I snowboard down a volcano?

Well, you can—but it's not a very good idea. (Especially if the volcano is still smoldering and active!) Strapping snowboards to their feet or squatting on wooden sleds, volcano surfers race down the slopes of Cerro Negro, an active volcano in Nicaragua. They reach speeds of 30 miles an hour (48 km/h), which makes for skinned knees and bloody elbows if they bail on the gravel-size grains of volcanic rock. Even scarier: Volcano surfers have very little steering control.

Why don't Sherpa guides
on Mount Everest pass out
from lack of oxygen?

When mountain climbers reach altitudes of 26,000 feet (7,925 m) on the world's tallest mountain above sea level, they enter a region cheerily named the death zone. Up here the air holds only a third of the oxygen we inhale at sea level; climbers without portable air tanks suffer from "hypoxia," or lack of oxygen, which causes them to pass out in half an hour. Fewer than 6 percent of people can make the climb without oxygen, even after acclimating themselves to the thin air for weeks and months. The Sherpa people of Nepal, however, have a natural advantage in extreme altitudes. After living high up in the Himalaya for generations, their bodies evolved with a superpower we sea-level dwellers lack: Their cells have adapted to make the most of the thin air, drawing more energy from less oxygen (like how a fuel-efficient car can squeeze more go from a tank of gas). Sherpa expertise and superhuman endurance have helped save many Everest expeditions from disaster.

WHY don't ANIMALS' SOUNDS

sound the same in other languages?

Cows go "moo" and roosters go "cock-a-doodle-doo," right? Only if you learned those animals' noises in English and in your particular corner of the world. People in other cultures and countries have their own versions of common critter speak in their own languages. Ask a Dutch person to imitate a cow, for instance, and she'll say, "Boo, boo!" Rooster calls in Spanish, German, and Dutch sound more like "key-kirra-key!" Dogs in Chinese go "wan-wan" instead of "woof-woof." It's not that the animals sound any different or speak in different languages in other parts of the world. Every culture interprets and speaks animal sounds a little differently based on the nuances of the local language and how often they encounter each critter. In Japanese, which doesn't have a *zzzz* sound, bees go "boon-boon" instead of "buzz-buzz." Americans have many more variations of barking sounds because dogs are more popular in the United States than most other countries. People in different parts of the world settled on their animal sounds a long time ago; then they shared them with each other and passed them down to their children as a part of their culture. Just as you learned that a duck goes "quack, quack," kids in France learned to say "kwan, kwan." Have a look—and listen—at how cultures interpret animal noises from around the world ...

What THE HECK IS THIS THING?

Impress your pals by dropping the genuine names of everyday thingamajigs and doohickeys.

The plastic bit at the end of a shoelace: **AGLET**

The wire loop that holds a lampshade: **HARP**

The loop on a watch band that holds the excess strap: **KEEPER**

The cardboard sleeve for a cup of hot coffee: **ZARF**

The metal tube at the eraser end of a pencil: **FERRULE**

The food-stabbing points on a fork: **TINES**

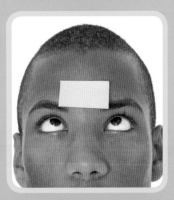

The smooth spot between your eyebrows: **GLABELLA**

The fleshy bit hanging above a turkey's beak: **SNOOD**

International ANIMAL SOUNDS

DOG
ENGLISH: Woof-woof
TURKISH: Hev-hev
HINDI: Bow-bow
ROMANIAN: Hom-hom

CAT
ENGLISH: Meow
JAPANESE: Nyah
CHINESE: Meemee
RUSSIAN: Meahh

PIG
ENGLISH: Oink-oink
JAPANESE: Boo-boo
DUTCH: Nor-knor
GERMAN: Groonz-groonz

MOUSE
ENGLISH: Squeak-squeak
JAPANESE: Choo-choo
SWEDISH: Pip-pip
RUSSIAN: Pee-pee

FROG
ENGLISH: Ribbit-ribbit
KOREAN: Kegull-kegull
GERMAN: Kwok-kwok
ITALIAN: Crah-crah

SAY WHAT?!

ALL THESE ANIMAL SOUNDS ARE EXAMPLES OF ONOMATOPOEIA (ON-OH-MOT-OH-PEE-AH), or words that mimic the sound of whatever they're naming. If you come across a word that sounds a lot like the noises of the thing it describes, you've found an example of onomatopoeia! It's both a mouthful and a tricky concept, so here are a few more examples of onomatopoeia in action: "splash," "snore," "crunch," and "rustle."

WHY don't VAMPIRES

sleep in beds instead of coffins?

Pick a place and period in the past and locals will share tales of creatures out for blood. Lilith, the mother of all vampire legends, was a winged demon that terrorized children 4,000 years ago in Mesopotamia, one of the oldest civilizations. The ancient Romans feared the stryx, an owl-like demon that feasted on human flesh. Romanians in the Middle Ages were wary of strigoi, restless spirits that rose from the grave to feed on the living. Imagine contemplating such frights each night before the invention of the night light! But, although terrifying, none of these ancient bloodsuckers resemble the smooth-talking, sharp-dressing, dirt-napping creatures of modern vampire myth—because most of those vampire ground rules were dreamed up by one man: Irish novelist Bram Stoker.

The word "vampire"—from the Serbian term *vampir*—entered the English language in the 1700s to describe the myth of recently deceased villagers who rose from their graves and fed on the living. Drawing from this fearsome folklore and historical facts, Stoker concocted a tale of the most famous vampire of all in his 1897 book *Dracula*. His Transylvanian terror, Count Dracula, set the style for all vampires to follow. He's a nocturnal nobleman who weakens in the sunlight, transforms into a bat, cringes from a crucifix (a holy cross), and casts no reflection. But Drac's habit of sleeping in a coffin wasn't introduced until Hollywood retold the tale in the classic 1931 horror film *Dracula*. In the book, Dracula prefers napping in the dirt of his native Transylvania.

Why can't a werewolf transform anytime instead of only during a full moon?

Just like their creepy cousins the vampires, werewolves are creatures of ancient folklore, and their legend has changed much with the times. They were considered a real threat to society in Europe—and particularly France—in the 16th and 17th centuries, when thousands of alleged human "werewolves" were arrested and put on trial. But these older shape-shifters have only one thing in common with the modern myth: They suffered from lycanthropy (from the Greek words for "wolf" and "human"), a mythical condition that transformed them from ordinary humans into shaggy monsters. European folklore offers many triggers for transformation: curses from the gods, magic creams, wolf-pelt belts, or pacts with the devil. Some people simply chose to become lycanthropes! You might think it takes a chomp from another werewolf and a full moon to unleash a lycanthrope's inner beast, but those are only relatively recent additions to the legend. The classic 1941 movie *The Wolf Man* and its sequel established nearly every modern werewolf rule. The movie's star catches a mean case of lycanthropy after surviving a werewolf attack. The flowering of a poisonous plant called wolfs-bane triggers his change, although in later films it's the light of the full moon.

Why aren't sailors still afraid of the kraken?

Ancient mariners feared this tentacled beast, said to wreck ships and drag crewmen to their doom using suckers the size of pot lids. Accounts from the 18th century describe a creature large enough to be mistaken for an island. Sailors off the coast of Africa claimed a kraken wrapped its tentacles around their vessel and began pulling it under. Wielding cutlasses, the crew hacked off the tentacles and narrowly saved their ship. But whereas yesterday's mariners dreaded a kraken encounter, today's marine biologists would do anything to see one up close! They suspect that the giant squid—known by the scientific name *Architeuthis dux*—is the inspiration for the kraken legend. As big as a school bus, this true sea titan is elusive and far from aggressive, at least toward ships and sailors. The giant squid prowls the lightless depths of the ocean preying on other squids and even whales. Until recently, scientists had never seen a living giant squid. They only knew it existed from *Architeuthis* carcasses that washed up on beaches (the longest ever found measured 59 feet [18 m]). In 2006, Japanese scientists reeled in a living specimen: The 24-foot (7.3-m) beast put up quite a fight as they hauled it aboard—and it was only a baby.

BRUTE FORCES

Mythical
MONSTERS FROM AROUND THE WORLD

THE BUNYIP (AUSTRALIA)

Australia's most feared river critter isn't the crocodile. The continent's original residents recount tales of the bunyip, a seal-like water spirit that lunges from water holes to snatch unwary bathers in its tusks. An Australian museum displayed a supposed bunyip skull in the 1840s (although experts claimed the bone was from a baby cow).

THE CHUPACABRA (MEXICO)

Four feet (1.2 m) long from head to tail, this Mexican monster has leathery skin, eyes that shine like headlights, and a back lined with spines. According to sightings, it slinks into barnyard pens in the dead of night and drinks the blood from frightened chickens, cows, and goats—hence its nasty nickname (chupacabra is Spanish for "goat sucker"). Theories for the chupacabra's origin abound. Some believe it's the runaway pet of an alien who dropped by Earth for a pit stop. Others insist it's an escapee from some mad scientist's lab.

THE KAPPA (JAPAN)

A mythical water monster known for making mischief, the kid-size kappa has the body of a turtle and lizardlike limbs. Legend has it that kappa suck the blood of swimmers in ponds and rivers and occasionally challenge them to feats of skill. This pond-lurking prankster also loves passing gas. Next time you accidentally make some bubbles in the pool, blame it on the kappa!

THE RAKSHASA (INDIA)

This hulking demon from Hindu mythology poisons its victims with its toxic claws before chowing down with saber-sharp fangs. Said to have bottomless bellies, rakshasa are always on the prowl for fresh flesh. They're also able to alter their size and appearance. They can take the form of any animal or person.

WHY can't I live in a HOUSE made of LEGO BRICKS?

Spaceships, castles, speedboats, fire stations—the list of objects you can assemble from those colorful Danish bricks is nearly endless, so why can't you build a full-size house? Oh, it's been done—although the end result was proof that a house built from snap-together toys wouldn't be a very good home. In 2009, British television star James May, along with about a thousand helpers, assembled a

two-story house in Surrey, England, U.K., built from more than three million bricks. The colorful casa had windows and skylights, a kitchen complete with dishes and snacks, a king-size bed topped with pillows and sheets, and even a bathroom with a working shower and toilet—all assembled from Lego bricks (yep, even the toilet paper). But May learned after a sleepless night that his bed wasn't comfy and the ceiling leaked when it rained. The house was later demolished brick by brick after the Lego company determined it would be too expensive to move the house to its Legoland theme park.

Building BLOCKS

Lego bricks might be too teeny to use for house-building material, but budding locking-block architects still have options for assembling their living spaces piece by piece. A company called EverBlock makes shoebox-size Lego-like bricks that snap together to build temporary walls, closets, forts—whatever you want, really—inside your home. And a company named Kite Bricks has come up with blocks similar to Legos for use in actual construction. Called Smart Bricks, they're made of concrete instead of plastic, but they snap together like Legos and even have removable panels for the installation of electrical wiring, plumbing, and insulation. The idea behind Smart Bricks is to make constructing buildings faster and more efficient. Simply design the structure in a computer program, buy enough Smart Bricks to build it, and hire a team of builders trained to work with the blocks. You'll have your dream Lego-like house much sooner than with conventional construction—as long as the workers don't lose any pieces.

Why can't
I live in a tree house?

Who says you can't? Six million years after the common ancestor of humans and chimpanzees climbed down from the trees and began walking on two legs, we're once again making our homes in the treetops. From sprawling multitrunk mansions to chic hotel rooms with views from the tallest branches, tree-based living has become a trend in rural spots across the world. There are even several tree house associations that hold annual conferences and share building techniques. Treetop living began to boom in 2010 with the invention of the "Garnier Limb," a heavy-duty anchor that bolts into a living tree and provides support for all sorts of fantastical houses up high. These aren't the simple tree forts your mom or dad might build in the backyard, either. They have electricity, bathrooms with showers and toilets, kitchens, HDTVs, Wi-Fi, fireplaces, air conditioning—all the comforts of home.

SAY WHAT?!

THE WORLD'S MOST EXPENSIVE TREE HOUSE, the seven-million-dollar straightforwardly named Treehouse in the United Kingdom, has its own restaurant and suspension bridges that connect wings perched in a forest overlooking a medieval castle.

HIGH LIFE

THREE LEVELS OF
treetop living

TREE HOTEL

Check into the Treehotel in Harads, Sweden, for luxury among the leaves. Each room is suspended in towering pines and offers funky design features, such as mirrored walls that blend in with the forest (but still have all the frills—including Wi-Fi!). One room is even shaped like a flying saucer!

TREE MANSION

Cradled in the branches of a massive white oak and six other trees in the forests of Crossville, Tennessee, U.S.A., the "Minister's Treehouse" has 80 rooms

spread throughout 10 floors that rise 97 feet (29.6 m) into the sky. Horace Burgess, an ordained minister, began building the house in 1993 as an act of his devotion. Nearly 260,000 nails later, his creation towers above the tree's tallest branches. It even has a basketball court!

TREE CITY

What better place for a sprawling tree house community than the rain forest canopy of Costa Rica? Finca Bellavista is a sky-high town of nearly 50 tree houses connected by zip lines and suspension bridges above a river and waterfall near the Pacific Ocean. Adventurous residents and guests wave out their windows to their neighbors: capuchin monkeys, sloths, and toucans perched high in the canopy. The eco-friendly community relies on renewable energy for its power needs.

FRONT COVER: (golf ball), Photodisc; (lightning storm), Igor Zhuravlov/iStockphoto; (dinosaur), Franco Tempesta; (rabbit), Andrew Walmsley/Nature Picture Library; (cupcake), Ivonne Wierink/Shutterstock; (brain), VLADGRIN/Shutterstock; **SPINE:** Ivonne Wierink/Shutterstock; **BACK COVER:** (astronaut), iurii/Shutterstock; (penguins), Gentoomultimedia/Dreamstime; (dog), Susan Schmitz/Shutterstock; (Stonehenge), Filip Fuxa/Shutterstock

FRONT MATTER: 1, pandapaw/Shutterstock; 2-3, Diane Collins and Jordan Hollender/Getty Images; 4 (LE), WENN US/Alamy Stock Photo; 4-5 (LO/L-R), urbanbuzz/Alamy Stock Photo; 5 (UP RT), Roos Koole/Getty Images; 5 (CTR RT), David Ducros/Science Source; 5 (LO RT), Kiko Jimenez/Alamy Stock Photo; 6 (UP LE), Brittny/Shutterstock; 6 (CTR LE), Castleski/Shutterstock; 6 (LO LE), Chendongshan/Shutterstock; 7, Regien Paassen/Shutterstock

CHAPTER 1: 8-9, Gérard Lacz/Biosphoto; 10, Suzi Eszterhas/Minden Pictures; 11 (UP LE), TongRo Images RF/Getty Images; 11 (LO LE), stable/Shutterstock; 11 (UP RT), Liumangtiger/Dreamstime; 11 (CTR), NHPA/SuperStock; 11 (CTR RT), Animals Animals/SuperStock; 11 (LO RT), Stefan Sollfors/Alamy Stock Photo; 12 (LE), Michel Gunther/Science Source; 12-13 (LO/L-R), M. Watson/Science Source; 13 (UP LE), D.P. Wilson/FLPA/Science Source; 13 (UP LE), Mark Bowler/Science Source; 13 (CTR), Viter8/Dreamstime; 13 (CTR LE), Alamy Stock Photo; 13 (LO CTR), Jose Manuel Gelpi Diaz/Dreamstime; 13 (LO CTR LE), Adam Fletcher/Science Source; 13 (LO RT), Bruce Morser/National Geographic Creative; 13 (UP RT), Science Source; 14 (UP RT), Eric Isselee/Shutterstock; 14 (LO LE), Damedeeso/Dreamstime; 15 (UP LE), ArchMan/Shutterstock; 15 (CTR LE), Ana Gram/Shutterstock; 15 (UP RT), Suzi Eszterhas/Minden Pictures; 15 (CTR RT), Joel Sartore/National Geographic Creative; 15 (CTR RT), redbrickstock.com/Alamy Stock Photo; 15 (LO RT), Matthew Studebaker/Minden Pictures; 16 (CTR LE), Eric Isselee/Shutterstock; 16 (LO RT), Pedro Luz Cunha/Alamy Stock Photo; 17 (UP LE), Photomyeye/Dreamstime; 17 (CTR LE), Paul Nicklen/National Geographic Creative; 17 (CTR), Mark MacEwen/Minden Pictures; 17 (UP RT), Robert McGouey/Wildlife/Alamy Stock Photo/Alamy Stock Photo; 17 (CTR RT), Juniors Bildarchiv GmbH/Alamy Stock Photo; 17 (LO RT), M. Watson/Science Source; 17 (LO RT), PA Images/Alamy Stock Photo; 18 (LO RT), Mark MacEwen/Minden Pictures; 18 (CTR LE), Steve Bloom/Biosphoto; 18 (CTR RT), MYN/Jerry Monkman/Minden Pictures; 19 (CTR LE), Birgitte Wilms/Minden Pictures; 19 (UP LE), Murray, Patti/Animals Animals/Earth Scenes/Animals Animals; 19 (LO LE), Auscape International Pty Ltd/Alamy Stock Photo; 19 (UP RT), Alex Mustard/Minden Pictures; 19 (CTR RT), Peter Charlesworth/LightRocket via Getty Images; 19 (LO RT), Yann Hubert/Minden Pictures; 20, HILDEBRAND photography/Getty Images; 21 (LO LE), Serge Montagnon/Minden Pictures; 21 (UP RT), Rosa Jay/Shutterstock; 21 (LO RT), Mitsuyoshi Tatematsu/Minden Pictures; 22 (UP RT), Shutterstock/Mirvav; 22 (LO LE), Ardea/Stefan Meyers/Biosphoto; 22 (LO CTR), Satoshi Kuribayashi/Minden Pictures; 22 (LO RT), Alain Mafart-Renodier/Biosphoto; 23 (UP RT), P. Bagavandoss/Science Source; 23 (CTR), BSIP/Science Source; 23 (LO RT), Mint Images/Frans

Lanting/Biosphoto; 24 (UP LE), Jacek Chabraszewski/Shutterstock; 24 (CTR RT), WaterFrame - Agence/Daniela Preissler-Dirscherl/Biosphoto; 24 (LO LE), Dave Fleetham/Design Pics; 25 (UP LE), ostill/Shutterstock; 25 (LO LE), Gerald C. Kelley/Science Source; 25 (UP RT), Matthijs Kuijpers/Biosphoto; 25 (CTR RT), Connie Bransilver/Science Source; 25 (CTR LE), Arterra Picture Library/Alamy Stock Photo; 25 (LO LE), UIG/Getty Images; 26, Mike Parry/Minden Pictures; 27 (UP RT), Colin Parker/National Geographic My Shot/National Geographic Creative; 27 (UP CTR), Jeff Rotman/Alamy Stock Photo; 27 (LO LE), Bidouze Stéphane/Dreamstime; 27 (CTR RT), Norbert Wu/Minden Pictures; 27 (LO RT), Eric Isselee/Shutterstock; 28, Cimmerian/iStockphoto/Getty Images; 29 (UP RT), Farlap/Alamy Stock Photo; 29 (CTR LE), Brendon Cremer/Minden Pictures; 29 (LO CTR), zsolt_uveges/Shutterstock; 29 (LO RT), Denis Crawford/Alamy Stock Photo; 30 (LO LE), Claudius Thiriet/Biosphoto; 30 (UP RT), Life on white/Alamy Stock Photo; 31 (UP LE), Gerry Pearce/Science Source; 31 (UP RT), Gabriel Barathieu/Biosphoto; 31 (CTR RT), Daniel Heuclin/Biosphoto; 31 (LO LE), Franco Banfi/Biosphoto; 32, Credit: Life on white/Alamy Stock Photo; 33 (UP LE), Gerard Lacz/Science Source; 33 (CTR LE), Steve Bloom Images/Alamy Stock Photo; 33 (CTR RT), Svetlana Foote/Alamy Stock Photo; 33 (LO RT), Life on white/Alamy Stock Photo; 34 (LO LE), Pavlina Sanborn/Alamy Stock Photo; 34 (LO RT), Viorel Sima/Shutterstock; 35 (UP LE), UpperCut Images/Alamy Stock Photo; 35 (LO LE), Katrina Brown/Alamy Stock Photo; 35 (UP RT), Life on white/Alamy Stock Photo; 35 (UP RT), Jean-Michel Labat/Science Source; 35 (CTR RT), GlobalP/iStockphoto/Getty Images; 35 (UP RT), bonzami emmanuelle/Alamy Stock Photo; 36 (LO RT), Voren1/iStockphoto/Getty Images; 36 (CTR LE), Tierfotoagentur/Alamy Stock Photo; 37 (UP LE), Danielle Donders - Mothership Photography/Flickr Open/Getty Images; 37 (LO RT), Sandra van der Steen/Alamy Stock Photo; 37 (UP RT), Tierfotoagentur/Alamy Stock Photo; 37 (CTR LE), Ken Gillespie Photography/Alamy Stock Photo; 37 (CTR LE), Juniors Bildarchiv GmbH/Alamy Stock Photo; 37 (CTR RT), Mark Taylor/Science Source; 37 (CTR RT), John Daniels/Science Source; 37 (LO RT), Tierfotoagentur/Alamy Stock Photo; 38 (UP LE), vvvita/Shutterstock; 38 (LO LE), TrainedPetPhotos/Alamy Stock Photo; 38 (UP RT), WilleeCole/iStock/Getty Images Plus; 38 (LO RT), David Lawson/Alamy Stock Photo; 39 (CTR LE), DBURKE/Alamy Stock Photo; 39 (CTR RT), Minerva Studio/Alamy Stock Photo; 39 (LO RT), Unchalee Khun/Shutterstock

CHAPTER 2: 40-41, Digital Vision; 42, Oliver Furrer/Getty Images; 43 (UP CTR), Vasko/iStockphoto/Getty Images; 43 (LO LE), Panoramic Stock Images/National Geographic Creative; 43 (LO LE), Blanko; 43 (CTR RT), Ivonne Wierink/Shutterstock; 44 (CTR RT), valio84sl/iStockphoto/Getty Images; 44 (LO RT), Hamiza Bakirci/Dreamstime; 44 (UP LE), luplupme/iStockphoto/Getty Images; 45 (LO LE), Mark Garlick/Science Source; 45 (UP RT), irra_irra/Shutterstock; 45 (UP LE), Wiki user Tttrung; 45 (UP RT), Naeblys/Alamy Stock Photo; 45 (UP RT), Images/Alamy Stock Photo; 45 (CTR RT), AP Photo/Frank Victores/REX/Shutterstock; 45 (LO RT), Rob Marmion/Shutterstock; 45 (CTR LE), Jan Smit/Minden Pictures; 46 (CTR RT), MasPix/Alamy Stock Photo; 47 (UP LE), nexus 7/Shutterstock; 47 (CTR LE), Richard

Kotch/iStockphoto/Getty Images; 47 (UP RT), Regien Paassen/Shutterstock; 47 (CTR RT), Vietnam Stock Images/Shutterstock; 47 (LO RT), Terry Chea/AP/REX/Shutterstock; 48, Phil Pauley; 49 (LO LE), joakant/Shutterstock; 49 (UP RT), Vlad61/Shutterstock; 49 (CTR RT), Jesper Anhede; 49 (CTR LE), Planetpix/Alamy Stock Photo; 49 (LO RT), Stewart Armstrong/National Geographic Creative; 50 (LO LE), Charlie Bennett/AP/REX/Shutterstock; 50 (CTR RT), Gary Hincks/Science Source; 51 (UP LE), Henning Dalhoff/Science Source; 51 (UP RT), Science History Images/Alamy Stock Photo; 51 (CTR), W.Haxby, Lamont-Doherty Earth Observatory/Science Source; 51 (LO CTR RT), Claus Lunau/Science Source; 51 (LO CTR RT), Julie Dermansky/Science Source; 51 (LO CTR), DanielPrudek/iStockphoto/Getty Images; 52, hepatus/Getty Images; 53 (UP LE), ttsz/iStock/Getty Images Plus; 53 (UP RT), Pictorial Press Ltd/Alamy Stock Photo; 53 (LO CTR), John Valley, University of Wisconsin-Madison; 53 (LO CTR), NASA/JPL/USGS; 53 (LO LE), Miguel (ito)/Shutterstock; 53 (LO CTR), NASA; 53 (LO RT), NASA; 54 (LO LE), Sergey Lavrentev/Dreamstime; 54-55 (CTR RT), Atiketta Sangasaeng/Shutterstock; 55 (UP CTR), Vvoevale/Dreamstime; 55 (CTR), Ken Backer/Dreamstime; 55 (LO CTR), Prim91/Dreamstime; 55 (UP CTR), Sharpshot/Dreamstime; 55 (CTR), Losmandarinas/Dreamstime; 55 (LO CTR), Sakdinon Kadchiangsaen/Dreamstime; 55 (UP RT), lgorius/Dreamstime; 55 (CTR RT), Pancaketom/Dreamstime; 55 (LO RT), Lars-ove Jonsson/Dreamstime; 55 (LO RT), Andrei_M/Shutterstock; 56 (UP RT), de-kay/iStockphoto/Getty Images; 56 (LO LE), Image Wizard/Shutterstock; 56 (UP RT), Dimjul/Dreamstime; 57 (UP RT), AnatolyM/Getty Images; 57 (CTR RT), Annette Shaff/Shutterstock; 57 (LO LE), The Alchemist, 1853 by Douglas, William Fettes (1822-91)/Victoria & Albert Museum, London, UK/Bridgeman Images; 58 (UP RT), yellowsarah/iStockphoto/Getty Images; 58 (CTR RT), Digital Vision; 58 (LO RT), Molly Williams/Dreamstime; 58 (LO CTR), Stock Connection/REX/Shutterstock; 58 (CTR RT), Dr. Juerg Alean/Science Source; 59 (UP RT), Mark Williamson/Science Source; 59 (LO ALL), Stuart Armstrong; 60 (UP RT), David Aguilar/National Geographic; 60 (LO LE), Carsten Peter/Speleoresearch & Films/National Geographic Creative; 60 (CTR LE), Denis Radovanovic/Shutterstock; 60 (LO RT), Africa Studio/Shutterstock; 61 (CTR LE), Roy Palmer/Shutterstock; 61 (LO LE), John Cancalosi/Alamy Stock Photo; 61 (CTR RT), Madlen/Shutterstock; 61 (LO RT), Francois Gohier/Science Source; 62, Juice Images Ltd/Getty Images; 63 (UP CTR RT), lkordela/Shutterstock; 63 (CTR RT), Greg Brave/Shutterstock; 63 (LO CTR RT), Johan W. Elzenga/Shutterstock; 63 (LO LE), bogdanhoda/Shutterstock; 63 (LO RT), Jan Martin Will/Shutterstock; 64, otsphoto/Shutterstock; 65 (UP CTR), NGS Image Collection; 65 (LO RT), Arcady/Shutterstock; 65 (UP RT), David Ducros/Science Source; 65 (CTR RT), Denis Tabler/Dreamstime; 65 (LO CTR RT), Florin Brezeanu/Alamy Stock Photo; 66, FloridaStock/Shutterstock; 67 (UP CTR), Chones/Shutterstock; 67 (UP CTR RT), FreshPaint/Shutterstock; 67 (CTR RT), gyn9037/Shutterstock; 67 (LO CTR), Tony Moran/Shutterstock; 67 (LO RT), Alex Mit/Shutterstock; 67 (LO RT), Gyuszko-Photo/Shutterstock

CHAPTER 3: 68-69, Andrey Armyagov/Shutterstock; 70 (CTR LE), Science Lab/Alamy Stock Photo; 70 (LO RT), Robert Gendler/Stocktrek Images/SCIENCE SOURCE; 70-71 (UP CTR), mrtom-uk/iStockphoto/Getty Images; 71 (UP CTR), NASA/GSFC/Solar Dynamics Observatory; 71 (CTR), NASA/GSFC/Solar Dynamics Observatory; 71 (LO CTR), NASA/GSFC/Solar Dynamics Observatory; 71 (UP RT), PRISMA ARCHIVO/Alamy Stock Photo; 71 (LO RT), Mark Garlick/Science Source; 72 (CTR LE), NASA/JPL/USGS; 72 (LO RT), Daniel BOITEAU/Alamy Stock Photo; 73 (CTR LE), Carl D. Walsh/Aurora Photos; 73 (LO), Science Source; 73 (UP RT), Kuki Waterstone/Alamy Stock Photo; 73 (LO RT), NASA/Caltech-JPL/MIT/SRS; 74, Corey Ford/Alamy Stock Photo; 75 (UP LE), Science Source; 75 (UP RT), Matt Gibson/Shutterstock; 75 (CTR LE), Classic Image/Alamy Stock Photo; 75 (LO RT), NASA; 76, NASA/JPL/Cornell University; 77 (UP CTR), 3quarks/iStockphoto/Getty Images; 77 (CTR LE), NASA; 77 (CTR), NASA/JPL/USGS; 77 (CTR RT), NASA/JPL; 77 (CTR RT), NASA/awrence Sromovsky, University of Wisconsin-Madison/W.W. Keck Observatory; 77 (LO RT), Detlev van Ravenswaay/Science Source; 78 (UP LE), NASA/JPL-Caltech/NRL/GSFC; 78-79, BSIP SA/Alamy Stock Photo; 78 (UP CTR), NASA/Johns Hopkins University Applied Physics Laboratory/Carnegie Institution of Washington; 78 (UP RT), NASA/JPL; 78 (CTR), Science Source; 78 (LO RT), NASA; 78 (LO LE), NASA/JPL-Caltech/MSSS; 79 (UP LE), NASA/JPL; 79 (CTR), NASA; 79 (LO CTR), NASA/JPL; 79 (LO CTR), Lynette Cook/Science Source; 79 (CTR & UP RT), NASA/Johns Hopkins University Applied Physics Laboratory/Southwest Research Institute; 79 (CTR), Friedrich Saurer/Science Source; 79 (CTR), John R. Foster/Science Source; 79 (LO CTR RT), John R. Foster/Science Source; 79 (LO CTR), NASA/JPL-Caltech/UCLA/MPS/DLR/IDA/PSI; 80 (UP RT), RapidEye/Getty Images; 80 (LO LE), NASA/JPL-Caltech/STScI; 81 (CTR LE), Laurent Laveder/Science Source; 81 (UP RT), ESA/Hubble; 81 (LO CTR LE), NASA/JPL-Caltech/UCLA; 81 (LO RT), Agsandrew/Dreamstime; 81 (LO LE), NASA/Ames/JPL-Caltech; 82 (CTR RT), NASA, ESA, the Hubble Heritage Team (STScI/AURA), A. Nota (ESA/STScI), and the Westerlund 2 Science Team The original observations of Westerlund 2 were obtained by the science team: Antonella Nota (ESA/STScI), Elena Sabbi (STScI), Eva Grebel and Peter Zeid; 82 (UP LE), Feng Yu/Shutterstock; 82 (UP RT), Shariffc/Dreamstime; 83 (UP LE), MatViv23/Shutterstock; 83 (UP CTR LE), vchal/Shutterstock; 83 (UP CTR RT), Allexxandar/Shutterstock; 83 (UP RT), NASA, ESA, the Hubble Heritage Team (STScI/AURA), A. Nota (ESA/STScI), and the Westerlund 2 Science Team The original observations of Westerlund 2 were obtained by the science team: Antonella Nota (ESA/STScI), Elena Sabbi (STScI), Eva Grebel and Peter Zeid; 83 (CTR RT), Jonathan Irwin; 83 (CTR LE), NASA Goddard; 83 (CTR RT), sciencepics/Shutterstock; 83 (LO CTR RT), NASA/JPL-Caltech; 83 (LO LE), Artwork Credit: NASA, ESA, and G. Bacon (STScI). Science Credit: NASA, ESA, A. Kowalski (University of Washington, USA), R. Osten and K. Sahu (STScI) and S. Hawley (University of Washington, USA); 83 (LO RT), NASA/JPL-Caltech/UCLA; 84, 3DSculptor/iStockphoto/Getty Images; 85 (UP LE), David Ducros/Science Source; 85 (CTR RT), NASA; 85 (LO RT), Christian Darkin/Science Source; 86, Image Source/Getty Images; 87 (UP CTR LE), NASA; 87 (CTR LE), Science Source; 87 (UP RT), Angie Knost/Alamy

Stock Photo; 87 (LO RT), NikoNomad/Shutterstock; 88, Francis DEMANGE/Gamma-Rapho/Getty Images; 89 (UP CTR RT), Syfy/NBCUniversal/Getty Images; 89 (UP LE), BrendanHunter/iStockphoto/Getty Images; 89 (CTR LE), © Buena Vista Pictures/Courtesy Everett Collection; 89 (CTR RT), © 20thCentFox/Courtesy Everett Collection; 89 (LO RT), CTRPhotos/iStockphoto/Getty Images; 90, Science Source; 90 (LO RT), ESO/Martin Kornmesser/Science Source; 91 (CTR RT), NASA/SOFIA/Lynette Cook; 91 (CTR RT), NASA/Northrop Grumman Corporation; 91 (LO RT), NASA; 91 (LO LE), NASA/JPL-Caltech; 92 (LO LE), David Aguilar; 92 (CTR RT), Dr. Seth Shostak/Science Source; 93 (UP LE), NASA/JPL/University of Arizona/Los Alamos National Laboratories; 93 (CTR RT), Lynette Cook/Science Source; 93 (UP RT), NASA/JPL-Caltech/Space Science Institute; 93 (LO LE), NG Images/Alamy Stock Photo; 93 (CTR LE), NASA/JPL-Caltech/SETI Institute; 94 (CTR RT), Provider: ESA (C. Carreau); 94 (LO RT), NASA; 95 (CTR RT), NASA/JPL-Caltech; 95 (UP RT), ESO/spaceengine.org; 95 (LO RT), Provider ESA/NASA, the AVO project and Paolo Padovani; 95 (CTR LE), Mark Stevenson/Stocktrek Images/National Geographic Creative

CHAPTER 4: 96-97, Franco Tempesta/NGS; 98, Franco Tempesta; 99 (UP LE), Yuriy Priymak/Stocktrek Images/Science Source; 99 (UP CTR RT), Valentina_S/Shutterstock; 99 (CTR LE), Stocktrek Images, Inc./Alamy Stock Photo; 99 (UP RT), Franco Tempesta; 99 (LO LE), Eric Isselee/Shutterstock; 100-101, Herschel Hoffmeyer/Shutterstock; 102, Stocktrek Images, Inc./Alamy Stock Photo; 103 (UP CTR RT), Sylvain Entressangle & Elisabeth Daynes/Science Source; 103 (CTR), Mauricio Anton/Science Photo Library/Science Source; 103 (LO CTR), Kennis & Kennis/MSF/Science Source; 103 (CTR RT), denisgo/Shutterstock; 103 (LO LE), David Gifford/Science Source; 104-105 (LO/L-R), Tom Stewart/Corbis/Getty Images; 105 (UP RT), Esteban De Armas/Shutterstock; 105 (CTR), bhofack2/iStockphoto/Getty Images; 105 (LO RT), Mauricio Anton/Science Source; 106 (CTR), Armando Frazao/Shutterstock; 107 (UP CTR RT), Hemis/Alamy Stock Photo; 107 (UP CTR LE), Keremgo/Dreamstime.com; 107 (CTR RT), sculpies/iStockphoto/Getty Images; 107 (LO LE), Sarin Images/The Granger Collection; 107 (CTR RT), Photodisc; 107 (LO RT), Panther Media GmbH/Alamy Stock Photo; 107 (UP RT), PaulaConnelly/iStockphoto/Getty Images; 108 (UP RT), kiankhoon/iStockphoto/Getty Images; 108 (CTR LE), Science Source; 108 (LO RT), MR1805/iStockphoto/Getty Images; 109 (UP LE), Steve Oehlenschlager/Shutterstock; 109 (CTR), The Granger Collection; 109 (CTR LE), Zoonar GmbH/Alamy Stock Photo; 109 (CTR RT), Berents/Shutterstock; 109 (LO RT), North Wind Picture Archives/Alamy Stock Photo; 109 (UP RT), Dja65/Shutterstock; 110 (CTR), Raymond Wong/National Geographic Creative; 110 (LO RT), akg-images/Pictures From History; 111 (CTR LE), Joseph E. Barrett/National Geographic Creative; 111 (CTR RT), Tom Lovell/National Geographic Creative; 112 (LO LE), Vince Clements/Shutterstock; 112 (UP RT), You can more/Shutterstock; 113 (UP LE), World History Archive/Alamy Stock Photo; 113 (UP RT), Christian Jegou/Publiphoto/Science Source; 113 (LO RT), David Wall/Alamy Stock Photo; 114 (LO LE), izusek/iStockphoto/Getty Images; 114 (UP RT), Vova Shevchuk/Shutterstock; 115 (UP RT), Mrs.Blondy/

Shutterstock; 115 (UP RT), kaanates/iStockphoto/Getty Images; 115 (UP CTR), Landscape Nature Photo/Shutterstock; 115 (UP CTR), Corbis; 115 (UP RT), akg-images/De Agostini Picture Lib./G. Dagli Orti; 115 (CTR), s-ts/Shutterstock; 115 (UP CTR RT), Nikola Spasenoski/Shutterstock; 115 (LO RT), chris brignell/Alamy Stock Photo; 116, catalinr/Getty Images; 117 (LO LE), Africa Studio/Shutterstock; 117 (UP RT), The Advertising Archives/Alamy Stock Photo; 117 (CTR RT), akg-images; 118 (CTR LE), gt29/iStockphoto/Getty Images; 118 (LO RT), Science Source; 119 (UP RT), Niday Picture Library/Alamy Stock Photo; 119 (UP RT), Rena Schild/Shutterstock; 119 (LO RT), B Christopher/Alamy Stock Photo; 119 (LO LE), ClassicStock/akg-images; 119 (CTR), Christian Mueringer/Alamy Stock Photo; 120 (UP RT), Stephen French/Alamy Stock Photo; 120 (UP LE), Skystorm/iStockphoto/Getty Images; 120 (LO LE), chainarong06/Shutterstock; 120 (LO RT), Babiina/Shutterstock; 121 (UP CTR LE), Daniel Mogan/Alamy Stock Photo; 121 (CTR LE), Imgorthand/Getty Images; 121 (CTR), Coprid/Getty Images; 121 (LO LE), Vadim Sadovski/Shutterstock; 121 (UP RT), De Agostini/G. Cigolini/Getty Images; 121 (CTR RT), Tony Cordoza/Alamy Stock Photo; 121 (CTR), Rawpixel.com/Shutterstock; 121 (LO CTR RT), Kletr/Shutterstock; 121 (LO RT), GoodMood Photo/Alamy Stock Photo

CHAPTER 5: 122-123, Hero Images/Getty Images; 124, Dragon Images/Shutterstock; 125 (UP LE), Rost9/Shutterstock; 125 (LO LE), Laurence Monneret/Getty Images; 125 (CTR RT), ERproductions Ltd/Getty Images; 126 (UP CTR), Africa Studio/Shutterstock; 126 (LO LE), Daxiao Productions/Shutterstock; 127 (UP RT), Janine Wiedel Photolibrary/Alamy Stock Photo; 127 (LO RT), Siri Stafford/Getty Images; 127 (lo le), Pixel 4 Images/Shutterstock; 128 (CTR RT), Jose Luis Pelaez/Getty Images; 128 (LO LE), m Studio KIWI/Shutterstock; 129 (UP LE), Gelpi/Shutterstock; 129 (UP RT), Flashpop/Getty Images; 129 (CTR), ERproductions Ltd/Getty Images; 129 (LO RT), Sonja Foos/Shutterstock; 129 (LO LE), Nattakit Khunburan/iStockphoto/Getty Images; 130 (UP LE), Klaus Tiedge/Getty Images; 130 (LO RT), Eric Isselee/Shutterstock; 131 (UP CTR), nito/Shutterstock; 131 (CTR), Vectomart/Shutterstock; 131 (LO LE), India Picture/Shutterstock; 131 (UP RT), stopabox/Shutterstock; 131 (UP CTR RT), Adrian_am13/Shutterstock; 131 (CTR RT), Samuel Borges Photography/Shutterstock; 131 (LO RT), Elnur/Shutterstock; 132 (UP LE), Dorottya Mathe/Shutterstock; 132 (LO RT), David Mack/Science Source; 133 (UP LE), Evan Oto/Shutterstock; 133 (LO LE), Lightspring/Shutterstock; 133 (CTR RT), ifong/Shutterstock; 133 (LO RT), Luis Molinero/Shutterstock; 134 (UP), ober-art/Shutterstock; 134 (CTR RT), Tuzemka/Shutterstock; 134 (LO LE), Monica Martinez Do-Allo/Shutterstock; 135 (UP LE), Jason Stitt/Shutterstock; 135 (CTR), Dave Pot/Shutterstock; 135 (LO LE), AiVectors/Shutterstock; 135 (UP CTR RT), HBRH/Shutterstock; 135 (CTR RT), Jurgen Falchle/Alamy Stock Photo; 135 (CTR RT), Tetra Images/Alamy Stock Photo; 135 (LO RT), Dewald Kirsten/Shutterstock; 136 (CTR RT), AFP/Getty Images; 136 (UP LE), juan moyano/Alamy Stock Photo; 137 (UP RT), VikramRaghuvanshi/Getty Images; 137 (UP LE), Pasieka/Science Source; 137 (LO LE), WDC Photos/Alamy Stock Photo; 137 (LO CTR LE), DFree/Shutterstock; 137 (CTR), Paolo Bona/Shutterstock;

Shutterstock/Africa Studio; 202 (LO RT), Photodisc; 203 (UP RT), Sean Pavone/Shutterstock; 203 (CTR RT), itographer/iStockphoto; 203 (LO LE), Stephen Dunn/Getty Images; 203 (LO CTR), Jonathan Daniel/Getty Images; 203 (LO RT), John Tlumacki/The Boston Globe/Getty Images; 204 (UP), Hero Images Inc./Alamy Stock Photo; 204 (LO RT), Paul Fearn/Alamy Stock Photo; 205 (UP CTR RT), Lane Stewart/Sports Illustrated/Getty Images; 205 (CTR RT), AP Photo/Lynne Cameron; 205 (LO RT), AP Photo/Daniel Hulshizer/REX/Shutterstock; 205 (UP RT), Blend Images/Alamy Stock Photo/Alamy Stock Photo; 205 (LO LE), Erik Pendzich/REX/Shutterstock; 206, mikeinlondon/iStockphoto/Getty Images; 207 (UP RT), Michael Baynes/Getty Images; 207 (CTR LE), Barcroft Media/Getty Images; 207 (LO RT), Cory Richards/National Geographic Creative; 208 (CTR LE), Bill_Anastasiou/iStockphoto/Getty Images; 208 (UP RT), Bill_Anastasiou/iStockphoto/Getty Images; 209 (CTR LE), Yury Shirokov/Dreamstime; 209 (UP CTR LE), Lumi Images/Alamy Stock Photo; 209 (CTR LE), MarFot/Shutterstock; 209 (CTR LE), Kaesler Media/Shutterstock; 209 (UP LE), Wilfredo Lee/AP/REX/Shutterstock; 209 (UP CTR RT), Norasit Kaewsai/Alamy Stock Photo; 209 (LO CTR RT), wildphotohunter/Alamy Stock Photo; 209 (UP RT), efetova/iStockphoto Getty Images; 209 (LO LE), Vitaly Titov & Maria Sidelnikova/Shutterstock; 209 (LO LE), Picture Partners/Alamy Stock Photo; 209 (LO CTR), Life on white/Alamy Stock Photo; 209 (LO CTR RT), Eric Isselee/Shutterstock; 209 (LO RT), PaulBull/Getty Images; 210, Dorling Kindersley/Getty Images; 211 (UP LE), rudall30/Shutterstock; 211 (UP RT), ART Collection/Alamy Stock Photo; 211 (CTR RT), Jaime Chirinos/Science Source; 211 (LO RT), Lysogor Roman/Shutterstock; 211 (LO CTR LE), Aloysius Patrimonio/Alamy Stock Vector; 211 (LO LE), Koji Sasahara/REX/Shutterstock; 212 (CTR RT), Steve Parsons - PA Images/Getty Images; 212, urbanbuzz/Alamy Stock Photo; 213 (UP RT), Courtesy EverBlock Systems; 213 (CTR RT), Christian Kober/robertharding/Alamy Stock Photo; 213 (LO LE), Tony LeMoignan/Alamy Stock Photo; 213 (LO RT), James Lozeau, Courtesy Finca Bellavista; 213 (LO CTR LE), Kerry Woo

BACK MATTER: 215 (UP RT), AnatolyM/iStockphoto/Getty Images; 216 (LO LE), Tony Cordoza/Alamy Stock Photo; 218 (LO RT), PaulBull/iStockphoto/Getty Images; 219 (LO RT), Shutterstock/Martina Osmy

Since 1888, the National Geographic Society has funded more than 12,000 research, exploration, and preservation projects around the world. The Society receives funds from National Geographic Partners, LLC, funded in part by your purchase. A portion of the proceeds from this book supports this vital work. To learn more, visit natgeo.com/info.

For more information, visit nationalgeographic.com, call 1-800-647-5463, or write to the following address:

National Geographic Partners
1145 17th Street N.W.
Washington, D.C. 20036-4688 U.S.A.

Visit us online at nationalgeographic.com/books

For librarians and teachers: ngchildrensbooks.org

More for kids from National Geographic: natgeokids.com

For information about special discounts for bulk purchases, please contact National Geographic Books Special Sales: specialsales@natgeo.com

For rights or permissions inquiries, please contact National Geographic Books Subsidiary Rights: bookrights@natgeo.com

Designed by John Foster

Hardcover ISBN: 978-1-4263-3191-6
Reinforced library binding ISBN: 978-1-4263-3192-3

Printed in China
18/PPS/1

The publisher would like to acknowledge the following people for making this book possible: Becky Baines, executive editor; Jen Agresta, project editor; Crispin Boyer, author; Amanda Larsen, design director; Lori Epstein, photo director; Liz Seramur, photo editor; Alix Inchausti, production editor; Anne LeongSon and Gus Tello, production assistants.

FOR MY WIFE, RAMAH, WHO YEARS AGO GAVE ME THE BEST ANSWER I GOT
—CB

WHY NOT

check out these other AWESOME books, too?

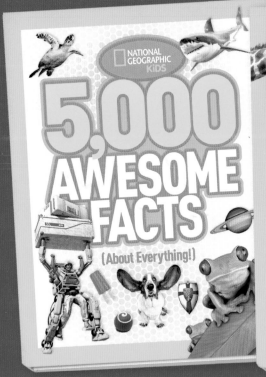

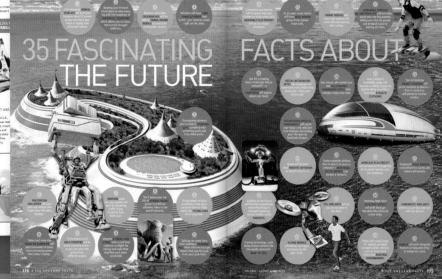